FV.

WITHDRAWN

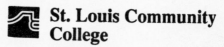

Women and Film: A Sight and Sound Reader

In the series
Culture and the Moving Image,
edited by Robert Sklar

Edited by Pam Cook and Philip Dodd

Women and Film
A Sight and Sound Reader

Temple University Press
Philadelphia

This book is dedicated to the staff of 'Sight and Sound': Charlotte Housden,
Caroline Moore, Colette O'Reilly, Jonathan Romney and Rebecca Russell.

Temple University Press, Philadelphia 19122
Published 1993

First published by Scarlet Press
5 Montague Road, London E8 2HN

Library of Congress Cataloging-in-Publication Data
Women and film: a Sight and Sound reader / edited by Pam Cook and
Philip Dodd.
p. cm. — (Culture and the moving image)
Collection of essays previously published by Sight and Sound.
Includes filmographies, bibliographical references, and index.
ISBN 1-56639-142-3 (cl). — ISBN 1-56639-143-1 (pb)
1. Women in motion pictures. 2. Sex role in motion pictures.
3. Lesbianism in motion pictures. 4. Feminism and motion pictures.
5. Women motion picture producers and directors. I. Cook, Pam.
II. Dodd, Philip. III. *Sight and Sound*. IV. Series.
PN1995.9.W6W63 1993
791.43'082—dc20   93-31694

Sight and Sound is published by the British Film Institute

Printed in Great Britain by Borcombe Printers Ltd

Contents

Philip Dodd

Foreword

The contributions that make up *Women and Film* are taken from the new *Sight and Sound*, which was relaunched as a monthly magazine by the British Film Institute in 1991. While the book has its own logic and force, its range and address derive from the particular intellectual trajectory of the magazine, and it may be helpful to readers of this anthology to sketch that in.

When it was relaunched, *Sight and Sound* had the conviction, unusual in Britain, that it is possible to be both popular and serious, and that it is necessary to address all kinds of cinema, at a moment when – as Linda Ruth Williams' introductory essay argues – the received categories, including feminist ones, seem increasingly inadequate for understanding cinema, past and present. Clearly the magazine has not jettisoned the past, but it has put past arguments to work in the present, acutely aware that new circumstances – whether the emergence of new arguments around Aids, or around nationalism and ethnicity – will often find old positions wanting and will require the elaboration of new aesthetic and cultural ideas. It has been one of the pleasures of editing the magazine that such a wide range of contributors from a wide range of cultures have been willing to write for it, and have found its pages a welcoming place in which to be published.

In direct opposition to those who believe that a small circulation is a test of seriousness, the magazine set out to capture a new popular readership, confident in the knowledge that, historically, fresh ways of thinking have been developed in relation to new groups – whether cultural studies evolving within the adult education movement or feminist studies in relation to the women's movement. This commitment to a new popular audience has guarded the magazine against the temptation to look backwards nostalgically to some earlier 'golden age' of either cinema or writing on cinema, since to have done so would have been to tell its readers – a growing number of whom are between the ages of 18 and 35 – that the present is just a feeble echo of the past.

The new *Sight and Sound* has been suspicious of the grand narratives of the past, knowing who and what they excluded, and has embraced a determined pluralism, as this anthology attests. We have been equally convinced that the magazine should show that intellectually dexterous writing can be pleasurable (in the face of the puritanical British belief that only if it hurts is it good for you); and that the magazine should look visually literate rather than pretend that black and white Letraset is a guarantee of seriousness.

Wanting to be in thrall neither to the 'movies' nor to 'theory', *Sight and Sound* set out to recognise and elaborate connections between cinema and major contemporary cultural debates. This anthology endorses the logic of what the magazine is attempting to do and celebrates its achievement. With the exception of the essay on Hattie McDaniel, which was prompted by a letter to the magazine, and the two introductory essays, all material in this book first appeared in *Sight and Sound*. The two complementary introductory essays offer, respectively, reflections on the development of women and film and reflections on the prospects for women and film.

Philip Dodd
Editor, 'Sight and Sound'

Pam Cook

Border crossings: women and film in context

In 1911, the militant suffragette Mary Richardson, outraged by the force-feeding of Mrs Pankhurst in prison, slashed Velasquez's *Rokeby Venus* in the National Gallery with an axe in protest against the idealised version of femininity it represented. Her act was one of politicised vandalism, congruent with the suffragettes' aim of drawing attention to their cause through attacks on state property. With hindsight, it also comes over as an act of revenge, and as a way of leaving an indelible mark, ensuring that history would never be able to forget the struggle of these women to be recognised as equal members of society. Mary Richardson's willingness to take risks for her beliefs makes her sister to the wayward girls and wicked women populating the pages of this collection, whether as writers, stars, characters or film-makers.

Today's feminists might view Velasquez's painting a little less censoriously. Twenty years of film theory has taught us that representation is not so simple. Idealised she may be; but the hint that the Venus might look back at the viewer via her reflection in the mirror held up to her by Cupid unsettles the system whereby the nude is contemplated privately and proprietorially by the male spectator. A sexual invitation, and an assertion that the woman also looks, Venus' gaze reminds us that woman is more than a body to be looked at; she participates. The articles assembled here are evidence of that will to participate. Their authors share a preoccupation with breaking open patriarchal histories and language to expose and overturn the ways in which women are positioned. These 90s feminist writers and film-makers insist that their assault on traditional cinema be seen and heard. If their acuity, energy and persistence are anything to go by, the days of male cultural ownership could now be numbered.

Yet this book is also a reminder that history is a process of ebb and flow rather than linear progression. We may seem to have travelled some distance from Mary Richardson's angry iconoclasm, but it finds an echo in many of the essays that follow – in B. Ruby Rich's indictment in 'Queer alternatives' of new queer cinema's exclusion of lesbian film-makers, for example. The writing in this anthology testifies to the gains made by feminist theory and politics, but it also reveals ideological shifts which have brought new 'post-feminist' problematics. The notion of post-feminism is nothing if not double-edged: on one hand, a celebration of undeniable victories achieved; on the other, registering the occlusion of women's issues as other political priorities take precedence.

The 70s, when 60s liberation politics came together with the wholesale revision of Marxist theory and new materialist approaches to language influenced by psychoanalysis, provides both links and breaks between earlier feminisms and the 90s. 70s feminists, like those before them, viewed the canons of literature, painting and cinema with somewhat jaundiced eyes. Art historian Linda Nochlin's 1971 ironic question, 'Why have there been no great women artists?', resonated through all the arts, pinpointing with precision not only the exclusion of women from male pantheons, but the ideologically loaded criteria which perpetuated their marginalisation. Nochlin's question implied a need for a multi-faceted political strategy: an assault on the bastions of male power in cultural institutions and the establishment of autonomous spaces for women's work; a rewriting of conventional histories to include the considerable contributions of female artists; an interrogation of the standards which determined what qualified as good or bad art; a critique of the dependency on the figure of woman as spectacle in prevailing systems of representation; and the development of new forms of expression through which women might articulate their own, different aspirations.

The feminists of the 70s set out an ambitious programme. But, in those heady days of the newly revived women's movement, they launched themselves into the task with vigour, not least in the area of film. Women's independent film-making and distribution groups were founded and women's film festivals burgeoned. Small magazines dedicated to women and film sprang up, while feminist writing found its way into the pages of left magazines from the theoretical journal *Screen* to the listings magazine *Time Out*. Publishing houses began to bring out books on neglected women film-makers and feminist critiques of Hollywood, perceived as patriarchal cinema *par excellence*. And articles were written questioning the assumptions of male-dominated film theory and criticism; the new feminist film theory was born. It has become fashionable these days (as it was then, in some quarters) to dismiss 70s film theory for its inaccessibility, its addiction to 'high' modernism and puritanical refusal of the pleasures of popular cinema. Certainly, much feminist theory of the period was afflicted by cultural pessimism. It seemed to allow little space for women to position themselves as active producers or consumers of critical meanings and pleasures, except as a kind of heckling from the sidelines.

But – impenetrable though much of that writing, and many of the associated independent films, now appear – 70s theoretical work has left an undeniable legacy, most obviously in the academy, where theory finds a natural home. Women's studies, in its own right and in the wider arena of media and cultural studies, now has a reasonably secure foothold, which has enabled the production of exciting and provocative intellectual work. But the transformation of feminism from a political movement into a cultural phenomenon has brought its own problems. Women are still marginalised both intellectually and creatively. Their work is given token value rather than the proper recognition accorded male intellectuals and artists. Twenty years on, books about women film-makers are few and far between.

Yet there is significant evidence of trickling up. There are more women working in British film and television than ever, and, if many find themselves ghettoised in 'minority' slots, others, such as Sally Potter or scriptwriter Lynda LaPlante, have received due acknowledgment. In the US, the independent production facilities of the 60s and 70s allowed some women to enter the industry, albeit at its borders, and though, unlike their male counterparts, they have often had to compromise their distinctive voice to cross over into the mainstream, there is now a considerable female presence in and outside Hollywood. The European film scene, east and west, boasts an increasing number of women directors – notwithstanding the fact that many of the movies will not get distribution outside their own countries. A new wave of female Australasian voices clamour to be heard and accepted on their own terms. And if one knows that Julie Dash's *Daughters of the Dust* will never receive the exposure afforded *Malcolm X*, one can celebrate the fact that it was made at all.

There are also more women film critics today. As well as film theory, the 70s saw the rise of a new breed of committed young journalists. Unafraid of special pleading, these writers, several of whom were women, put their political allegiances on the line in reviews which were both cineliterate and opinionated. Writing with confidence and verve, they brought a new perspective to film journalism, drawing attention to feminist work ignored by the middle-of-the-road, middle-aged male reviewers who dominated the scene at the time – and still do. In their ability to pick up on current and emerging trends, to make waves in the stagnant pools of established film culture and to insist on the importance of the new and the different, these reviewers performed an invaluable service. Their dissonant voices can be heard in the columns of today's newspapers, weekly journals and magazines.

The 80s brought distinctive cultural and intellectual shifts. A significant number of features directed, produced and written by women, mostly from the US, Europe and Australia, were released. Television, as funder, producer, distributor and exhibitor, became a prominent player in the British film scene, re-energising a moribund industry. Britain's independent black workshops generated provocative and stylish work on the subject of sexual politics and race. New national cinemas from China and Africa received international recognition. For what now looks like a very brief period, the possibility of a genuinely hybrid film culture was in the air. At the same time, new theoretical work began to take issue with the 70s tendency to 'fix' spectators in abstract, closed positions and to argue that identification was far more fluid than had previously been thought, and that feminist questions were inseperable from those of gender and race. This was a momentous shift, heralding the age of 'post-feminism', regarded with suspicion by many, who saw the appropriation of feminism by gender studies as a guise for letting in male power through the back door and the beginnings of a major backlash.

These misgivings were not entirely without justification. Certainly, mainstream 80s cinema abounds in images which betray profound anxieties about female sexuality, from *Fatal Attraction* to the 'baby boom' movies and *Alien*. Nevertheless, it would be a mistake to underestimate the extent to which male sexuality is also under scrutiny in these films, or to ignore the fact that they project a crisis in male authority, in much the same way as did postwar *film noir*. It is not often recognised that women such as Glenn Close's Alex or Sigourney Weaver's Ripley are presented as besieged characters, victims of the renewed ascendancy of 'family values' and the erosion of their control over their reproductivity. The feminisation of popular genres and the return of the 'women's picture' during this period is as much a recognition of the cultural power of feminism (and of women as significant members of the cinema audience) as it is an attempt to capitalise on and control it. It is a symptomatic response to historical changes which produced contradictory results: on one hand, a proliferation of powerful female figures, from Margaret Thatcher to Cat Woman; on the other, a retraction of women's hard-won political rights.

Though the mid-80s eruption has subsided somewhat, the tremors are still being felt. In the early 90s, while masculinity-in-crisis movies from *Godfather Part III* to *Falling Down* are everywhere, femininity-in-crisis pictures from Kathryn Bigelow's *Blue Steel* to Maggie Greenwald's *The Ballad of Little Jo* are making their mark. The opening up of Hollywood to young black film-makers and the move of queer cinema into the art house circuits, both hopeful signs, have not as yet proved of much benefit to women, though there is a new generation waiting impatiently in the wings. As the pages that follow indicate, women are still out there, working away in the mainstream and the margins to produce challenging ideas and formally inventive movies.

Indeed, it is a film made by a woman – Sally Potter's *Orlando*, a co-production which wears its dual British/European identity on its spectacular sleeve – that suggests a positive way forward for British cinema. No sad Europudding this, but an exploration of the borders of identity itself, *Orlando*, like Jane Campion's *The Piano* and Julie Dash's *Daughters of the Dust*, rewrites its national history from the perspective of the women caught up in it, displaying a deep suspicion of the forms conventionally used to express that history and a profound sense of alienation from national culture. Where new black or queer cinema asserts the necessity for oppositional identities, these new feminist movies transgress boundaries – between national and international, home and abroad, art and entertainment, masculine and feminine – finding their identities in the very act of transgression. All of them are about travelling – through time, to new shores, between island and mainland – in a restless search for a fulfilment which can only be imagined, never realised. In their ambivalence towards 'home', the place where women are traditionally meant to find themselves, they echo longstanding feminist concerns; but in their engagement with post-imperial and post-colonial histories, their embracing of spectacle and masquerade, and their forging of new forms of cinematic expression, they are very much of the 90s.

In the articles that follow, the reader will find new thoughts on old problematics, the latest developments confronted with time-honoured questions, reassessment mingled with provocation – and fresh ideas. The opening section, 'Icons', looks at stars and their function in mainstream cinema from the perspective of 90s internationalism. The essays range from historical material – studies of Marlene Dietrich, Hattie McDaniel, Lillian Gish and Audrey Hepburn – to new takes on black star Whoopi Goldberg, Chinese actress Gong Li, and radical gender-bender Tilda Swinton, and a celebration of Jodie Foster's success as an actress and director in contemporary Hollywood. Richard Dyer, who writes here about the construction of Lillian Gish's star persona as an ideal of 'whiteness', was a pioneer in the field of star study – one of the first to attempt to theorise a phenomenon often thought to be indefinable: star 'charisma' and our fascinated response to it. At a time when film theory was heavily weighted towards textual analysis inspired by literary models, Dyer's work emphasised the links between stars as clusters of contradictory meanings and society. It also, by highlighting the identification of gay men with female stars such as Judy Garland and Bette Davis, drew attention to the heterosexual bias of much film study.

In *Stars* (1979), Dyer argued that star charisma – that extra something which leads us to experience certain performers as special – could work against the relentless drive of the narrative towards ideological closure. Although stars performed a function in the story, encouraging identification with key protagonists, their charisma produced an excess of meaning which, by captivating the spectator's gaze, disrupted involvement with narrative progression. Even if the story made sure that a strong female character got her comeuppance, her dazzling image lingered in the spectator's mind, over-riding the knowledge of her punitive destiny. Marlene Dietrich, considered here by Gertrud Koch and Marjorie Garber, is a clear case of charisma working in this way. Her spectacular, often perverse image, particularly in the films she made with von Sternberg, hijacked the movies in which she appeared, endowing her charac-ters with a presence which often belied their fate.

The star's persona, carried across and between individual movies, can also work against the grain of negative stereotypes – as Stephen Bourne points out in his account of black actress Hattie McDaniel's career. In spite of being restricted to demeaning mammy roles, McDaniel's flamboyant and defiant image lent a sub-versive edge to her interpretation of them. A key element in Dyer's argument was the notion of star performance militating against the smooth passage of ideology. This is an idea which could be applied to Whoopi Goldberg as an example of a contemporary black actress who appears to have crossed over, even if, as Andrea Stuart claims here, she is permitted to do so only in a limited capacity. Goldberg's comic persona carries within it a whole history of black performers which surfaces in almost parodic fashion, undermin-ing attempts to confine her to playing black characters whose black-ness and/or politics are not an issue.

Many of the pieces explore the role of stars in focusing the aspi-rations of their national cultures. Dietrich and Deneuve, Gong Li and Goldberg, Audrey Hepburn and Jodie Foster are all considered for the way they project, however contradictorily, national ideals. In some cases, as with Dietrich and Foster, who both faced hostil-ity in their own countries, they are a target for disappointment as much as hope. Yet what comes over most strongly in 'Icons' is the notion that while these female performers have all played a crucial part in projecting the utopian desires of their cultures, they also resist the role assigned to them. Perhaps this is where true star quality resides.

The theme of female resistance is explored in the next section, 'Women against the grain'. In the low-budget and mainstream exploitation movies under scrutiny here, women characters are dri-ven to extremes in heroic bids for freedom. Like Mary Richardson, they risk everything, including their lives, for recognition and iden-tity. Like Thelma and Louise, they take revenge on men for aeons of oppression. Feminist critics travel with them into taboo territory –

the exploitation arena which, like pornography, also the subject of recent reassessment, has traditionally been deemed too 'low' to merit serious critical attention. Although exploitation genres, with their high quotient of sex and violence and apparent pandering to sadistic male fantasies, seem at first glance to be unredeemably misogynist, a closer look reveals that all is not as it appears. Not only have women film-makers worked successfully in exploitation, but feminists take exploitation movies seriously, defending their potentially pleasurable appeal to female audiences. With their strong heroines battling against all odds, these films offer women of the 90s satisfying daydreams of endurance and escape.

Low-budget exploitation was born with the rise of US drive-in cinema and was a blatant attempt to capitalise on a youth audience for the most part disinterested in reading about movies – though the films also had a student following on the college campus circuits. During the late 60s and 70s, independent production companies such as Roger Corman's New World turned out low-cost exploiters with the declared aim of making a fast buck. While these cheap and cheerful efforts conformed to requirements in containing nudity, violent action and sex, they also did more than this. They were often re-makes of more upmarket mainstream productions which they parodied mercilessly. Their appeal to the youth market, and the fact that many of them were made by film school graduates getting their first break, meant that they often picked up on contemporary political issues. A popular version of 'women's lib' was celebrated in sexual role reversals in which strong, assertive women, often brandishing weapons, took their destiny in their own hands, and a significant number of the movies dealt with social problems such as rape and unwanted pregnancy, performing a delicate balancing act between the demands of exploitation and politics.

In the 80s, exploitation entered the mainstream as the major Hollywood studios began to penetrate the exploitation market, a development deplored by quality critics, who bemoaned the birth of the blockbuster and the prevalence of 'slasher' movies of the *Nightmare on Elm Street* and *Friday the Thirteenth* variety. Unfortunately, most of the women directors who cut their teeth on low-budget exploitation have failed to cross over into mainstream production – though this was not the case with their male counterparts. Jonathan Kaplan's 1988 *The Accused*, for example, which is the subject of Carol J. Clover's examination of the relationship between big-budget exploitation and its disreputable low-brow cousins, has clear roots in movies he made for Corman in the early 70s, such as *Night Call Nurses*, in which rape was sympathetically handled. One cannot help but wonder why one of the many women directors with similar credentials was not given the job. Nevertheless, as Amy Taubin's piece on recent serial killer movies attests, the move of exploitation material from margins to mainstream has resulted in women's issues being brought to the fore in feminist-influenced blockbusters such as the hugely successful *The Silence of the Lambs*.

There are several reasons for feminist critics to be wary of exploitation cinema, in both its 'high' and 'low' manifestations. Its response to the women's movement is nothing if not ambivalent – on one hand, bringing to centre stage feminist and gay sexual politics, on the other, churning up the cultural panics surrounding these groups. Yet, as the articles in 'Women against the grain' testify, there is much enjoyment to be had from watching alienated female protagonists stalk inimical landscapes in which male abuse of power has gone out of control, looking for survival and retribution. Sigourney Weaver's Ripley character in the *Alien* trilogy and girls-on-the-run Thelma and Louise have become cult heroines for today's feminists, who see them as role models in the struggle against renascent nuclear family ideology and mandatory maternity. Even the ambiguous endings, in which death is chosen as a way out, can be seen as a triumph – Ripley and Thelma and Louise leap over the edge in what is at once a utopian gesture of defiance and a recognition of the impossibility of freedom for women under patriarchy.

The contributors to 'Deconstructing masculinity' follow the feisty heroines of 'Women against the grain' in turning the tables on male power. The articles in this section are the result of a significant shift that took place as 80s feminist film theory turned its attention towards the construction of gender. In the mid-70s, the idea that cinema had systematically exploited the image of woman in the interests of the expression of male desires, while women themselves were by and large excluded from the processes of production, surfaced in a number of theoretical articles. The best known of these is probably Laura Mulvey's 'Visual Pleasure and Narrative Cinema', which argued that Hollywood cinema was constituted by a system of looks dominated by a controlling male gaze at the highly fetishised figure of woman, thus confirming the traditional active male/passive female dichotomy. An associated argument took up the idea of femininity as masquerade, claiming that the image of woman in mainstream cinema did not represent woman at all, but was simply a vehicle for man's anxiety about his own extinction. Both these positions left little room for women as active contributors to, or consumers of, cinematic pleasures. What is more, they seemed to hanker after a 'true' femininity which was waiting in the wings.

The search was on to define the female spectator's pleasure. During the 80s, interest developed in the critically maligned but popular genres of melodrama and the women's picture, which not only had narratives predicated on female desire, but seemed to offer women the opportunity to contemplate highly enjoyable images of feminised men. Parallel work began to look at portrayals of flawed masculinity in contemporary US cinema. Perhaps unsurprisingly, these investigations revealed that male power was neither as monolithic nor as stable as had been argued; but more than this, the regimes of looking in mainstream cinema, so overwhelmingly characterised in terms of male control, were in fact more contradictory, and identification more fluid than had previously been thought. It was discovered that cinema abounded in images of masculine punishment and defeat, and the idea gained ground that masochism was at least as potent a source of aesthetic pleasure as the sadistic voyeurism that had been stressed.

The essays in this section reflect this shift of interest towards female pleasure in woman-made masculinities. They reformulate the master category 'masculinity' as a specific historical and social construct, and as a shifting entity whose dominance can no longer be taken for granted. A common theme is the lure of the feminised male – a paradoxical figure whose power, as Ginette Vincendeau notes in her analysis of Jean Gabin's role in *La Bête humaine*, seems to reside in his impotence. Yet male characters can incorporate feminine, nurturing qualities without relinquishing control, as Vincendeau's account of French cinema's father-daughter narratives and Lizzie Francke's piece on the rash of recent Hollywood movies about childhood demonstrate. And feminisation can be used to shore up masculine authority, as my own discussion of Scorsese's *Cape Fear* shows. Carol J. Clover on *Falling Down* brings the debate bang up to date: white average male D-Fens' masculinity crisis is seen as intimately linked to the collapse of US national identity.

There is clearly much for women to relish in these narratives of male identity crisis and images of men stripped of phallic power. They are a visible response, however phobic, to gay and feminist politics and the perceived empowerment of women. They provide symptomatic evidence of social change, even as they attempt to recast the roles of victim and oppressor. And they open up the question of identity itself, testing its limits and exposing its mutability. The articles in 'Queer alternatives' approach this question from a different perspective, one which asserts the necessity for political identities defined against the ideologies of ruling groups – in this case, compulsory heterosexuality. The contributors to this section celebrate the visceral energy and lack of respect for political correctness characterising the new queer movies, even though they detect a residual misogyny in their privileging of male desire. But they deplore the fact that, despite the wealth of talented lesbian film and video-makers, there is little sign of a new dyke cinema. German director Monika Treut, who predates queer cinema, yet whose humorous S/M scenarios and pro-sex stance certainly qualify, is something of an exception. As Julia Knight points out, the emergence of queer cinema and new lesbian and gay distribution companies has worked in her favour, providing a context for her otherwise hard-to-place movies.

The recent explosion of queer cinema on to the art cinema and festival circuits is evidence of the post-Aids increased visibility of gay politics and the funders' and distributors' recognition of these developments. Paradoxically, Aids has brought a new urgency, motivation and confidence to gay film-making, shaking up old debates. Gay and feminist theory grew up side by side, but each has its own history and distinct lines of development; there are areas of overlap, particularly when it comes to lesbian film-making, but there are areas of conflict as well.

The crucial importance of cinema in the process of forming and transforming identities, particularly in the case of socially isolated sub-cultures, has been a central element in gay debates. In the face of the absence of positive representations of homosexuality, gay people in the cinema audience have operated a form of *bricolage*, pilfering straight images to put to their own uses – whether in film-making or in critical responses which camped up those images.

There is an element of disguise in this formulation, which suggests that gays are particularly liable to 'try on' different identities. This, and the fact that recent theory has claimed that identification is in any case a flexible process, raises the issue of whether positive images of homosexuals and lesbians are either possible or desirable. These arguments revolve around the question of what a gay sensibility, or identity, might be, and echo controversies within feminism about the virtues of a politics based on woman-centred essentialism. The debates are not closed, and probably never will be, since the tension between what is specific to a certain group or individual, and what is shared with those against which it defines itself, is endemic to the very process of identity formation.

If in 'Queer alternatives' a cacophony of female voices clamours to be heard, the film-makers discussed in 'Women direct' could be said to have made the difficult leap from margins to mainstream. Yet the feature films included here represent a significant drop on the numbers for the mid-80s mini-boom. The reasons are partly economic, as worldwide recession forces cut-backs; but, as the existence of new black and queer cinema testifies, they are also ideological. Cinema is still a boys' playground, and girls have difficulty making the team – after all, they play the game differently, and changes have to be made to accommodate them. This section bears witness to the remarkable resilience of women film-makers who are not just determined to survive in adverse circumstances, but who refuse to allow their distinctive voices to be compromised. The 90s has brought a new maturity to feminist cinema, with veterans such as Chantal Akerman, Doris Dörrie and Sally Potter updating and rethinking past concerns. It has also seen the emergence of a generation of younger directors hustling their way into boys' territory and irreverently reclaiming genres such as the thriller and Western for themselves.

In the 70s, the search for a feminist aesthetic revolved around questions of authenticity and realism. Many argued that documentary was more suitable than Hollywood-style artifice to express the 'truth' of women's oppression effaced in mainstream cinema. Others disputed the claims of documentary to have access to 'truth' and made a case for a feminist counter-cinema which, through playful juggling of dominant forms, would de-naturalise the myths of women on which they depended. The films of Dorothy Arzner, Nelly Kaplan and Stephanie Rothman, among others, were seen as examples of the latter. Simultaneously, ideas were appropriated from the anti-narrative strategies of the avant-garde, which could be deployed to deconstruct the fictional codes of mainstream cinema and the roles they allotted to women. Akerman, whose films were key players in the quest for new forms of expression, and Potter belong in this counter-cinema tradition, though neither has allowed herself to be constrained by it. Akerman and others such as Yvonne Rainer went on to receive international acclaim on the festival circuit, and international distribution, while Hollywood, not to be outdone, produced its own spate of feminist-influenced women's pictures from *Julia* to *An Unmarried Woman* and *Alice Doesn't Live Here Any More*.

Out of the shoestring cinema of the 70s were born the confident feminist features of the 80s, from Marleen Gorris to Margarethe von Trotta, Lizzie Borden and Donna Deitch. And a new group of women directors coming from low-budget exploitation – Amy Jones, Penelope Spheeris *et al* – seemed to be poised on the brink of mainstream success. The move into feature film-making produced variable results, particularly in the US. The stylish early efforts of the likes of Susan Seidelman and Kathryn Bigelow are to be remembered with pride, as are the ingeniously off-kilter achievements of new Australian cinema's Jane Campion, Ann Turner and Tracey Moffatt. In Britain, women's features were less in evidence: Sally Potter's *The Gold Diggers*, Pat Murphy's *Maeve* and *Anne Devlin*, and Lezli-An Barrett's *Business As Usual* spring to mind. One should also look to television and to black independent workshops such as Sankofa for examples of inventive feminist film-making in this period.

One of the projects of 70s feminist film criticism was the reassessment of the work of women film-makers who had been neglected by traditional male-oriented histories. The aim was not only to create alternative pantheons, but to gather ideas for new forms of expression. The work of Dorothy Arzner, for example, was investigated not just to claim for her the auteur status accorded her male counterparts, but for the way the formal strategies of her movies appeared to subvert the conventions of 30s and 40s classic Hollywood cinema. Leni Riefenstahl, whose relationship to National Socialism and attachment to what is perceived by many as a fascist aesthetic make her an uncomfortable figure for feminists, has not yet been afforded revisionist treatment. Thomas Elsaesser's review of Riefenstahl's uneasy position in Nazi cinema, and of her role in focusing national guilt, suggests that she might be ripe for feminist re-evaluation.

Like Riefenstahl, most of the film-makers featured in 'Women direct' are at odds with their cultures, so it is hardly surprising that their work manifests common themes of identity and alienation and an interest in finding appropriate languages to articulate their concerns. Chantal Akerman and Doris Dörrie, discussed by Angela McRobbie and Carole Angier respectively, are both given outsider status. While feminism has made their films possible, neither is totally assimilable within it. Mira Nair, the subject of Andrea Stuart's article, is another figure who is both inside and outside her culture. Her film *Mississippi Masala* goes against the grain of black nationalism by looking forward to a new, hybrid social order based on ethnic mixing. In its focus on the dialectical process of exile and return, *Mississippi Masala* echoes the preoccupation of all the film-makers in this section with venturing beyond fixed boundaries. This is certainly the trajectory of Sally Potter's *Orlando*, which not only takes giant leaps through time and space, but journeys to the very hinterland of sexual identity. In the course of the movie, Tilda Swinton's Orlando tries on a number of roles, the most significant of which is his transformation into a woman.

Jane Campion's *The Piano* and Julie Dash's *Daughters of the Dust* are also, like *Orlando*, concerned with rewriting history from a 90s perspective, and both also reinvent the costume drama in the process. Stella Bruzzi's article describes how Campion uses costume in an entirely original manner to express the sexual and emotional awakening of her mute Victorian heroine, while Dash, as Karen Alexander reveals, in developing new ways of telling based on West African oral traditions, has transformed the historical costume drama in much the same way as Toni Morrison, Alice Walker *et al* have revolutionised the historical novel. In their confidence, ambition and innovative flair, these movies are more than a match for anything produced by the male black and queer new waves.

The 90s film-makers included in 'Women direct' are influenced by feminist debates without being in the least inhibited by them. The overriding impression is of remarkable creative diversity. Each of the women directors featured here has distinct concerns arising out of their different contexts. Yet they share common ground. They are all motivated by an iconoclastic desire to break with traditional cinematic forms and subject matter. They all speak from a position outside their cultures and hold fast to their renegade status. Yet they all see women as central figures in the transformation of society. They speak for themselves and not necessarily for all women; but they insist on their right to speak differently, and for that difference to be recognised.

Linda Ruth Williams

Everything in question: women and film in prospect

Virginia Woolf's *Orlando* begins with a provocative lie: 'He – for there could be no doubt of his sex.' As one might expect of perhaps the key masquerading text of this century, of 'his' sex there can *only* be doubt. Sex is also the central question in Sally Potter's 1993 film of *Orlando*, and Potter doubles the deed of disguise, casting not only a woman as a man (posing the question of what Orlando really is – a man? a woman? and how do we identify Tilda Swinton?), but a man as a woman (Quentin Crisp as Elizabeth I). The man is a queen, the director a woman, and the gender-fuck art-film crosses to the mainstream.

Indeed, doubt is not only all there can be of Orlando's sex, but, in these post-Freudian, post-consciousness-raising times, all we can know of any sex. Sex, as Woolf argues again in *A Room of One's Own*, is not to be known and identified in measurable 'nuggets of pure truth'. Sex is an anxious, unfinished question, and upon the exquisite trauma of our incomplete sexualities, pleasure fitfully rests. The sex of feminism and its cultural products – writing, films, images – is as dubious as Orlando's, but not because, like him/her, it swaps gender or alliance, but because it has helped to pull the carpet of fixed and fitting gender identity out from under us. Women's filmmaking and film-writing today take place in a minefield of questions: detonate one and you blow a whole range of given 'truths' (Woolf's nuggets) to the winds. This, then, is as much a time of questions and experimental uncertainty – not only for the low-budget avant-garde, but in mainstream cinema and criticism too – as it is of consolidation and shoring-up of political and aesthetic gains.

What *is* true is that the stories are changing – only now does a 400-year-long tale of a man becoming woman find its £1 million budget. The master narratives may be rewritten, unpicked, their subjects reinvented, but this does not herald the death of story-telling. There are other stories to be told. One of the big issues of cinema in the late 80s and early 90s has been women's appropria-tion or reassessment of these narratives and motifs: the feminist road movie (*Thelma & Louise*), women with guns (a sub-genre stun-ningly well armed with examples, from *Nikita* to *The Silence of the Lambs*), the fluidity of sexual identity (*Orlando*, *Salmonberries*, even *Just Like a Woman*), or the deconstructed or reinvented family. New family romances are legion, with a number of anxiously reworked Oedipal narratives coming to the fore, and here I am thinking not only of the infantilism of Hollywood's obsessive return to a range of contradictory images of childhood in recent baby boom films, but of any number of masculinity-in-crisis films, as well as the conflict of Ripley and the Alien queen as good and bad mother images, or Linda Hamilton's central speech in *Terminator 2*, which bleakly posits Arnie the cyborg as the perfect father. As Manohla Dargis puts it, 'On this trip, when women drive, Oedipus spins out of control.'

So what happens when marginalised or repressed stories come to the fore? What happens when fantasies of power or tales of dif-ference which have hitherto been subtextual figures in the carpet of older film-making styles become the conscious, overt, mar-ketable stuff of mainstream cinema? We need to ask this question not because 'women have arrived' (as the pathetic celebration of women in film at the 1993 Oscars ceremony evidences), but because feminism has itself become to some extent respectably established elsewhere. Women's studies is now a legitimate academic area in many institutions, while feminist components on courses in film, literature, media, history, law and the social sciences are standard fare. The voices of 'soft' feminism can be heard across the cinematic spectrum, from the soft-porn erotic thriller to the British Board of Film Classification's appropriation of the arguments of liberal fem-inism to justify censorship decisions on the grounds that the films in question might be pernicious to women. Even Michael Winner has entered the fray, with the release of his adaptation of Helen Zahavi's feminist vigilante fable, *Dirty Weekend*. Clearly the insur-gent edge has been lost, but in tandem with this institutionalisation has come a radical sense of all identities and identifications being fundamentally open to question. Feminism has always been disrespectful of institutions, but it is arguably only recently that it has learned to be disrespectful of itself, and that the identity 'feminist' has been questioned along with all other fixed identities. The general move has, then, been from calling for a voice, a space, an integrated and publicly powerful subjectivity, to calling that subjectivity itself into question. There is no longer a single feminist (or misogynist) view (was there ever?); the notion of an essential way of viewing or directing as a woman came into doubt almost as soon as it was suggested.

So something has shifted with this growing cultural prominence of women's issues, as the images of the underground or repressed of women's history begin to leak through into the mainstream. This is partly the work of a growing band of women such as Kathryn Bigelow, Penelope Spheeris, Gale Anne Hurd and Lizzie Borden, who, having begun in the margins producing and directing avant-garde shorts or low-budget exploitation movies, moved through to command bigger budgets and took the marginal concerns with them. But it is also the effect of the filtering into mainstream thrillers, horror and erotic films of the questions of sexuality and identity raised undiluted in 70s rape-revenge exploitation films and (what have been called in Britain) 'video nasties', as well as some of the imagery of hardcore pornography, all of which at root address the anxieties of an increasingly demanding and militant feminism. The new identifications these images demand of us are taking place not only in the art houses and avant-garde, but in the narratives of the mainstream, whether we are viewers of the revealing contradictions of the exploitation flick or sex film, desiring against the grain of 'normal' identifications, or of the spectacle of an erotically charged feminist machismo.

Which all adds up to a sense of issues coming slowly out of the closet, a move which suggests a significant shift in the conscious and unconscious life of cinema. Post-modern cinema might rest upon a reversal of the categories 'mainstream' and 'marginal' (with marginal questions and stories becoming mainstream and vice versa), setting up the possibility that the opposition itself is deconstructed by this reversal, thus ceasing to operate. And when the marginal becomes mainstream, the mainstream is pushed to the margins. Masculinity or whiteness are forced to shift over in films such as *Thelma & Louise* or *Mississippi Masala*, a move which radically redefines these dominant identities.

This model of a mainstream collapsing against the growth of its tributaries suggests another discourse which has been extremely important to women writers and film-makers, that of psycho-analysis. Indeed, psychoanalysis relies upon a system of symbolic substitution or metaphorics, wherein that which the unconscious cannot speak leaks through into consciousness. What, then, is at stake once those leakages become the self-consciously fore-grounded stuff of women's cinema, no longer the dark secrets of sex, but the spoken substance of new narratives? What shifts then take place in cinema's unconscious? Metaphors for the unspoken-ness of sex cease to have currency when we all recognise that sex speaks all the time and everywhere, and when its stories are laid bare without suggestion. The leaking, disintegrating boat of the family at the end of Scorsese's *Cape Fear* is now too heavy-handed an image of those splintering structures of repression, the failures and powers of which are by now as familiar as the Freudian slip. We do not need metaphors for things which can be spoken in plain lan-guage, which are becoming the images of prominence, yet it is per-haps in women's cinema more than anywhere else that a new imagistic language is being coined, providing the metaphors for other currents and anxieties which remain beneath.

Our old image of the unconscious figure in the carpet of film or text, to be discovered only if that text is read against the grain, needs radical re-reading once the subtext becomes text, the unconscious conscious, the formerly unspeakable the subject of public dis-course. The essays in this collection look forward to a conscious real-isation on screen, and in the working practices of women in film, of what feminist critique has so far found buried in the contradic-tory images of cinema history. An example lies in the overt repre-sentations of incestuous ties, particularly father-daughter relationships, which have featured recently in French cinema. Here the 'familiar', unconscious reworking of Oedipal themes comes out of the closet through overt, playfully self-conscious representations and storylines. While the results are hardly liberating, their impor-tance lies in their audacity in laying bare structures which under-pin our psychic life.

These shifts in cinematic imagery and emphasis have them-selves taken place in the context of a wider shift in feminist thinking, which might be likened to the differences between the Marquis de Sade's two most famous heroines, Justine and Juliette, the violated puritan and the indulgent libertine. While Justine's identity is constructed around her revulsion and horror of those who oppress and subjugate her (characterising women as victims and arguing through rank opposition), Juliette experiences with pleasure, embracing as intimately as possible the structures of power upon which sexual difference rests, deconstructing the difference from the inside. The analogy, of course, can be most directly mapped on to the debate within women's criticism and film practice around sado-masochism and pornography, with Justines and Juliettes coming out for and against the powers and pleasures of bondage, domination and visualised sex. From an early critique of woman as sex object has come a reassessment of objectification and an indulgent self-definition through sexuality (even the question, 'what's wrong with being a sex object when you're having sex?'), in the work, for instance, of writer Susie Bright, performer Annie Sprinkle, or young queer film-maker Sadie Benning. Women have long been making a spectacle of themselves in film; a new liberationist strain is embracing the move to make that spectacle more gloriously disgraceful on women's own terms.

A more general shift in thinking from Justine's defence of achieved identity to Juliette's willingness to have identity dismembered has also taken place. Whether we are willing to rest in Juliette's amoral, all-questioning shoes is currently under review. From the crisis articulated by the aesthetic relativism of post-modernism and a larger sense of ethical aporia, perhaps a single question is formed: what is *not* questionable? Is there an ethical or sexual bedrock which cinema should rest upon or try to uncover? Are there any 'truths' which can or will never be up for grabs?

This is clearly a question posed on the cusp of cultural change, as one set of concerns pushes towards a limit. The historical shift from J. Lee Thompson's original 1962 *Cape Fear* to Scorsese's 1991 remake traces this erosion of fixed values, so that by the second version, good and bad are more or less relative terms. The definitively bad Robert Mitchum is replaced by the indefinitely amoral Robert De Niro, and cinema seems to catch up with Nietzsche, a hundred years later and somewhere beyond good and evil.

What lies beyond that is the issue of the moment. There is a turn in *Orlando* where our heroine enters a maze in the eighteenth century and emerges from it in the nineteenth. The difficult transition of a century's change, and how to represent that cinematically, is at stake, both in the film itself and in a feminist film practice encountering an apocalyptic *fin de siècle*. Our own moment's maze, and the route it offers forward, is being currently played out not between cuts, through the witty convenience of an elegant puzzle, or in the margins of the industry, but on the screens of contemporary women's cinema and writing.

Richard Dyer

The colour of virtue: Lillian Gish, whiteness and femininity

Stars are things that shine brightly in the darkness. The word 'star' has become so taken for granted as meaning anyone who's a little bit famous in a little bit of the world that we're apt to forget just how appropriate the term was for people who did seem to be aglow on stages and screens in darkened halls. And no star shone more brightly in that firmament than Lillian Gish.

We may well mistake Gish's importance in film history. In the silent period, other women stars were bigger – Mary Pickford especially, but also Theda Bara and names still less familiar now such as Blanche Sweet, Norma Talmadge, Clara Kimball Young and Anita Stewart, all of whom often eclipsed Gish's place in the public imagination. It is partly because she was a star for so long that we now accord her such importance: she was still making it impossible for you to take your eyes off her in the 40s (*Duel in the Sun*, 1946), 50s (*The Night of the Hunter*, 1955), 60s (*The Unforgiven*, 1960), 70s (*A Wedding*, 1978) and 80s (*The Whales of August*, 1987) and she was always a wonderful interviewee who could bring early cinema to life. Our enthusiasm may also have to do with the fact that her acting seems so minimalist compared to that of many of her contemporaries, closer to a later aesthetic of screen performance in which not betraying the fact that one is acting is deemed such a virtue. And it is certainly because of her association with D. W. Griffith and the heroic place in the development of film that even the most revisionist histories accord him. Yet perhaps none of that would carry much weight if, when you see her in the Griffith films or *La Bohème* (1926), *The Scarlet Letter* (1926) or *The Wind* (1928) she did not radiate the screen. She is the apotheosis of the metaphor of stardom, a light shining in the darkness.

There is a scene in *True Heart Susie* (1919) which encapsulates the relationship between stardom and light, a relationship at once technical, aesthetic and ethical. The film tells of a country girl, Susie (Gish), who puts her true love William (Robert Harron) through college, only to have him marry a city girl, Bettina. Susie has to go to the party at which William announces his marriage; she knows that Bettina is also carrying on with a city boy, Sporty Malone. The establishing shot of the sequence has the party in full swing and Susie/Gish entering and sitting on a chair down screen right, where she remains throughout the sequence, looking at the party, at William and Bettina. The sequence cuts to other characters, to reactions to the wedding announcement, but keeps coming back to Susie/Gish, in close-up or in the original establishing set-up. This is lit from the front, with some extra fill and back light on Gish; she is more in the light.

The light is firstly an adjunct to storytelling: it emphasises Gish's narrative importance as the star and main character of the film; it enables us to see her better. The fill and back light create depth by making Gish stand out a little from the party further back in the image, while also placing her clearly in relation to what is unfolding. Fill and back light also beautify her, creating a subtle halo effect and bringing out the fairness of her hair; the use of make-up too gives her face a seamless white glow. This beauty is in turn a moral value, the aura of her true heart. There is, in other words, a special relationship between light and Gish: she is more visible, she is aesthetically and morally superior, she looks on from a position of knowledge, of enlightenment – in short, if she is so much lit, she also appears to be the source of light.

Such treatment is the culmination of a history of light that has many strands. The association of whiteness and light – of white light – with moral values goes far back. In classical Greek art, female figures are paler than male, as befits those whose proper place is in the home, a notion taken to angelic extremes in Victorian domestic ideology and imagery. Christian art has long emphasised the radiance of the pure white bodies of Christ, the Virgin, the saints and angels. Enlightenment and post-Enlightenment philosophy stressed the intrinsic transcendent superiority of the colour white, notions that were grafted on to nineteenth-century biological accounts of racial difference. The celebration of women in painting during the same period etherealised the body, drawing upon the translucent imagery of Madonnas, angels, nymphs and sprites.

Photography brought a special quality to such imagery – as images printed on white paper, photographs always show people as partly transparent, as ghost-like, a characteristic readily capitalised upon in nineteenth-century portraiture and fairy set-pieces. Some of this imagery was found in the theatre too, in the romantic ballet, the féerie and pantomime. Here the star metaphor really begins to take hold. With the introduction of gas lighting, the difference between the auditorium and stage was emphasised, with all light in the latter. Developments in make-up, costume (notably the tutu) and directional lighting made it possible to make the female performer the focus of light, to be suffused with light or to reflect and thus apparently emanate it. Film took all of this and intensified it; the halls could be darker and the images on the screen were always of people with light shining through them. Provided they were white people.

Film developed its own codes of lighting, with the female star as centrepiece and Lillian Gish as a supreme yet typical example. By the 20s the norm for correct lighting in Hollywood was what was known as 'North' lighting, light from the land of white people. The tendency for fair hair to look dark (too dark) in black-and-white photography was overcome by using back lighting. Three-point lighting, soft light, gauzes and focus could all be employed to create the haloes and glows of feminine portraiture.

Even in contemporary cinema, if you look for it, and quite noticeably in silent cinema, there is often a change of lighting between a general shot of a scene and a close-up or two-shot within it. It is here particularly that the specialness of stardom, or of the experience of romance, is signalled. There is a scene in *Way Down East* (1920), for instance, where Anna (Gish) comes to the Bartlett family farm; she has been wandering the country, having been abandoned by the man who married her in a false ceremony and having lost her child at birth. She enters at the back of the set, which in the establishing shot is in even, outdoor light. But when the film cuts to a close-up of her, a gauze over the camera, side lighting and an iris all create the beauty of pathos. There is cross-cutting between her and the Bartlett son (Richard Barthelmess), whom she will eventually marry. Both are gorgeous and treated to special, glamorising lighting – but he is shot against a dark background with a close black iris, leaving little light around him, whereas she is fully in the light against a light background and wearing a hat that suggests a halo. When she speaks to father Bartlett, who is suspicious of this waif, both stand in the full sunlight and wear hats of much the same size – but his casts his face in shadow, whereas her face, with some extra fill light no doubt, remains radiantly white, with the hat still a halo, not a shade.

Many lighting set-ups were developed for the depiction of the heterosexual couple, frozen to perfection in production stills (a neglected factor in the construction of film-historical memory). There is the soft haze that envelops the couple, with often a subtle fill radiating the woman's face so that the man appears to be wrapped up in her glow. Or there is the head-and-shoulders close-up, with the man darkly dressed and only his shirt collar and face white and light, while the woman is lightly dressed, but even lighter around the face. He rears up out of the darkness, but she is already in the light. That light comes from behind his head, magically catching the top of his hair but falling full on her face, itself an unblemished surface of white make-up which sends the light back on to his face. Barthelmess and Gish in *Way Down East*, Harron and Gish in *True Heart Susie*, Lars Hanson and Gish in *The Scarlet Letter*: she is the angel of light who can redeem his carnal yearning.

Lillian Gish could be considered the supreme instance of the confluence of the aesthetic-moral equation of light, virtue and femininity with Hollywood's development of glamour and spectacle. She may also be its turning point. Very soon the radiance of femininity came to be seen as a trap for men, not a source of redemption – Louise Brooks in *Pandora's Box*, Rita Hayworth in *Gilda*, Sharon Stone in *Basic Instinct*. Even when it wasn't that, its artifice, its materiality, its lack of spirituality have become more and more evident, taken to a post-modern apogee by the so artfully named Madonna. Lillian Gish, however, simply was a Madonna, as indeed Monte Blue observed: 'She is the madonna woman, and greater praise no man can give.'

Gish's place in this history of light is not mere chance. The weight of association and the careful assemblage of light have to 'take' on the figure to which they are applied. One could throw all the light one wanted on any number of attractive and talented young white women and not come up with Lillian Gish. This does

**Darkness and light: Lars Hanson and
Lillian Gish in 'The Scarlet Letter' (1926)**

not mean that no one else could have held an equivalent place in the history, but that nonetheless there had to be qualities which could carry these light values.

Gish's face and body have characteristics that suggest both the steeliness and the simplicity of virtue, which is to say that she embodies the values of feminine white light. Because having eyes larger than one's mouth was a touchstone of female beauty, and because this was not the case with Gish, she purses her mouth, keeps it closed – not intensely (which would suggest anxiety or neurosis) but poisedly – eliminating the lasciviousness of the opened mouth and suggesting primness or purity, according to taste (people found her both). Her carriage is erect, worthy of a ballet dancer, recalling the dictum of turn-of-the-century deportment (stand up straight, shoulders back) – to me a very New England look suggesting Quaker piety, Puritan simplicity. If it didn't seem ungracious, I would compare her aesthetically to a Shaker chair.

Thus her appearance has a sinewy and unfrilly quality that has its own particular historical and cultural resonances. These are carried equally by her performance style. She is thin and small, and sometimes that also means painfully frail, not least in *Broken Blossoms* (1919) as she cringes away from her abusive father or from the moment of lust that passes over the face of the Yellow Man before his own goodness reasserts itself. Yet her toughness is at least as legendary, braving the ice flows without a double in *Way Down East*, facing up to the remorseless sand blows of *The Wind*, facing down Robert Mitchum in *The Night of the Hunter*. Her body and face are mobile and flexible when necessary, an astonishing range of nuances may play over her face in a single shot: she can if need be let herself go to heights of joy, abjection or dementia – yet the formal means used remain small and uncomplicated. I want to put her alongside Willa Cather, Margot Fonteyn or Ella Fitzgerald, artists able to imply depths of feeling through spare, limpid means. With Gish, this toughness and limpidity, this steeliness and simplicity, is of a piece with the prevalent conceptions of light, virtue and femininity. Her body and performance can seem to emanate the same qualities the light is moulding. This is why all that white light took so breathtakingly, why she shines so compellingly in the dark.

There is one film that acts like a hiccup in accounts of Lillian Gish's career. It cannot be avoided – it makes a loud noise – but it is quickly passed over. This is *The Birth of a Nation* (1915). It certainly is not her finest hour – *True Heart Susie*, *Broken Blossoms*, *Orphans of the Storm* (1921), *The Scarlet Letter* or *The Wind* among her silent features may vie for that honour – but it does make explicit the concatenation of gender, race and light that is key to her stardom.

The Birth of a Nation recounts the history of the Civil War and the Reconstruction period through the intertwined stories of two families, the Southern Camerons and the Northern Stonemans. Gish plays Elsie Stoneman, who becomes the sweetheart of Ben Cameron (Henry B. Walthall). It is tempting to treat the relation between the history and the love story in terms of the former disrupting the latter, lovers torn apart by ideology and reunited by the triumph of right (in this case, white supremacy). In part this is undoubtedly correct. Elsie and Ben do not meet until after the war, but her father is a Northern congressman committed to civil liberties in the South; when she discovers Ben's involvement with the Ku Klux Klan, she has to break off the relationship; it is only when the black population have been revealed to Elsie and her father in their true colours (as it were), and Ben and the KKK have routed the population, that the couple can be reconciled.

Yet there is more to it than this. Gish as Elsie represents the white womanhood that must be won for the South, she incarnates the ideal that the South is presented as fighting to defend. What is most evidently at stake in *The Birth of a Nation* is not an economy based on slave labour or even hatred of black people, but an ideal of purity as embodied in the white woman.

Ben first sees Elsie in a miniature her brother Phil shows him. As an inter-title puts it, she is 'the ideal of his dreams'; before she is a real person, she is an essence. When he meets her, she is in an iris shot which echoes the oval of the miniature. He shows her this, saying that he has carried her about with him 'for a long, long time'. She figures for Ben, the representative of the South, as the embodiment of an ideal.

Her goodness is established for us before this, from the first shot of her in the film. She is with her father and is the very model of a dutiful daughter, tending to his needs, making him the centre of her attention. Stoneman represents white liberalism; in this most biological of films, he is therefore bald and lame and has a 'weakness' for a woman of mixed race. In the first shot of Elsie and him, most of her energy is put into fussing with his toupee, endlessly drawing attention to his lack of hair (and, by contemporary implication, of virility). There is something both comic and perverse about this image of filial devotion, this ministering to what the film constructs as crippled. When Elsie rides with Ben in the KKK parade at the end and in the final lovers' tableau, she has passed from her father's helpmate to being her husband's, which in part signifies that Ben (the South) has rescued her (purity) from the sickness of the North.

But he has also rescued her from something else, a fate worse than death: marriage to a man of mixed race (Silas Lynch). This itself can be seen as a product of her father's weakness, for he has promoted Lynch politically and even looks pleased when Lynch tells him he wants to marry a white woman – until he realises that the woman is his own daughter. He has created the conditions which put her in jeopardy and too late learns the error of his ideas. In the famous and thrilling climax, three elements are intercut: Lynch menacing Elsie into a forced 'marriage'; the Cameron family besieged in a small log cabin by rebellious blacks; the gathering and riding of the Klan to the rescue. Elsie and the Camerons clearly symbolise the Southern ideals the Klan is about to redeem. The focus on Elsie, on the sexualisation of her plight in the race war, not only intensifies the drama – giving Ben, the leader, a personal investment in the situation – but also makes it clear that what the Klan stands for is the protection of white femininity.

The manipulation of light is less elaborated than in some of Gish's later films, but she and Ben do get the enveloping romantic treatment and she is picked out in scenes and has altered lighting for close-ups. What is at first sight surprising is that it is she, a Northerner, who is so glorified and not either of the Cameron daughters. Margaret (Miriam Cooper), the elder of these, is dark and oddly (indeed interestingly) sour looking. The younger, Flora (Mae Marsh), is excitable and nervy. Neither has Elsie/Gish's stillness and sureness, something brought out amusingly by her startled reaction to Flora's excessively affectionate greeting when they meet for the first time. It is these qualities – Gish's Northern steely simplicity of purity – that the film lauds, not the more debilitating forms of Southern femininity.

Yet this is, in fact, crucial to the film's project, which is, as we tend curiously to forget, to depict the birth, the coming into being, of a new entity, a nation. The fact that Elsie is a Northerner, quite apart from the association of the North with white light, is important in achieving a healing of the breach opened up by the Civil War. When she rides in the KKK parade, the nation is finally born, its unity assured under the banner of Southern values. She is the prize exhibit in the new white nation.

Gish's demeanour and style catch and reflect a way of seeing light that has deep roots in western tradition, roots distinguishable but not extricable from ways of seeing racial (and gender) difference. She is a great white star from a period when you had to be white to be a mass-market star. Paul Robeson or Lena Horne, Whoopi Goldberg or Wesley Snipes are routinely referred to as black stars, yet I still feel I am going to be thought out of order when I start talking about Lillian Gish as a white star. What it suggests is that a white star's magic is no less socially particular than a black star's. Yes, indeed, and the sooner white people accept the particularity of their image ideals the better – but that doesn't mean there's no magic, white or black. It takes nothing away from Gish – not her talent and intelligence, not the spell of her shining up there in the dark – to say that her special glow is nonetheless a specifically white one.

First published in August 1993 (volume 3, number 8).

Gertrud Koch

Exorcised: Marlene Dietrich and German nationalism

The unification of East and West Germany, which ushered in the last decade of the twentieth century, was followed by two remarkable events that brought Berlin back into the limelight. The mortal remains of two famous Prussians were to be returned to their native soil: Frederick the Great (1712–1786) and Marlene Dietrich (1901–1992).

'Old Fritz' might have been dead for over 200 years, but he lived on in popular memory in the dual incarnations of the strong military leader who fought fiercely to defend the conquests made at the beginning of his reign, and as an *homme de lettres*, musician and correspondent of Voltaire. During the Second World War his remains were transferred to a safe place as a 'national monument' and were then stored in the west for safe-keeping during the Cold War. Their ceremonial return to Sanssouci Castle in Berlin was staged like a set from Disneyworld, with the nineteenth-century railway train carrying his remains chugging its way through the reunited German lands.

The same firm of undertakers was also responsible for the interment of Marlene Dietrich. Both celebrities enjoy a definite, if different, place in the political symbolism of German culture, with a common low point between 1933 and 1945, when Frederick featured largely on the cinema screens of the Nazi era, played chiefly by Otto Gebühr, as the great advocate of tenacity on the battlefield, while Dietrich went over to the other side and became an American citizen whose first return to Germany was in the company of US combat troops.

When Frederick's remains were brought to Berlin as the 'common legacy' of the reunited German states, the event sparked debates about his desirability as a popular symbol. But unity seemed at least to ensure that the feared (or desired) reaction to the funeral was not too vociferous, and public enthusiasm seemed decently restrained. All the more astonishing, then, was the discord that accompanied Dietrich's burial. 'The reactions to this funeral are extreme,' an employee of the undertaker told Berlin's *Tageszeitung*. 'Our company buried Old Fritz as well. But it wasn't like this. There have been ugly letters and threatening phone calls.' When, to many people's surprise, she asked to be laid to rest in Berlin, next to her mother, Marlene Dietrich, who proudly cited the Prussian virtues as the secret of her success and who had never played down her origins in the family of a Prussian officer, was hounded to the grave.

The attitude of the people of Berlin to Marlene Dietrich – if not the attitude of Marlene Dietrich to Berlin – has been subject to much interpretation. Berlin's city council promised a dignified memorial and funeral service, at which it would be clearly expressed that it was proud to give the international star a final resting place, and which would obscure the memory of the vituperative welcome given Dietrich by the people of Berlin in the 60s. But the promised flowers – metaphorical and real – were missing. Admittedly some florists had ordered up large numbers of red roses, which they distributed themselves to passing mourners, but the public ceremony to which friends and fellow-stars were to be invited was called off at the last minute.

According to dissenting diplomatic statements, the reasons lay not with the Cannes Film Festival, which supposedly meant that the major stars were too busy to attend, but rather in the political arena. The vox pops included voices that still considered Dietrich a 'traitor to her country', a star who had pledged allegiance to the Stars and Stripes and come back to Germany in an American uniform. The politicians hid their anxiety behind excuses about the lack of time for preparation, which were dismissed by the theatre management commissioned to stage the event. They complained that at the last minute the city politicians were simply unprepared to put enough money into the event, as the financial commitment would have required a greater degree of political legitimation than German history was willing to bestow on the émigrée. In the end, in a form of political victory for the emergent right, it did not appear prudent for as much money to be spent on Dietrich as on the Prussian king.

But why did Dietrich remain an effective political symbol for so many years? Why should she be regarded so ambivalently, despite the official desire for her merits as a committed opponent of National Socialism to be acknowledged? The few returning émigrés and politically active resistance fighters were treated after 1945 with suspicion and hatred, and ostracised. They included both Willy Brandt and Marlene Dietrich. To anyone who remembers the smear campaigns that afflicted Willy Brandt as Mayor of Berlin and Federal Chancellor, it will come as no surprise that Dietrich too provoked ambivalent reactions on her few visits to the Federal Republic. Her political involvement touched a raw nerve; she had, after all, taken sides against Nazism on the simplest possible grounds: that it did not take any great knowledge or insight to be opposed to a regime that gassed little children and presented the fact as a heroic deed. When she fought beside the American troops during the war, she did so because she believed that all Germans were guilty for this war, and so felt obliged, as a German, to shoulder responsibility for it by standing side by side with the Allies and helping to bring it to an end.

What Dietrich did was to highlight the incomprehensible scandal that the overwhelming majority of Germans, if they had not actively supported the National Socialist regime, had nonetheless condoned it. The fact that they had in the process broken fundamental rules of humanity and humaneness, a crime formulated by the judges at the Nuremberg trials, was given a new form in Dietrich's repeated reference to Kant's Categorical Imperative ('Act only on that maxim through which you can at the same time will that it should become universal law'), in a manner so plain, a child could have understood it.

One of the ideas current in the 50s, designed to make the fearsome learning process psychologically easier, was of the entire, childlike German people in thrall to an all-powerful seducer whom they were helpless to oppose. And the fact that Dietrich, the glamorous seductress, had remained immune to Nazi offers to return to the greater glory of Germany on her homeland's cinema screens, and instead greeted the German Jewish emigrants from the studios in Babelsberg and the Berlin theatre with open arms, divided her more deeply than anything else from the German audience. Not only did she embody the idea of the 'better Germany' and a counter-force to the rigid marches of Leni Riefenstahl's *Triumph of the Will*, but also, unlike Riefenstahl, she was not Hitler's 'relative being', almost his favourite daughter, but instead the ruler of a different Empire, with different needs.

Prussia's martial fantasies are clearly influenced by an imaginary 'topography of the sexes' (Sigrid Weigel): a pole of paranoid male purity, in relation to which women are grouped either as 'relative beings' of the male (Sartre), their function determined in relation to him, or as exotic invaders and seducers whose sensuality is a destructive threat. Dietrich played a historical part in this projective topography of nations, races and sexes, and the coincidence of her departure for Hollywood with the rise of National Socialism turned her portrayal of Lola in Josef von Sternberg's *The Blue Angel* (1930) into an image iconic of both memory and leaving: the image of a woman as openly sexual and lascivious as she is motherly; an image that died, along with the Weimar Republic, in National Socialism.

The intensity with which this image affected contemporary viewers as a *promesse de bonheur* is readily apparent in reviews and descriptions of the film. It is no coincidence that Berlin's *Tageszeitung* printed a previously unpublished text by Franz Hessel from the 20s on the occasion of Dietrich's death. It contained the following passage: 'Those dangerous women incarnated by Marlene Dietrich do not give one the feeling that they mean too much harm. As cheery Lola from the Blue Angel, she takes the schoolteacher's ruffled, bearded head in her kind and maternal hands, pats the cheeks of this man so tenderly enchanted by her as though he were a child, looks up at her poor victim with a bridal smile when he makes this supremely unworthy woman his wife, and smiles him his dream of pure happiness.'

The strong maternal aura described by Hessel could only work with an image of motherliness that did not eschew sexuality. A highly ambivalent image, certainly, just as most of Dietrich's images are ambiguous, playing with sex without repressing it. In Sternberg's *Blonde Venus* (1932) she also plays a mother-whore figure, who becomes the projected ideal of her own son and of a series of other men. And later, Orson Welles works with the same image in *Touch of Evil* (1958): older now, and somewhat the worse for wear, she holds a cooking pot in her shabby room with the same nonchalant expression with which she wears her sensational dress.

If we read, against Hessel's yearning description from the 20s, a post-war review of one of Dietrich's London appearances from a German-language newspaper, it is striking how strongly eroticism is now portrayed as betrayal, prostitution as business, Dietrich as an old procuress, as if a clearly pejorative attitude had to be enforced to counteract the ambivalence of the old maternal image: 'To hear Marlene's "whisky-tenor" and get a glimpse under her skirts, sent soaring by a sophisticated wind machine,' complained a tabloid article, 'you pay a good 1400 Schillings a ticket... Marlene, not only "the most charming grandmother in the world" but also dazzlingly good at calculation, is well aware of this. In the end, her life was not led only for "falling in love again" but just as much for money' (*Der Mittag*, 16 October 1956). These lines reveal not only their hatred for the successful woman, but also overflow with anti-British and misogynist sentiment. The woman with the 'whisky- tenor' was clearly not a real woman (with a proper soprano voice); her appearance and charm were all calculated, a mechanical means of seduction from Britain's foreign shores.

Dietrich's discovery was not the secret sexuality of the mother figure, but an image of bisexuality which, counter to all her assertions, was part of her aura from Berlin of the 20s – in her performances with Margo Lion, for example. So it should come as no surprise that much of her audience throughout was drawn from various subcultures. That her funeral in Berlin became a catwalk for the city's transvestites transformed it into a lively affair, while her appropriation by the lesbian and feminist subcultures has sought to release her from the image of a female icon designed for the male gaze.

But the fact that Dietrich could be received in this way, regardless of what she might have thought of it herself, together with the ironically fragmented non-identity of her roles and portrayals, led to accusations of ambivalence in Germany. She might have been a star during the regrettably short-lived Weimar Republic; she might have been a star in 20s Berlin; she might always have stressed her German origins – but she did not become a German star in her lifetime: Germany had exorcised images of women like her from its culture at least by the time of National Socialism. And Marlene's homecoming, too, was ambivalent. What was at issue is not so much her motives and intentions, her identity or her career, as the internal constitution of the culture from which she derived her formative images.

When a German critic attending a concert by Dietrich in London during the 70s irritably noted that she was singing in German, he invented some adventurous constructions in which, drawing on his Prussian legacy, he experienced the sensuality of her aura as German, and interpreted its Germanic qualities as a kind of 'catalogue of masculinity': 'Whatever the case may be – since that evening it has been clear how incredibly important for Marlene Dietrich's authentic sound is that gutturally hard and sibilant language, the rhythm of those teutonic accents, the aggressive mixture of nuance and command. Perhaps it was only the exotic appeal of hearing the seductress of German singing – still so very German – that made the English audience rapturously applaud her German songs. More important to me was the certainty, both patriotic and depressing, that what Marlene Dietrich expresses in terms of melancholy, brazenness and corrupt pride, she can express only in the German language, and that every English version from "The Blue Angel" to "Where have all the flowers gone?" sounds like a thin copy of the wonderfully strong German original' (*Frankfurter Allgemeine Zeitung*, 12 February 1975).

First published in September 1992 (volume 2, number 5).

Marjorie Garber

From Dietrich to Madonna: cross-gender icons

In the opening moments of Josef von Sternberg's *The Blue Angel,* a complacent Professor Immanuel Rath (Emil Jannings) chirps hopefully towards a corner of his breakfast room, cuing his pet bird into song. Receiving no answering chirp, he advances towards the cage, food morsel in hand. Sorrow and surprise cross his face; without a word he withdraws the body of the dead bird and hands it to his housekeeper, who receives it matter-of-factly and drops it in the fire. 'No more singing,' she says. 'No more singing.'

The death of Marlene Dietrich, the glamorous and seductive star whose international career as a singer and sex symbol was launched by *The Blue Angel*, has called forth eulogies and tributes from every corner of the globe. No caged bird, Dietrich gained her fame through a combination of good looks, good timing, wartime gallantry, unerring professionalism and an indefinable star quality. The singing itself was not so much the point – although *The Times* of London described her voice as 'reminiscent of boots on crushed leaves', an image that suggests the elegant dominatrice she played to such effect in her cabaret scenes. Rather, her fascination lay in the entire ensemble: aloof, indifferent, unapproachable, self-knowing, not a sex object but a sexual and sexualised subject, the narrative and enigma of sex itself.

Critic Kenneth Tynan, whose appreciative words were cited in virtually every obituary, commented that 'She lives in a sexual no-man's land – and in no woman's either. She dedicates herself to looking, rather than to being, sexy. The art is in the seeming.' 'She has sex but no positive gender,' Tynan noted in his most quotable – and

**Unsettling powers: Marlene Dietrich
performs in 'The Blue Angel' (1930)**

quoted – phrase. 'Her masculinity appeals to women and her sexuality to men.'

Tynan had an eye for cross-gender representations and their relationship to star quality and theatrical power. He once described Laurence Olivier's portrayal of Richard III as that of a 'bustling spinster', and characterised Lady Macbeth as 'basically a man's role', for which it would 'probably be a mistake to cast a woman at all'. But his appraisal of Dietrich has a particular resonance. 'Sex but no positive [that is, determinative] gender.' A 'sexual no-man's land – and no woman's either.' A 'masculinity' that appeals to women, and a 'sexuality' (not a 'femininity') that appeals to men.

Dietrich's reputation, Dietrich's image, is built on this structure of cross-gender representation. There is the nightclub singer Amy Jolly in *Morocco* (1930), who performs in top hat and tails, insouciantly kisses a woman in the audience on the lips, and offers legionaire Gary Cooper a rose, which he tucks behind his ear. Then in *Blonde Venus* (1932), entertainer Helen Faraday – because she is a devoted mother and, intermittently, wife – resumes her stage career and in effect 'quotes' her own performance in *Morocco*, although this time the hat and tails are light-coloured rather than dark, and the flirtation with women takes place onstage rather than off, as a slinky line of 'Arab' dancing girls makes its way past her and she takes one by the sleeve, pinching her on the cheek, all the while waving her long cigarette holder in a parody of phallic power. In *Seven Sinners* (1940), the itinerant, incendiary singer Bijou dons a naval officer's uniform, complete with cap, epaulets and necktie, to sing 'The Man's in the Navy' to an enraptured crowd of officers, patrons and sailors. 'Mister, watch your wife/The man's in the navy,' she croons – and the seductive danger of the 'man' in question is posed, pre-eminently, by the cross-dressed figure before us, rather than by the officers to whom she is, deliberately and calculatingly, addressing her flattering words.

No wonder, then, that Dietrich became so quickly, and so completely, the index both of gender crossover and star power. She is quoted and copied everywhere, from mainstream movies to female impersonators. Her presence – or even her evocation – has itself become a sign of the provocative destabilisation of gender that is the very signature of the erotic.

In Luchino Visconti's *The Damned* (1969), for example, Helmut Berger in the role of the decadent Martin von Essenbeck appears as

Dietrich in her *Blue Angel* role, complete with top hat, feather boa, garter belt and stockings, and the obligatory bentwood chair tilted back, scandalising his staid relatives at a family entertainment as he belts out a torch song about 'ein Mann'. When news of the burning of the Reichstag is announced, forcing him to break off his performance, he petulantly strips away his blonde wig; this is the first time the cinema audience learns that he is not a woman. Is Dietrich more 'ein Mann', in the song's terms, than Martin? The film will tacitly test this out, at the same time as it will show the 'healthy' homosexuality of young boys in a Nazi youth camp. Martin/Marlene is made the signifier of perversity, not merely of sexuality. But then this has always been her paradoxical – and enigmatic – power.

Liza Minnelli as the wannabe-decadent Sally Bowles in *Cabaret* (1972), set in Weimar Berlin, straddles an identical chair, and brandishes her legs and her bowler hat. The stage show in which she appears, MC-ed by the sinister Joel Grey with his rictus of a smile, contains another, less predictable and far more offensive crossover representation – the 'heroine' of Grey's mock love song, 'If You Could See Her with My Eyes', a bashful girl-gorilla in a pink tutu. (The song's punchline, a reminder of the anti-semitism already rife in pre-Nazi Germany, completes the refrain 'If you could see her with my eyes... she wouldn't look Jewish at all.') Any Dietrich fan would be reminded not only of Lola in *The Blue Angel*, but also of the famous gorilla suit in *Blonde Venus*, from which, in the course of a song called 'Hot Voodoo', the cool and incontrovertibly Aryan Marlene skilfully emerges.

Or consider yet another moment of screen homage, Raquel Welch's appearance as a transsexual in *Myra Breckinridge* (1970), Michael Sarne's over-the-top film of Gore Vidal's novel. As the seductive and meretricious Myra (formerly Myron), Welch appears in a naval uniform that is the twin of Dietrich's in *Seven Sinners* – and, in fact, is introduced in this regalia, to ensure the legibility of the quotation, by a clip from the earlier film, a few frames and bars of 'The Man's in the Navy'. The few frames are enough to disclose and (disclothe) the difference between one 'man' and another: where Welch's Myra – now employed as a teacher of 'posture and empathy' to aspiring actors she seduces and humiliates – seems merely camp, the compelling elegance and eroticism of Dietrich comes through even – or especially – in the grainy clip.

But perhaps the most effective recent homage to Dietrich has been that of Madonna, another 'blonde Venus' and mega-entertainer, whose name rivals the earlier singer's own for paradox, pertinence (or impertinence) and power. Maria Magdalena was Dietrich's given name – Mary Magdalene – a name she shortened to Marlene in part because her family objected to her going on the stage. Mary Magdalene, the whore with the heart of gold – and Madonna, the virgin, as 'hot' as Dietrich is 'cold', as funky as Dietrich is glamorous, yet each in her own way, and for her own time, cheekily, effectively seductive.

Madonna has over and over again quoted from Dietrich's great performances. The classic bentwood chair moment from *Blue Angel* is recreated as a solo porn peek-show for 'Open My Heart'. The double-breasted, man-tailored suit, complete with monocle and dominatrice disdain in 'Express Yourself' is the essence of Dietrich. Even the Madame de Pompadour hoop-skirt (complete with naughty ruffled panties) in which Madonna performed her 'Vogue' dance number for the 1990 Music Video Awards show quotes Lola in her dressing room – just as the song's lyric lauds 'Greta Garbo and Monroe, Dietrich and DiMaggio' as icons of glamour for today's woman – and man.

A hit song of the pre-Madonna era that still resonates for fans and adepts of transgender performance tells the story of the singer's encounter in a club in London's Soho with a figure who 'walked like a woman and talked like a man.' 'Girls will be boys and boys will be girls,' runs the lyric. This 1970 hit by The Kinks was called – and was about – the erotic power of 'Lola'. 'It's a mixed-up muddled-up shook-up world – except for Lola.' The Lola of the Berlin club called the Blue Angel is still very much alive, extolling the ambivalent and terrifying pleasures of falling in love again.

No more singing? *Au contraire.* See what the boys in the back room will have... and tell them I'm having the same.
First published in September 1992 (volume 2, number 5).

Berenice Reynaud

Glamour and suffering: Gong Li and the history of Chinese stars

A bride is carried in a traditional red palanquin along the road that leads to the winery. Aware that the groom is a leper, her young porters jolt and make fun of her. The procession is stopped by a highwayman, who robs the porters and musicians and lifts the red veil that covers the bride. The unexpected, lustful smile of the heroine illuminates the screen, revealing, in her perfect face, two irregularly shaped front teeth like large pearls encased in velvet. With this smile, 22-year-old Gong Li became an overnight star.

To cast the female lead of his 1987 feature *Red Sorghum*, director-Pygmalion Zhang Yimou interviewed scores of theatre students before he met Gong Li. He then spent three days spying on her while Gong, unaware, performed for her teacher. Their subsequent romance delighted the readers of the scandal sheets from Beijing to Hong Kong, as Zhang's wife noisily refused him a divorce. For years Zhang and Gong lived miles apart, in their respective work units, together only when they made movies.

Zhang obsessively cast Gong in a series of melodramatic situations (*Ju Dou*, 1990; *Raise the Red Lantern*, 1991) in which his camera lingered on her beauty and the exquisite mixture of pain and sensuality she expressed. The international success of the three films turned Gong into a celebrity abroad as well. Meanwhile, she had her teeth fixed to conform to the standard Hollywood smile and posed for pin-up calendars. The first Chinese star to appear in *Elle*, she is mobbed in the streets at home – Chinese spectators want to touch their idols – and wooed by Hong Kong producers. Her fourth major film with Zhang Yimou, *The Story of Qiu Ju* (1992), in which she plays an unglamorous, heavily pregnant, touchingly obstinate heroine, displays another facet of her talent. Happy in love as in her work – Zhang is now divorced – the woman whose face 'makes men weak and women longing' (Scarlet Cheng, *South China Morning Post*) has become hot property indeed.

Mainland China has no shortage of talented actresses, but in spite of the pressing adoration of Chinese audiences, few can be considered 'stars' in the western sense of the term. In the west, stardom is associated with glamour, fashionable clothes, exotic locations and scandalous love affairs that daily life in Communist China hardly permits. After 1949 film actors, paid a proletarian salary by their work units, were cast as 'cultural workers' involved in the enormous task of turning cinema into a popular art. From this point of view, they were extremely successful: in 1949, 90 per cent of Chinese had never seen a film, whereas by 1982 cinema attendances were as high as 25.5 billion. To enable them to portray working-class or peasant heroines, actresses would work in the fields or factories for months at a time. This in turn contributed to their popularity: identification worked particularly well for audiences able to recognise themselves in the drawn-from-life characters. Stars toured villages and factories for the opening of their films, where they would be surrounded by large crowds who would hail them familiarly by the name of the character they portrayed.

Famous actresses of the period are remembered not for their idiosyncrasies, tragic life stories or extravagant lifestyles, but for their appearance in some masterpiece of Chinese revolutionary cinema: Tian Hua in Shui's *White-Haired Girl* (shot in 1950 and attracting audiences of more than 150 million), Qin Yi in Xie Jin's *Girl Basketball Player No. 5* (1957) and Lin Yang's *Red Seed* (1958), Xie Fang in Xie Tieli's *Early Spring in February* (1963) and Xie Jin's *Two Stage Sisters* (1965). Both *Early Spring* and *Stage Sisters* were violently attacked during the Cultural Revolution, a period when it was no easy thing to be a movie star. Jiang Qing (Mrs Mao), a former second-rate actress, was especially virulent in prosecuting talented performers as 'rightist' or 'decadent'. A tragic case was that of the exquisite Xin Fengxia, an opera star since the age of 14, whose 1951 wedding to film director and playwright Wu Zuguang made the front pages. In 1963 Xin made her film debut as star of *The Rose of Wouke*, a romantic musical written by her husband. In 1966 she was sent to a re-education camp; her health failed and she became paralysed. Wu used

ARTIFICIAL EYE

Glamour and suffering: Gong Li plays the golden-hearted yet bitchy prostitute in 'Farewell to My Concubine' (1993)

her memoirs in one of his plays, *Up Hill and Down Dale*, brought to the screen by Cen Fan in 1984. The plot – abject poverty, impossible love, forced marriage – would fit in a 30s Chinese melodrama.

Even today, Mainland Chinese actresses are unable to reach what we would recognise as stardom except through co-productions. Gong Li would have remained a salaried performer if Japanese, Taiwanese and Hong Kong money hadn't been poured into her career. And as a result of the open door policy instated in 1978, a few other actresses have also managed to reach that goal.

Liu Xiaoqing, who was revealed in Wang Yan's *About Xu Mao and His Daughters* (1981), and went on to star in Ling Zifeng's *Chun Tao* (1987) and Xie Jin's *Hibiscus Town* (1988), is a character larger than life. Still attracting attention for her romance and partnership with the great actor Jiang Wen (he is slightly younger than her, still a taboo in Chinese society), Liu is now in a position to call the shots. When a Hong Kong production company asked her to star in a costume drama, she imposed Fifth Generation director Tian Zhuangzhuang. For the film, *Li Lianying, the Imperial Eunuch* (1991), she aged herself to give a moving performance as the Empress Dowager Cixi – the stuff legends are made of. Less flamboyant, Siqin Gaowa, star of Xie Fei's *Women from the Lake of Scented Souls* (1993) has gradually emerged as one of the strongest actresses of her generation. Yet her hard-won achievements seem possible only through a schizophrenic life: she left behind the children of a previous marriage for seclusion in Switzerland.

The combination of glamour and tragedy is not a new concept for the female star of Chinese cinema. In March 1935, in Shanghai, Ruan Lingyu, a star of the silent era nicknamed 'the Chinese Garbo', committed suicide at the age of 25. The procession following her funeral was five kilometres long, and half a century later she is still remembered with nostalgia. Like Gong Li, Ruan became famous for her portrayal of suffering women. In her most famous film, Wu Yonggang's *The Goddess* (1934), she plays a tough, chain-smoking streetwalker forced into the job to earn money to raise her child. In Sun Yu's *Little Toys* (1933) she is a tough, tender and patriotic 'mother courage' who sacrifices her love interest to her family and becomes mad after losing her children. In Cai Chusheng's *New Women* (1935) she plays a writer who refuses to prostitute herself to pay her daughter's hospital bill. The child dies and, a victim of malicious gossip, the heroine kills herself. The film was inspired by the recent suicide of another female star, Ai Xia, and was Ruan's last screen appearance.

Unlike Gong, who knows how to project a mask of pain while remaining an uncomplicated modern middle-class girl, Ruan – who started her film career as a teenager to avoid the abuse and humiliation of her situation as a maidservant's daughter – did not 'act', but really experienced the feelings she projected on screen. Hence the unaffected emotional charge, poignancy and feistiness of her performance – unable to separate acting from reality, she was consumed by the tragic dimension of her roles.

As the capital of Chinese cinema, Shanghai produced a series of unequalled masterpieces until the Japanese occupation in 1938. The emergence of strong female stars was a result of the fierce competition between the 50-odd production companies. Under contract for a monthly salary, stars became the studios' trademarks. This in itself was a small revolution: in the first Chinese film, *An Unhappy Couple*, directed in 1913 by Zhang Shichuan for an American company, Asia Motion pictures, male theatre actors were cast in the female parts. When Zhang created his own company, he gave the leading role of *The Orphan Saves His Grandfather* (1920) to a 'westernised' secretary, who became the first Chinese female movie star: Wang Hanlun. Zhang also 'discovered' Ruan Lingyu, but his main star was Hu Die, who graced such classics as Zhang's *Tenderness Market* (1933) and *A Bible for Girls* (1934). Another great star was the vivacious Li Lili, who played Ruan's daughter in *Little Toys* and a resilient entertainer in Sun Yu's *Blood on the Volcano* (1932). Stars posed for fan magazines and even for commercial advertisements. Chinese critics claim that unlike their modern counterparts, Shanghai actresses of the 30s have *xiuyang* – a subtle mixture of education, refinement and elegance.

With the Japanese invasion, the war, and the Communist revolution, many film professionals emigrated to Hong Kong. There a new genre was soon born, the Mandarin musical, that was to flourish until the 60s and to generate a new kind of female star: the songstress. Divided between 'sweet' and 'sour' beauties (a picturesque metaphor for the good girl/bad girl dichotomy), songstresses carried the traditional burden of female suffering. Thought to be no better than prostitutes, they were often forced into the profession by unhappy circumstances – poor, raped, pregnant, exploited by cads, forbidden to marry for love.

The sweetest was Zhou Xuan, a singer nicknamed 'the Golden Throat', who had a huge following and starred in many first-rate melodramas in Shanghai, including Yuan Muzhi's masterpiece *Street Angel* (1937). After the war she emigrated to Hong Kong, where her real-life misfortunes inspired the plots of such musicals as *An All-Consuming Love* (1947) and *Orioles Banished from the Flowers* (1949). Bai Guang, the sexiest and sultriest of the Hong Kong 'sour' beauties, became famous as one of the most wicked *femmes fatales* in Chinese cinema. In *Blood-Stained Begonia* (1949), 'she does every despicable thing imaginable except murder. She spends lavishly, forces her husband into a life of crime, abandons her daughter, seduces men, pimps, hits her "girls", she is frequently shot in langorous poses, all the while dangling a steamy cigarette from her scarlet lips.' (Sam Ho, Hong Kong Film Festival.) Another famous 'sour' beauty, Li Lihua, played a series of glamorous singing bitches of the 40s and 50s.

Beyond the sweet/sour dichotomy, the Mandarin musical produced in Hong Kong witnessed the blossoming of a certain form of modernity. As in Hollywood, pop music and dancing embodied the values of youth, as opposed to high art and traditional morality. Even as a 'fallen woman', the songstress was on the side of progress. The stage was set for the emergence of a woman who could sing and dance without having to suffer for it. That happened in *The Mambo Girl* (1957), hailed as 'the best Mandarin musical', which was tailor-made for its star, the spirited Ge Lan (aka Grace Chang). Definitely middle class – with the obligatory plot twist revealing that she was, after all, adopted – the heroine wards off men and the trouble they bring by teaching them to dance the mambo and the cha-cha.

With her dynamism, *joie de vivre* and casual sweaters, Ge's mambo girl echoed European and American youth culture of the late 50s. Even when playing a tragic heroine, she displayed an endearing humour and sense of parody, as in the exhilarating *noir* musical *Wild, Wild Rose* (1960), in which she crones about 'Meeen' and 'Loooove' to the most famous tune of Bizet's *Carmen*.

Ge Lan retired in the mid-60s, at the peak of her career. She left a double legacy. Melodrama, to survive, had to turn to comedy, so most female stars who followed combined acting and singing. The most successful currently is Hong Kong pop goddess Anita Mui. A soft-hearted courtesan-turned-ghost in Stanley Kwan's nostalgic melodrama *Rouge* (1988) and a gun-totting moll in Tsui Hark's thriller *To Live and Die in Saigon* (aka *A Better Tomorrow III*, 1989), she is also an extremely popular singer. Most starlets are 'discovered' through beauty contests, then jump to television and talk shows. Catering to a young audience and still influenced by the classical canons of Chinese beauty, Hong Kong cinema is even more obsessed with fresh, pretty faces than Hollywood. Yet some starlets become brilliant artists, as is the case with Sylvia Chang.

Born in Taiwan, living in Hong Kong and a mega-star in both, Chang appeared in more than 80 movies and worked with the greatest Chinese directors, from kung fu master King Hu in *Legend of the Mountains* (1978) to New Wave wonderkid Tsui Hark in *Shanghai Blues* (1984). Her excellent comic timing and smooth, adolescent beauty made her a queen of the Hong Kong action comedy, but her real love has been auteur films. Although 'almost retired' – despite a physique that would tempt many western performers to carry on playing teenagers – Chang recently made a stunning appearance in Lawrence Ah Mon's *Queen of Temple Street* (1990), shot in the red-light district of Kowloon. Without make-up or fashionable clothes, she plays a working-class madam, a woman who has loved and suffered and is not afraid to fight. Also in Hong Kong, Chang produced *The Secret* (1979), Ann Hui's first feature. In Taiwan she gave Edward Yang his first directing chance, thus contributing, with *That Day on the Beach* (1983) to the launching of a New Wave. She has also tried her hand at directing: the sophisticated portrait of two women in *Passion* (1986) and a comedy starring Gong Li, *Mary from Beijing* (1992).

Many other actresses have turned to producing, the most famous being former kung fu goddess Hsu Feng, discovered in her native Taiwan by King Hu, who gave her the second female role in *Dragon Gate Inn* (1966) when she was only 15. Admired for her cool, glamorous presence and breathtaking acrobatic skills, she was honoured in 1992 by a retrospective at New York's Lincoln Center. The star of many action films, including King Hu's celebrated *A Touch of Zen* (1969), she married a real-estate millionaire and retired – only to start a production company whose latest film is Palme d'Or winner *Farewell to My Concubine* by Fifth Generation director Chen Kaige, starring none other than Gong Li. In *Farewell* Gong starts as the conventional golden-hearted yet bitchy prostitute who gets her man, then ages to become a wife driven to suicide by her husband's betrayal during the Cultural Revolution.

When she works in Mainland China, Gong simply receives a

salary from her studio. In Hong Kong it is another matter. Yet while she is among the top actresses there, Gong is not the most highly paid – that honour falls to Brigitte Lin, who seduced audiences as a 20s heroine donning men's clothes in Tsui Hark's *Peking Opera Blues* (1986). Cast in many action films thanks to her acrobatic talents and beauty, she resumed cross-dressing when Tsui gave her the part of Master Asia, the villain who castrated himself to acquire supernatural kung fu powers, in *Swordsman II* (1992). Half man, half woman, Lin flirts with the hero underwater and in her bedchamber but fights him in the air and on the battlefield – thus suggesting a sexual ambiguity rare in Chinese cinema.

Gong Li – sometimes rumoured to be difficult with journalists – is not the most popular star in Hong Kong either. That would probably be Maggie Cheung – also the first Chinese actress to have won a major international award (Silver Bear in Berlin in 1992 for her portrayal of Ruan Lingyu in Stanley Kwan's *Actress*, aka *Centre Stage*, 1991). Yet in spite of Cheung's magnetism, beauty, winning personality and immense talent, her iconic value pales in front of Gong's. Is it because western audiences are Orientalist at heart, and Cheung is too much of a modern Hong Kong girl to make them dream? For what is remarkable about Gong is not so much her poise and versatility, but her ability to signify Chineseness, femininity and mystery outside her own culture.

There wouldn't be female stars without 'women's directors'. Zhang Yimou might be Sternberg to Gong Li, but Stanley Kwan is the Cukor of Hong Kong. Not only has he given Anita Mui, Sylvia Chang, Maggie Cheung and Siqin Gaowa some of their most fulfilling roles, but he has explored the seductions of female stardom by directing a complex video portrait of Siqin Gaowa and by paying homage to Ruan Lingyu in *Actress*, a film as alluring, fragile and mysterious as its subject.

'I wasn't interested in Ruan's love affairs, but in recovering the golden age of Chinese cinema,' Kwan claims. The film dwells lightly on the reasons that might have drawn Ruan to suicide – her tormented private life, the malicious gossip campaign against her – and leaves intact the myth of glamorised female suffering. If Ruan's memory continues to haunt Chinese viewers, it is both as a symbol of the lost splendour of Shanghai and as a victim of history – of the feudal oppression of women and the poor, Confucian morality and the Japanese invasion. Women suffer a lot in Chinese fiction, especially in troubled times when their pain becomes a metaphor for their country's fate. But Gong Li is fond of asserting that 'women's condition has changed in China', placing a distance between herself and the feudal heroines she plays – not unlike Madonna, who wants a career *à la* Marilyn, but without the barbiturates.

Gong symbolises the film-making of the Fifth Generation – and her collaboration with Zhang Yimou articulates a cultural dilemma. Gong is the same age as the students of the Democracy Movement that ended in the Tiananmen Square massacre; robbed of his adolescence by the Cultural Revolution, Zhang Yimou can vicariously relive his youth through his star/lover. The underlying nostalgia that can be read in the way Gong is framed, marketed and consumed is that of irretrievable loss. This alchemy, whereby Gong comes to represent what she is not, involves a double silence, foreclosing both the Cultural Revolution (his loss) and the 4 June 1989 massacre (her loss, or at least that of her generation).

If Gong Li learns to speak English, Hollywood might open its doors to her – as it did to another Chinese actress, Joan Chen. On the other hand, Ruan Lingyu and the screen goddesses of the 30s, who remain eternally silent, continue to make us dream. What makes a legend most? Good looks, gumption or *xiuyang*? I'll bet on *xiuyang* any day.

First published in August 1993 (volume 3, number 8).

Stephen Bourne

Denying her place: Hattie McDaniel's surprising acts

For playing Scarlett O'Hara's faithful mammy in *Gone with the Wind* (1939), Hattie McDaniel became the first black actress to win an Oscar – and the last for over 50 years until Whoopi Goldberg for her role as 'mammy' to Demi Moore and Patrick Swayze in the 1990 comedy *Ghost*. McDaniel has become closely identified with the role of the mammy – a passive, one-dimensional, comical, non-threatening caricature of black womanhood. Yet in the 70-odd films that made up her career, she also managed to extend, subvert and confound the Hollywood stereotypes of black women.

The mammy caricature found its first representation in the popular fiction, poetry and music of the nineteenth century. Aunt Chloe, the mammy in Harriet Beecher Stowe's novel *Uncle Tom's Cabin* (1852), who is described as having 'a round, black, shining face... Her whole plump countenance beams with satisfaction and contentment from under her well-starched checked turban,' is as good an example as any. Mammy first appeared in Hollywood films in the silent era, including nine versions of *Uncle Tom's Cabin* between 1903 and 1927. Bossy and cantankerous she may be, but her loyalty is never in question, as in D. W. Griffith's Civil War melodrama *The Birth of a Nation* (1915), where mammy, played by a white actress in blackface, continues as a faithful servant to her former white master even after the Civil War and emancipation.

In the silent era most black roles were played by whites in blackface, but with the coming of sound in the late 20s this began to change. Gertrude Howard played Aunt Chloe in the 1927 screen version of *Uncle Tom's Cabin* and subsequently found herself typecast as a mammy in a succession of films, including the first film version of *Show Boat* (1929), in which she played Queenie, and *Hearts in Dixie* (1929). Her most famous role was as Mae West's maid and confidante Beulah Thorndike in *I'm No Angel* (1933), where she is tossed one of the most famous racist remarks ever made to a black woman in the movies: 'Beulah, peel me a grape.' Sadly there is nothing in Howard's portrayal of the submissive, scatterbrained Beulah to counteract the racism of the film.

Following Howard's unexpected death in 1934, McDaniel inherited her crown as Hollywood's favourite mammy. But unlike Howard she defied convention and resisted the stereotype. In spite of her efforts, for some black Americans her presence in the movies was an embarrassment. The *Pittsburgh Courier*, a weekly black newspaper, denounced *Gone with the Wind* for presenting its black characters as 'happy house servants and unthinking, hapless clods'. And during the Second World War, several black film celebrities, including McDaniel, were criticised for perpetuating racist stereotypes. Walter White, executive secretary of the National Association for the Advancement of Colored People (NAACP) collected complaints from black men in the forces, one of whom accused McDaniel and other black actors of lowering the morale of black soldiers, making 'them wish that they were sometimes never even born... I don't like to see my people act as though they were just in America to take up space.' A wartime poll published in *Negro Digest* revealed that while 53 per cent of whites believed that films were fair to black people, 93 per cent of the black people questioned thought otherwise. Though not politically active like contemporaries such as Paul Robeson and Lena Horne, McDaniel responded to her critics by proclaiming that she would rather play a maid than be one. 'What would you expect me to play?', she asked. 'Clark Gable's leading lady?'

In fact, McDaniel often managed to breathe life into the mammy stereotype, and the characters she portrayed were rarely completely submissive or subservient. In film after film, especially in the screwball comedies of the 30s, she gave Aunt Dilsey, Beulah and Delilah a wide range of moods. Admittedly she was always cast as a helpful maid and confidante, a loyal, trusted friend to her white mistresses, but where possible she infused her roles with integrity and depth. Through a remarkable effort of interpretation, and with occasional support from directors such as George Stevens and James Whale, her mammies and maids appeared opinionated, defiant, hostile, flamboyant, camp, assertive and tough.

In her films of the 30s and 40s McDaniel matched just about every major Hollywood movie star. In 1932 in *Blonde Venus*, she hides Marlene Dietrich from a private detective – the first of many roles as friend and protector to a white movie heroine. Black women as confidantes (but not social equals) were featured in numerous Hollywood films of the time, the typical example being Louise Beavers as 'Aunt' Delilah Johnson in *Imitation of Life* (1934). But McDaniel's movie servants were different. In *Alice Adams* (1935) Katharine Hepburn plays a small-town social climber who wants to make an impression on the son of a wealthy family. She invites him to dinner and hires gum-chewing Malena Burns (McDaniel) to cook and serve the meal. Director George Stevens makes clever use of McDaniel to comment on, and make fun of, Hepburn and her family – as Donald Bogle describes it in *Toms, Coons, Mulattoes, Mammies and Bucks*: 'Thus was fixed, in this film, the nature of Hattie McDaniel's relations with her white masters. Through her uproarious conduct, she puts them in their place without overtly offending them... she struts about looking down on them, all the while pretending to be the model servant... thirties audiences knew Hattie McDaniel was putting them on.'

In most of these films McDaniel behaves familiarly with white players, a rare occurrence for a black actor in Hollywood movies at the time. For example, in *China Seas* (1935), when her employer Jean Harlow asks her if she looks like a lady, McDaniel replies: 'I've bin with you too long to insult you that way!' In *Saratoga* (1937) McDaniel reveals her sexual attraction to Harlow's leading man (Clark Gable). 'I'd fix up for him anytime,' she says. 'If he was only the right colour, I'd marry him!' In *The Mad Miss Manton* (1938) she roughly dismisses a (white) telegram boy from Barbara Stanwyck's apartment with the words: 'OK, child. You'd think they'd send an older man up to this apartment' – an assertive wit no real-life black maid would have risked. And there is nothing subtle about her delivery when she answers white people back, as in *Show Boat* (1936), where she turns on a docker who tells her to get out of his way with the retort: 'Who wants to get in your way?' In *The Shopworn Angel* (1938), as maid to Margaret Sullavan, she is incorporated into the narrative, functioning in the drama as well as in the comedy, a status attributed to no other contemporary black movie servant.

BFI STILLS, POSTERS AND DESIGNS

**Speaking out: Hattie McDaniel subverts the
stereotypes in 'Gone with the Wind' (1939)**

When directors encouraged it, McDaniel's acting revealed a camp side. To be camp is to behave in an outrageous, self-mocking and exaggerated way because of social displacement. As Queenie in *Show Boat*, for the flamboyant gay director James Whale, also a 'socially displaced' Hollywood figure, McDaniel shows many facets of her talent. Physically and temperamentally she is the opposite of her husband Joe (Paul Robeson): while she is small, rotund, quick tempered, tough and aggressive, he's a passive, towering presence, a tall, gentle giant. The two performances complement each other beautifully, with Robeson appearing relaxed and charming when he is supposed to look stupid and shuffling. McDaniel's campness comes through not only in her performance and posture (especially in the song 'Can't Help Lovin' That Man'), but in her appearance: the jewellery (brooch, rings, large dangling earrings), the gigantic, ludicrous bandanna, the carefully manicured fingernails. All this appears to be a deliberate attempt on the part of McDaniel and Whale to send up the stereotype. And in the duet 'I Still Suits Me', as she sits on Robeson's knee and chuckles with a suggestive look, the repressed sexuality of black women in Hollywood is released, if only for a few seconds.

When producer David O. Selznick was casting *Gone with the Wind* in the late 30s, McDaniel was the most versatile black actress working in Hollywood and the obvious candidate for the role of Scarlett O'Hara's mammy. In scene after scene she matches Vivien Leigh's spirited performance as the hot-tempered Southern belle, infusing the role with her own style of broad comedy and quiet dignity. As McDaniel herself said: 'I tried to make her a living, breathing character... to glorify Negro womanhood; not the modern, streamlined type of Negro woman who attends teas and concerts in ermine and mink, but the type of Negro of the period which gave us Harriet Tubman, Sojourner Truth and Charity Still.'

In the comedy scenes audiences laugh with her, not at her, recognising that she is in charge and will always have the last word, almost as if she were trying to reverse the slave-mistress roles. In her final scene she has a rare opportunity to parade her ability as a dramatic actress. When she describes the tragedy surrounding the death of Scarlett and Rhett's young daughter, bossy, cantankerous mammy unexpectedly reveals deeper emotions. Her expression of pain and grief is very moving: rarely in Hollywood films did black actresses have the opportunity to show an emotional range, and here McDaniel reveals that she can do much more in her roles than play the clown.

By the mid-40s, the roles McDaniel played had become embarrassingly sentimental. For example in Walt Disney's *Song of the South* (1946), she is reduced to a one-dimensional mammy caricature. Only one post-*Gone with the Wind* assignment offered her a brief departure from the stereotypes: as Minerva Clay, the soft-spoken mother of Parry, a law student wrongly accused of a murder in John Huston's *In This Our Life* (1942). When her employer (Olivia de Havilland) visits her after the charge, the grief-stricken Minerva convinces her that Parry is innocent. 'Police just come and took him off... they don't listen to no coloured boy,' she says. The scene is not long (80 seconds) but McDaniel conveys real emotion.

Though her work has all too often been ignored by feminist historians, several black American film writers of the 70s acknowledged the limitations imposed on McDaniel while at the same time celebrating her success. Donald Bogle described her as 'one of the screen's greatest presences, a pre-Fellini-esque figure of the absurd and a marvel of energetic verve and enthusiasm.' Perhaps her appeal is best summed up by Eileen Landay in her book *Black Film Stars*: 'As a fiercely protective, hard-to-please, devoted black mammy, she was the first to "talk back," thus defining herself as a human being. Although the standards she defended so fiercely were applied only to her masters and never to herself, although she seemed to have no life or desires other than to serve, the great talent and spirit of Hattie McDaniel overshadowed the parts written for her. Those who watched her knew that hidden behind the mammy was a real person.'

Elizabeth Wilson

Audrey Hepburn:
fashion, film and the 50s

The 80s retrospectively transformed the 50s of our imagination into a world of lost innocence, a world before drug abuse, a world in which it was safe to walk the streets. Films and television advertisements catered to this longing for lost youth with scenarios of blue jeans, country dancing and swinging ponytails (on girls, not boys), forgetting that the downside of this innocence was a stifling conservatism. But feminists are less likely to forget. They have reconstructed the 50s as the worst of times, when women were buried alive in their domestic interiors, and forced to resemble Marilyn Monroe or Elizabeth Taylor.

Audrey Hepburn reminds us that it was never that simple. Her startling – and startled – beauty may have been the embodiment of 50s innocence, but also anticipated a different and freer kind of 60s innocence. At the same time her films hinted at a continuing oppression. The waif is free, yet needs to be rescued. For me, growing up in those years, she offered hope from the moment I saw her portrait in *Vogue*. Her chrysanthemum fringe, huge eyes and poloneck sweater instantly created a different style. The cliff-like bosoms, heavy pouts and concrete curls of the beauties of the period were a million miles away from anything I could ever hope or want to look like; the hour-glass fashions simply didn't suit me. Of course I would never look like Audrey Hepburn either, but at least she demonstrated that there was, after all, another way to be.

She was described as 'gamine', but for me her charm lay not in the androgyny of simple hair and a boyish figure, but in a style that seemed the embodiment of sophisticated, existentialist Europe as opposed to the overripe artificiality of Hollywood. She might look like Bambi, but her casual style signalled student, not starlet; she proved that a woman could have brains and still be attractive. Years later, I was fascinated to read in the autobiography of Barbara Hulanicki, creator of that wonderful 60s dress emporium, Biba, how Audrey Hepburn had been her inspiration. Hulanicki wrote feelingly of her teenage despair at a time when even clothes intended for the young were based on *haute couture* fashions that had been designed for the middle aged. Then, at art college: 'Sabrina Fair made a huge impact on us all... everyone walked around in black sloppy sweaters, suede low-cut flatties and gold hoop earrings... Audrey Hepburn and Givenchy were made for each other. His little black dress with shoestring straps in *Sabrina Fair* must have been imprinted on many teenagers' minds forever.'

Audrey Hepburn and Leslie Caron, who had both trained as ballet dancers, created and popularised a look that disrupted class-bound British society without succumbing to American stereotypes. They made wit and intelligence seem sexy. Today, I can appreciate the wit and irony of the Hollywood sex icons: Doris Day in *Calamity Jane*, Kim Novak in *Vertigo* and the Marilyn Monroe comedies don't simply send up, but implicitly question the Hollywood sexual ideal. At the time, I was too young to see that, and found the sex and femininity in films such as *Niagara*, *From Here to Eternity* and *A Place in the Sun* humourless and negative.

Of all of Hepburn's films, *Funny Face* (1956) best demonstrates the way the industry could knowingly laugh at its own assumptions. Though the film satirises the world of fashion magazines rather than that of the film industry, the two held similar notions of glamour. Hepburn as 'Funny Face' wears glasses and a black sweater and works in a Greenwich Village bookshop where she dreams of meeting the great Parisian philosopher, Emile Flostre. When the editor of an upmarket fashion magazine (a satire on Diana Vreeland, who in her time edited both *Harper's Bazaar* and American *Vogue*) gate-crashes the shop for a fashion shoot, her photographer (based on Richard Avedon) 'discovers' Hepburn, who is whisked off to Paris as a model. There, all three get involved in a wonderful parody of existentialist café society, before Hepburn finds happiness as a model (and wife) with her Svengali.

The ending is conventional, but this has less impact than the ridicule heaped on the absurdities of the fashion scene. And although Hepburn does finally metamorphose into a fashion icon, the integrity of her earlier, intellectual self is endorsed, even if it is betrayed by the philosopher, who turns out to be a vulgar seducer. In *Funny Face*, Hepburn represents an innocence that is idealistic, but not stupid. In *Roman Holiday* (1953), too, her youthfulness has dignity, and though she returns in the end to her life as a princess, we are allowed to believe that her carefree interlude on the back of a moped has at some level more worth than the hypocrisies of pomp and spectacle.

Both films speak what Barbara Hulanicki felt: this was the beginning of the youth rebellion, which happened not in the 60s, but in the 50s. Hepburn's films, in however lighthearted a way, protest against the stuffiness and cultural conservatism of their times – not just in Eisenhower's America or Tory Britain, but in Adenauer's Germany, Christian Democrat Italy and France's post-war republic.

Truman Capote's short novel *Breakfast at Tiffany's* (1961) was an attempt to create in Holly Golightly a Sally Bowles who lives in post-war Manhattan rather than the Weimar Republic. But Holly Golightly was a gamine, a kooky character without the whiff of anarchy and madness which Christopher Isherwood brought to Bowles. The film version is so glossy that the viewer gets little sense of a genuine Greenwich Village bohemia, and Hepburn is too innocent to bring out the squalor and humiliation of Holly's life. Hepburn is incapable of being damaged or shop-soiled, yet there is a poignancy in her films that comes from the metamorphosis that invariably lies in wait: her passionate innocence is encased in *haute couture*, her beauty gets embalmed in happy endings that solve nothing. (*Roman Holiday* is the exception here, and to that extent more truthful.)

Hollywood stars such as Joan Crawford in the 30s were famous for their clothes, created by California-based designers such as Adrian. (Although Chanel had been invited to Hollywood briefly, her designs were considered too understated for the requirements of film.) A whole industry had been set up to market copies of the outfits of the stars, with department-store displays, special fashion magazines and even paper patterns. By the 50s this had waned. For one thing, Paris couturiers had begun to mass-market their designs, and there were in any case more sources of fashion inspiration. Also, European cinema was challenging the dominance of Hollywood. A number of films explored Left Bank style (Chabrol's *Les Cousins*, for

**Lost innocence: Audrey Hepburn
combines fashion, brains and beauty
in 'Funny Face' (1958)**

example) and Jeanne Moreau would soon create a fashion for a new, more offbeat look with *Jules et Jim*.

Since Audrey Hepburn was the forerunner of this trend, the extent to which her films are dominated by *haute couture* may seem surprising – and unrealistic, as when a chauffeur's daughter appears in a staggeringly glamorous evening dress, or a Greenwich Village waif visits Sing Sing dressed in the expensive chic of a little black dress, huge black hat and trailing beige scarf. And it is certainly the case that although she was celebrated as a girl in black drainpipe trousers and a Left Bank sweater, the clothes in many of her films were in fact designed by Givenchy, and her relationship with the designer was close, both artistically and in life (this made Hepburn even more exotic as an international star – to be dressed by a Paris designer was unusual). Yet despite his incontrovertible status as a *haute couture* designer, Givenchy, following his master Balenciaga, was the important forerunner of the minimalist designs of the 60s. And Hepburn's films played a crucial role in changing sensibilities, so that by 1960 the 50s stars seemed blowsy.

Nevertheless, the Hepburn/Givenchy style does send out contradictory messages. The Hepburn character of her contemporary films is both free and bound. To be a wilful, trouser-clad student type can only ever be a phase. In the end, she must 'grow up' and wear grown-up clothes.

In 1958, an article in *Twentieth Century* wondered at the way young women dressed like their boyfriends, in jeans and duffle coats, yet appeared uninterested in feminism or careers. Even when they rebelled, young women seemed more likely to be rebelling for artistic than for feminist reasons. Both *Funny Face* and *Breakfast at Tiffany's* allude to the choice faced by the hero between artistic integrity and commercial success. This occludes that other choice made by so many 50s women: between work and marriage.

Today, Audrey Hepburn has become the ghost of all those hopeful students, dancers, artists – a talented generation of young women, most of whom abandoned careers for the American suburban dream. We remember her like Henry James' heroine in *The Portrait of a Lady*, poised forever at her moment of momentous choice. Whatever the unexplored consequences, her beauty triumphs. She soars like a bird, forever on the wing, a wild creature who cannot be imprisoned.

First published in March 1993 (volume 3, number 3).

Ginette Vincendeau

Catherine Deneuve and French womanhood

In French town halls, two icons, one male and one female, symbol-ise the nation state. One is a photograph of the president, gazing down in a benignly patriarchal, or as the French might put it, avun-cular, way (François Mitterrand is often referred to as '*tonton*'). The other is a plaster bust of Marianne, the symbol of the French Repub-lic. But whereas the president's identity is self-evident, French may-ors have a choice when it comes to Marianne. They can order, among others, the 'traditional' version, a Brigitte Bardot model, or, since October 1985, the Catherine Deneuve model (FF2,908.94 plus tax).

The 1993 release of *Indochine*, directed by Régis Wargnier, looks set to bring back Deneuve as the top female French star of our time. This is noteworthy, because though Deneuve has received many prizes and her star image has shone for three decades, allowing her to command one of the highest salaries for a star in France, her film parts since Truffaut's *Le Dernier Métro* (1980) have tended to be acts of symbolic presence rather than actual leads, a little like Marianne in the town halls. This discrepancy between her status and the roles she plays brings up interesting questions about the make-up of Deneuve's star image and the place of women within the French star system.

For an international art-cinema audience, Catherine Deneuve is likely to evoke two things: French chic and 'perverse' sexuality. The first derives from the association of her beauty with prestigious French fashion houses; the second from her performances as the angel-faced schizophrenic murderer of Polanski's *Repulsion* (1965) and as Séverine, the shy bourgeois wife of Buñuel's *Belle de jour* (1967) who spends her afternoons as a prostitute in a discreet and luxurious Parisian brothel.

For French audiences, Deneuve set out in a different mode. After a few small parts with her sister Françoise Dorléac in light comedies such as *Les Collégiennes* (1958, at the age of 14) and *Les Portes claquent* (1962), she began her career proper as Virtue in Vadim's *Le Vice et la vertu* (1960, based on a novel by the Marquis de Sade), in which her bouffant hairstyle reflected Vadim's attempt to clone her, after Annette Stroyberg and before Jane Fonda, on Bardot.

But Deneuve did not pursue the libertine line for long, and her real breakthrough came with a better hairstyle in a better film: *Les Parapluies de Cherbourg* (1963), the first of Jacques Demy's sentimental, pastel-coloured musicals with all-sung dialogue. So while internationally Deneuve is associated with Polanski and Buñuel, at home she has paid tribute to the pivotal role of Demy in establishing her career. Against the background of the still repressive sexual mores of early 60s France, while Bardot continued her role as explicit sex goddess and dark-haired New Wave actresses such as Anouk Aimée, Anna Karina and Jeanne Moreau embodied 'intellectual' versions of French femininity, Deneuve triumphed as a sexy but innocent blonde, a persona reinforced by two further Demy films, the musical *Les Demoiselles de Rochefort* (1966) and the costume fairy tale *Peau d'Ane* (1970) as well as by several light comedies such as *La Vie de château* (Jean-Paul Rappeneau 1965).

The construction and perception of women's personalities always depend on their looks. And in the case of Deneuve, those looks are defined as much by grooming as by any physical attributes. Her hairstyles, for instance, have consistently been seen as an intrinsic feature of her persona and many writers have talked about changing her image in terms of messing up her hair. Like her hairstyle in *Les Parapluies de Cherbourg* (smoothed back in a neat half ponytail), Deneuve's image in the film is one of smoothness and restraint, a well-behaved middle-class girl (even if in the narrative she becomes pregnant out of wedlock). Unlike a number of prominent female European stars of the 50s and 60s who connoted unfettered, 'natural' sexuality – Silvana Mangano, Sophia Loren, Gina Lollobrigida, Bardot – through displays of (semi)nudity in close association with nature, Deneuve was positioned as a woman whose sexuality was always under control and under wraps, her hair impeccably lacquered, her body hidden by fashionable clothes, a creature whose habitat was the salon rather than the hayfield or beach. In *La Vie de château*, a comedy set during the German occupation in which she is the object of desire of most of the male characters, the peak of her sexual display is to frolic around the château in a white nightdress. Her ordeal at the end of the film, while the men are busy with D-Day, is to be forced to wade through a lake, sullying her immaculate tailored suit.

In this respect Deneuve was continuing a tradition of elegant French actresses modelling couture clothes, from Michèle Morgan to Edwige Feuillère, Martine Carol to Danielle Darrieux (at the beginning of her career she was even known as the new Darrieux). But whereas in the 50s such actresses and their films (*Adorables créatures*, *Mannequins de Paris*) celebrated women's fashions, in the 60s Deneuve's clothes played a more ambiguous role, particularly in auteur cinema. For example, Buñuel in *Belle de jour* used them as an index of bourgeois repression, and the film, which marked the beginning of a long-standing partnership between Deneuve and designer Yves Saint-Laurent, fixed her image for many years as the epitome of the *soignée* bourgeoise. The Saint-Laurent clothes – figure-hugging, tailored, with skirts cut just above the knee – included an element of sexual display, but a controlled and class-coded one, which acted as a foil to Séverine's 'true' sexuality, expressed through her masochistic fantasies and rough sexual encounters in the brothel. A great deal of writing on *Belle de jour* has pondered where the division between 'reality' and 'fantasy' in the film lies, but with feminist hindsight both sides of the Séverine character appear equally fantastic.

Belle de jour turned Deneuve into an international star. Creating a moment of perfect fit between performer, character and image, Buñuel's film successfully combined her existing, antagonistic, personae – the proper *jeune fille* of *Les Parapluies de Cherbourg* and the schizophrenic killer of *Repulsion* – into the ambiguous figure of the ice maiden whose intimidating beauty both covers and suggests intense sexuality. For an art film, *Belle de jour* was a box-office success, and the persona it established for Deneuve endured through Truffaut's *La Sirène du Mississipi* (1968), Buñuel's *Tristana* (1970), and Marco Ferreri's *Liza* (1971) – and in subdued form to *Le Dernier Métro* and *Indochine*.

Given her immense popularity both at home and abroad, it is worth pondering where Deneuve's appeal lies. One clue is that, as

Simone de Beauvoir has pointed out, female 'virginity' or 'frigidity' invite male conquest and suggest the need for a man to reveal to the woman her own sexuality (the Michel Piccoli character indirectly fulfils this function in *Belle de jour*). The young virgin (the older one is only ever an object of ridicule) is thus attractive because of her presumed incompleteness. It is not surprising to find her in the work of Buñuel, since the child-woman was a figure of fascination for the Surrealists, who wrote abundantly on her attractions.

There is a further, sadistic twist to this figure of male fantasy. The more immaculate and inaccessible the woman, the more she is deemed to invite profanation, which is then ascribed to her 'masochism'. The youthful Deneuve got a lot of that: she is flagellated and pelted with mud in *Belle de jour*, has a leg amputated in *Tristana* and is treated literally like a dog on a leash in *Liza*. Later, as a vampire in *The Hunger* (1983), she is covered with blood. Many actresses have been put through such ordeals on screen, but the characteristic specific to Deneuve is her simultaneous representation of extreme beauty and its defilement, from reverence to rape, in a single image. In a lighter vein, watching her peel potatoes in *Le Dernier Métro* causes a special frisson, as does seeing her cast as an 'ordinary', cardigan-clad provincial housewife in André Téchiné's *Le Lieu du crime* (1986).

Deneuve's mask-like face and understated performance style, her glamour and aloofness, her ice-maiden image and, as Truffaut put it, 'dream element', were a throwback to the great female icons of Greta Garbo and Grace Kelly, with both of whom she has often been compared. Such qualities marked her out as different from her French contemporaries: whether the Bardot-type sex goddesses, the existential New Wave heroines, or, later, naturalistic actresses such as Annie Girardot, Isabelle Huppert and Miou-Miou, or, again, the expressionist style of her rival in stardom, Isabelle Adjani.

Deneuve's international career has taken her mainly to Italy, though she has made four films in Hollywood, of which Robert Aldrich's *Hustle* (1975), in which she plays a high-class call girl, and Tony Scott's vampire movie *The Hunger* are the most notable. She has, however, long been known in the US as 'the most beautiful woman in the world', thanks as much to her commercials for Chanel as to her films. The exportability of Deneuve's image gives us another clue to her appeal. The combination of classy elegance and sexuality reflects precisely the two dominant clichés attached

BFI STILLS, POSTERS AND DESIGNS

**Intimidating beauty: Catherine Deneuve
has retained her status as an icon of
French womanhood since the 60s**

to French women: they dress well and they are highly sexed. Deneuve's success is linked to the way she has more or less willingly embraced these nationally coded values, both at home and abroad.

Acting as a semi-official ambassador for French fashion on and off screen, Deneuve did nothing to contradict the high-class mannequin image which emerged from *Belle de jour* and which informs all her film roles up to *Indochine* – where her exquisite frocks are a highlight. In terms of sexuality, the fit has been less perfect. While Deneuve was idolised as the perfect *jeune fille* in *Les Parapluies de Cherbourg*, her private life was considered scandalous, especially the fact that she had an illegitimate child with Vadim in 1963. Later both her screen image and public mores caught up with her. Her character in *Je vous aime* (directed by Claude Berri in 1980), for example, has a multitude of lovers and children by different fathers – a scenario not too far removed from the star's own life. And in her latest film, André Téchiné's *Ma saison préférée*, she plays opposite Chiara, her 20-year-old daughter with Marcello Mastroianni, whom she also did not marry.

Deneuve has acted in comedies throughout her career, but though a few have been successful, including *La Vie de château* and *Le Sauvage* (1975, with Yves Montand, also directed by Rappeneau), on the whole such roles have seemed at odds with her persona (*Zig-Zig*, directed by Laszlo Szabo in 1974 and her one attempt at producing flopped). She has retained the image established by her more serious films into the 80s and 90s, and as she has aged (extremely gracefully), the ice maiden has given way to the tragic *grande bourgeoise* – often a heroic mother whose sedate if glamorous life is disturbed by sexual passion, usually stirred up by a younger man. Two films in particular show the durability of the sexual (re)awakening theme: *Le Lieu du crime* (with Wadeck Stanczak as a young criminal) and *Paroles et musique* (directed in 1984 by Elie Chouraqui, with Christophe Lambert as a rock star). Both deal in the familiar screen conflict between a woman's sexuality and motherhood. In *Le Lieu du crime*, resolution is achieved in apocalyptic fashion (the young man is killed, Deneuve's son is estranged and she gives herself up to the police), while in *Paroles et musique* she returns to her husband and children. In *Indochine* too, Deneuve is allowed a relationship with a younger man (Vincent Pérez), only to be denied it when the young lover is paired with her adopted daughter.

Such narratives and the way Deneuve is used within them are

indicative of the unease of French film in dealing with sexually active, mature female characters and actresses. But they are also attempts at integrating into film specific features of contemporary French feminism, a task for which the later Deneuve persona is well suited. Deneuve's characters of the 80s and 90s, with their combination of glamour, independence and determination, have been much more pleasurable for female spectators than the male fantasies of the 60s and early 70s. Deneuve has increasingly been perceived as liberated (partly for the same reasons as she was regarded as scandalous in the 60s) both on and off screen, evidenced by Gérard Depardieu's remark: 'Catherine Deneuve is the man I would have liked to be.' She has taken overtly feminist positions in life. In 1982, when it was less fashionable, she still told *Le Nouvel Observateur*, 'Yes, I am a feminist.' And she is one of the actresses who makes recordings of women's novels for the feminist publishing house Editions des femmes.

But Deneuve is a very French feminist, which is to say that, like Julia Kristeva, Hélène Cixous and other prominent French writers, her feminism is combined with glamour and elegance in a way often perceived as utterly contradictory in Britain and North America. As the discourse of overt feminism has gradually disappeared from the French political and cultural scene, one of the ways its impact has endured is through the presence in public life of professionally and intellectually powerful women who are also glamorous: examples that spring to mind include previous Socialist government officials Elisabeth Guigou, Martine Aubry and Ségolène Royal, the charismatic television journalist Christine Ockrent (who looks not unlike the short-haired Deneuve), and successful film-makers Diane Kurys and Coline Serreau.

But if Guigou, Ockrent *et al* obey – and shape – the logic of the French job market and political scene, the logic Deneuve follows is that of the French star system. And within that system, her gender and looks are a double-edged weapon. As in her youth, they are a reminder of her to-be-looked-at-ness and of the burden of carrying the nationally coded signs of elegance and sexuality. But they are also a powerful source of pleasure, and, not negligibly, of revenue. If femininity is a masquerade, then the cool elegance of these professional French women is a sign of their being in control, rather than of being controlled as was the case back in the 60s.

Deneuve is powerful in other ways too. In the embattled financial and shifting genre structures of recent French cinema, major stars are more important than ever, not for their capacity to attract audiences to cinemas, but as a means of raising production funds, guaranteeing television and video sales and generating media coverage. The cult television cultural chat show *Bouillon de culture* devoted a whole programme to Deneuve to coincide with the release of *Indochine*, as if to prove that Wargnier could not have got the film off the ground without her, or at least not on such a scale. In return, she received a real leading part in a major production, a rare opportunity in recent years, when it has seemed as if her presence and looks were enough to signify a constellation of traits – career woman who remains feminine, determined but tragic mother, strong-willed but vulnerable lover – that allude to the changing roles of French women, but at the same time confine them to precisely this symbolic function. In films such as *Le Choc* (1981, with Alain Delon), *Le Choix des armes* (1981, with Yves Montand and Gérard Depardieu) and *Fort Saganne* (1984, with Depardieu), Deneuve featured in roles which were not cameos, but which occupied very little screen time and had little narrative importance compared to the roles of her male partners; yet the producers still claimed her as a major star.

This is not just clever marketing, but exemplifies a traditional gender imbalance in French casting going back to the 30s, whereby female stars may get leading parts in auteur cinema, but only exceptionally in the mainstream. It is also a perhaps unwelcome side-effect of Deneuve's elevated status. Because of her exemplary career in both auteur and mainstream film, and of her perceived embodiment of the values of French womanhood, she has become the symbol of a certain idea of French cinema as well as of France (it was perhaps inevitable that it was Deneuve who was chosen to accompany the Minister for Culture, Jack Lang, to open a festival of French film in New York in 1983). Indeed in *Indochine*, Deneuve's dominating narrative role could be ascribed as a symbolic representation of France, portrayed as the liberal colonising force.

It is a measure of the importance of cinematic culture in France that film stars are so strongly implicated in representations of national identity. Jean Gabin, as the train driver of Jean Renoir's *La Bête humaine*, became the key symbolic figure in the celebrations to mark the bicentenary of the French Revolution in 1989, in much the same way as Bardot and Deneuve literally personify France in the statues of Marianne. As might be expected, the male representation is historically grounded and actively social; the female one abstract and passive. Of course Gabin could model himself on Georges Clémenceau for *Le Président* in 1961, while Deneuve could only realistically be cast as a president's lover, as in *Le Bon Plaisir* (1984, directed by Francis Girod). But the difference goes beyond role models, since male stars such as Gérard Depardieu are offered a far wider range of roles encompassing a spectrum of characters from French social history, whether based on real or fictional sources (for example, *Danton* or *Germinal*). And the recently formulated French heritage genre does not seem to have altered this pattern, in that male stars still dominate in films such as *Jean de Florette*, *Cyrano de Bergerac* and *Tous les matins du monde*.

But perhaps the success of *Camille Claudel* (with Isabelle Adjani), *L'Amant*, and indeed of *Indochine* will herald better leads for female stars of Deneuve's stature. French history, society and literature, after all, are not devoid of tough, inspiring and glamorous women crying out to be embodied by Catherine Deneuve.

First published in April 1993 (volume 3, number 4).

B. Ruby Rich

Never a victim: Jodie Foster, a new kind of female hero

The iconographic significance of Jodie Foster as 'persona Americana' cannot be overstated. It is not simply that by her 30th birthday she had already had a career longer than many actors twice or thrice her age, in the process winning the loyalty that child actors inspire when they last. It is not just that, with the release of her debut feature *Little Man Tate* she has made the transition to directing that eludes many of her peers (and many of her gender). And it's not merely that the singular drama of her college years, in which a madman mistook the movies for life and used her as an excuse for political violence, has hopelessly confounded the filmic and extrafilmic for a nation of spectators. In the process the over-identification by the American public, the fandom raised to the level of obsession and idolatry, have as much to say about the power of movies as they do about the nature of acting – or, for that matter, about the articulation of the female in cinema.

Graduating from an entertainment industry that had been rescued for posterity by auteurist arguments of its artfulness, US cinema in the 70s responded to social change and to the French New Wave by initiating a kind of film-making that was more self-conscious about both its cinematic strategies and its home-grown subject matter. If Foster's presence came to suggest a different kind of film-making (as in the early Scorsese films), she also quickly came to represent a different kind of woman.

'[Jodie] was never a traditional-looking girl. And I think that has a lot to do with her success. It was just at the beginning of women's liberation, and she kind of personified that in a child. She had a strength and uncoquettishness. Maybe it comes from being raised without a father to say, "Turn around and show Daddy how pretty you look".' (Evelyn Foster, Jodie's mother, interviewed by Linda Miller, *American Film*, 1988)

Jodie Foster grew up in the movies. She was in basic training for celluloid from the time she was born; actually, even before. The publicity machine is full of stories: how she was already present in the womb when her film-publicist mother appeared in divorce court, made her first appearance at age three after falling into her brother's Coppertone television commercial try-out, nearly didn't survive her first film appearance (when a co-starring lion attacked her off-screen), contributed her wages to the upkeep of her family of a single mother and four kids, and, finally, was so smart that she became valedictorian of her French-language school and then went on to Yale University. The stuff of legend.

Raised in front of the camera, moving from childhood to adolescence to adulthood all on screen, Jodie Foster grew up as an image. By all rights, by the design of Hollywood, she should have become a predictable commodity as an actress. But she didn't. She didn't turn into the empty vessel that movies like a woman to be, so the director and the audience and the wet-dream critics can fill her up. But she didn't outgrow the movies, either, like so many childhood stars. Since she grew up right inside the image factory, she never had to stand outside it, trying to get in. No years of high-school plays, straining to look cute or prettier than the other girls.

Jodie Foster was there from the beginning, deep inside, imprinted by Hollywood as surely as Konrad Lorenz's duck. In her case, though, Hollywood functioned as its own immunisation: she became resistant to the artifices of glamour and the siren song of artificial femininity. She became her own woman, instead of theirs, with the unexpected result that women in the audience finally got to see on screen someone whose guts showed on her face.

'A while back I bought some acting books, because I'd started feeling very insecure about not knowing the terminology... So I looked at them, and I realised that most of it was common sense: if you're sitting at a table and it's cold, you're cold; or, if you're supposed to eat something, you actually eat it; if somebody's dead, you're upset. It's all about common sense and human behaviour and paying attention. Ultimately, I think I did probably do a lot of the things that acting classes and acting schools teach, but to me, it was just the way it was supposed to be. I had grown up that way and didn't really know anything else,' she commented in 1991.

Acting may well be the hardest element to define in film-making, since everyone from critics to directors to fans is eternally confusing the dancer with the dance. Actors who disappear into their characters are always suspect as novelty acts, or disdained as cool technicians pulling off star turns. Those who don't, who instead replicate their screen selves over and over, are dismissed as personalities lacking in skill, incapable of the craft of acting. On the other hand, actors who capture the attention and affection of the public (often, like Julie Christie or Diane Keaton, in conjunction with a particular historical moment) are forever memorialised, no matter the success of subsequent films or their own frequently ambivalent relationship to the media.

Foster is no exception to these rules. Thrust by talent and circumstance into the stratosphere of public obsession, she has struggled to keep her screen persona in perspective and to continue her lifelong preference for ensemble pieces, for a style of acting more collaborative than narcissistic, and for a kind of performance that might be termed the 'extraordinary ordinary' – a hyperrealism of character that mixes class traits and gender attributes into a singular but vulnerable strength.

The best example is probably her role in *Stealing Home* (1988), a forgotten film in which she gives one of her best performances as a troubled but carefree teenager, determined to have fun and to show the little boy she's annointed as her pal how to enjoy life. Everyone who missed that film had to wait until *Thelma & Louise* (1991) to see a woman drive a car or mouth off in quite this way. With movie sophistication, she instructs the boy how to smoke, how to look sexy for girls, and how to have an innocent kind of hellraisin' fun. In the process, Foster manages to fine-tune her trademark persona. She's sexy and confident, smart and brash, seemingly golden, but with tragedy waiting in the wings. The pattern would hold through a lot of films. She's never a dutiful daughter, never daddy's girl nor the apple of mommy's eye. In fact, she's almost never in a family at all.

The family is where little girls are made. In Foster's case, the family that Hollywood created for her is particularly striking. She wasn't given a nuclear family like so many other celluloid girls. No, from the start, her families are fractured – and when not fractured, dysfunctional. In film after film, she plays a girl with an absent dad, missing mom, hated parent, or a divorce survivor, or even an orphan. Today, Foster acknowledges that, since her mother picked her parts in those days, she very well may have responded to scripts that mirrored their own family portrait. Whatever the reason, the independence of the Foster character was usually matched by a narratively enforced self-sufficiency.

There are exceptions, of course: films in which Foster is contained within a traditional nuclear family. When the sexuality that inflects the Foster persona through most of her career meets up with a family context, however, the result is usually Oedipal perversity – most often played for laughs in an attempt at defusion. In an odd Disney vehicle, *Freaky Friday* (1976), she and her mom get to do a mind-body switch and the whole audience gets to hold its breath while the movie tiptoes around Daddy's game responses to the wife who now calls him 'daddy' and daughter who now calls him 'Bill'. This being Disney, we reach the end without full Oedipal rupture. In *The Hotel New Hampshire* (1984), however, there is no such restraint. The family goes nuclear. By the time the movie ends, mommy is dead, daddy is blinded, and Foster's Frannie has gone to bed with a woman in a bear suit (played by Nastassja Kinski) and her own brother (none other than Rob Lowe).

Foster grew up at a moment in US history when the notion of home as a sanctuary retreated into nostalgia (at least for the white middle class, since Latino and African-American families continued to hold their own). Girls were leaving home all over the country, and 'bad girls', the kind that Foster so often played, were moving out fast. If the nuclear family was dangerous, a truth hammered home throughout the 70s, then the world outside wasn't exactly safe, either. Certainly not for women.

'If I portray a victim, does that mean I'm not Wonder Woman? Well, I'm not trying to be. There are a lot of ugly things in our [women's] history, as in black history – and the truth has to be told. You can't censor art through political "correctness".' (Jodie Foster interviewed by Dan Yakir, *Interview*, 1987.)

To be sure, Jodie Foster does play characters who are abused, manipulated, pimped, set up, raped or nearly raped, even killed. However often she may be victimised, though, she never plays the victim. She brings bravado to her performances and prevents the demolition of her characters' subjectivity. Never submissive, she may be threatened or even overpowered, but always fights back, defends herself, gets even. However vulnerable at the level of the body, every Foster character is smart and tough and determined to prevail in the end. And bad things (jail, rejection, death) happen to the men who defile or humiliate her.

Foster never quite fits the damsel-in-distress role, even when the early scripts require her rescue. She always tries taking care of herself first, and sometimes even succeeds. As her filmography progresses and the actress Jodie Foster ages, her characters begin to act increasingly in their own self-defence, casting the damsel aside entirely. Sometimes, this is due to the script. But at other times, it's clear that the Foster persona has influenced the character far beyond the narrative's requirements.

In *Five Corners* (1987), which tries hard to be an American art film, she plays a character who goes down swinging, literally whacking her psycho pursuer with a board and knocking him flat, scoring a momentary victory. If he catches up with her later, well, it takes a whole townful of men to save her – no single man, neither sweetheart nor cop, can do it. Films like these decisively overturned the structuring presence of the male protector that used to characterise the action movie. As a result, a space opened up, extending even to mainstream genre films, wherein Jodie Foster could come of age, not merely alongside her characters, but in step with them.

The release of *The Accused*, virtually simultaneously with *Five Corners*, showed the new shape of gender relations: here, men are the problem, no longer the solution. Foster's Sarah Tobias character looks across class, not gender, for a saviour and finds her in the person of a yuppie woman assistant DA who takes on her rape case as a routine assignment. Even with a woman on her side – partially as a result of the class divide and partially due to the injustice of the legal system – the Jodie Foster character realises that she has to help herself. She may be dependent on another woman professionally (legally), but first she has to fight back, literally on her own.

Foster's portrayal of Sarah Tobias as a working-class woman picked up on a strain already present in earlier Foster performances and made it official, setting the tone followed by both her subsequent screen roles: the spunky proletariat gal who can take on anyone from a posse of rapists to a psycho killer to a manipulative genius. In *The Accused*, whether she's invading her attorney's dinner party and lashing her with anger or physically fending off an attack by one of the rape witnesses by destroying his truck with her car,

Tobias rejects any hint of victimisation. It is only when she is immobilised in a hospital room, with the assistant DA playing a classic bedside scene, that Jodie Foster as Sarah Tobias is willing to let down her guard and to speak the kind of lines that could have run as a postscript to *Taxi Driver*: 'I never got to tell nobody nothing. You did all my talking for me...' Sarah wants to defend herself, not just with action but with law; as a surviving victim, she wants to bear witness – an impulse that any reader who watched even a fraction of the televised Clarence Thomas confirmation hearings can certainly understand.

To think about Foster in *The Accused* is also, inevitably, to think about Foster's sexuality and the sexualised roles she has played since her earliest appearances, from the hooker-child in *Taxi Driver* to the *femme fatale* in *Hotel New Hampshire*. Strikingly, Foster has avoided the trade-off so common for women in Hollywood cinema, whereby actresses trade intelligence or strength for sexual appeal on screen. Foster gave up nothing, held on to it all, as a child, adolescent, and adult actress. The very fact of her sexuality (one that appeals to audiences across all kinds of generational, gender, and national boundaries, unifying her publics in a commonality of desire) is fused to her obvious personal authority, to create a fascinating tension, one that says as much about gender definition in late twentieth-century America as about her own career.

The child-sex frisson of her early roles indelibly marked Foster. In *Taxi Driver* (1976), she plays Iris as someone who's still a kid, adulthood pasted on to her like a cheap disguise, with her sexuality a commodity produced in her by adult men, for adult men. It's the shock of the disjunction – a child, sexualised, in an adults' world – that provides the tone of perversity. In *Bugsy Malone*, released in the same year, the assignment of sexuality to Foster has the opposite effect: it marks her as an adult in a world of children. Her expert integration of herself with the role of Tallulah, a worldweary and seductive gangster's moll, sets her apart from the world of children she inhabits and results in an inversion of the very perversity that Iris was marketing. Seen together, the films present an explicit critique of sexuality as a fixed element, demonstrating instead its variable nature. Sexuality, as attached to the Foster persona, moves across the pair of films like a floating signifier, cut adrift, shifting position like a word that means two very different things in two different languages.

Ever since, Foster's sexuality has been overdetermined. Certainly, female sexuality is always a double-edged sword, with power (and who's got it) hanging in the balance. And nowhere is this truer than in the movies. Foster presents us with characters who are strong-willed, not weak; active, not passive; direct, not coy; openly sexual, not repressed or puritanical. Of course, the parts are written by the screenwriter and not by her. But by now, if not actually scripted with her in mind, they are certainly transformed by her enactments. The change of sexuality makes these tough characters vulnerable, while giving them the strength to sustain that vulnerability. *The Accused* made this shatteringly clear. By now, the scene of gang rape on a bar-room pinball machine has been described over and over, until it has gathered a totemic significance equal to that of the original rape, perpetrated in an actual bar in New Bedford, Massachusetts, in 1983. But the scene of the rape, to my mind, is not the central traumatic event of the film, despite the unanimity of statements on the matter. Any viewer of the film today can notice, as Foster has pointed out, that the more fraught moment takes place before the rape, when Foster as Sarah Tobias flirts drunkenly in the bar and does her long sexy solo around the dance floor.

It is in this moment that *The Accused* becomes a metaphor for a woman's place, in cinema as in the world. Foster dances, and we see Sarah enjoying and indulging her own sense of self and sexuality, confident, projecting at once control and abandon. But the dance is played out under the sign of the tavern, a male gathering place, where the presentation of a female self is subsumed, first by a voyeurism that strips away her autonomy, and then by an invasion that transgresses the boundaries of passive voyeurism. The public display of a private self is an act of risk for a woman, and in this film, it's a risk with frightful consequence.

The male possession of public space is not limited to the tavern; cinemas, too, constitute a regime of power in which the viewer can assume ownership over that which he views and feel proprietary towards a female body captured only by his gaze. Sarah Tobias dancing in that bar becomes a metaphor for every actress performing on screen, for every woman sitting in the darkened cinema watching a dress rehearsal of her own conceivable fate. Foster's ability to embody in her characters the 'extraordinary ordinary' renews the pact of identification with her audience. The victory of the trial scene resonates beyond the film to claim, for Foster as for all of us, the right of a woman to the expression of a self-determined sexuality, free of punishment or invasion.

The Silence of the Lambs (1991) upped the ante: women were sought not for their sexuality but simply – literally – for their bodies, the killer's drive for possession stripped of any sexual impulse whatsoever. Buffalo Bill was just collecting skins. In the climactic scene, in which Foster's Agent Starling hunts the killer, only to become the prey, Buffalo Bill's use of infra-red glasses turns the drama in a peculiarly self-reflexive direction. Vision and the act of looking are the stuff of which movies are made; when that act is foregrounded, something's always up. Though the shot is the only one in the film to structure Clarice as victim, the point-of-view shot is not lined up with the audience's position of identification. Instead, it is here that Foster gets to reverse the outcome of the bar-room scene in *The Accused* by turning the tables on the killer, however improbably, and taking the audience with her. She may still be on view, may still be subject to the consuming gaze of the powerful male – this time a murderer with no intent to rape – but the deck is not stacked. Here, she can win, saving not only herself in the process but also the girl, trapped and panicked, screaming out 'help me' from the bottom of a well. Who does she represent? Every actress done for by a killer in a horror movie? Every woman assaulted? You? Me? Foster herself in other movies?

Infra-red vision or not, Clarice Starling seems to demonstrate that there are some male gazes – and male acts – that are not permissible and will not be tolerated. Significantly, director Jonathan Demme purged the horror genre that had been the favourite boy-toy of the 80s by rigorously desexualising the violence in *The Silence of the Lambs* and ensuring that Foster's character would face only death, not defilement. The movie offered a new kind of female hero, one whose vulnerability and emotions were seen as aid rather than impediment, one who could avenge an entire decade's genre sins in a single act.

'Obviously I wouldn't do softcore porn – it doesn't interest me. Nor do all those boys' films that have two minutes' worth of girl interest... I wouldn't do anything regressive or repressive or that advocates an old moral regime.' (*Interview*, 1987)

And she hasn't. But 1991 was a year in which she was taken to task as though she had. The paradox is worth examining. Even before *Silence* opened in the US, it was being denounced in the gay press as a work of pernicious homophobia for its Buffalo Bill portrayal. Foster was also being praised, in mainstream circles, for her strongest performance ever. She graced the covers of magazines from *Mirabella* to the *New York Times* magazine. But the controversy soon took over. Sides were drawn, and you had to pick one or the other. Critics were polled. Director Jonathan Demme was occasionally targeted for abuse. Actor Ted Levine, who'd played the Buffalo Bill character, was rarely mentioned. The full force of wrath descended, instead, on Jodie Foster herself. Was this star-fucking gone awry? Misogyny? Scapegoating? She was just an actress, playing another character. Simultaneously, a campaign gathered momentum, aimed at forcing Foster to break her prohibition on discussing her personal life and relationships. The campaign turned her life and career into a sinister prize in a new contest of so-called 'outing' that seemed more intent on gathering this private woman's skin for a trophy than even Buffalo Bill had been. A mere decade after the Hinckley debacle, Jodie Foster was again a public target.

Why? Or, as Foster herself had put it, writing in *Esquire* in 1982 about the hideous Hinckley episode: 'Why me?' For a complete answer, it's necessary to look at the autumn of 1991 as well, when Foster made her directorial debut with *Little Man Tate*, the story of a boy genius torn between nature and culture, between his simple emotional mom (Foster) and his emotionally crippled mentor (Dianne Wiest). It is a modest and competent movie, full of feeling but less adventurous than many films in which Foster has starred. But never mind that. Look at the reaction.

First out of the gate was *Interview* magazine, playing Foster on the cover in a pose that couldn't help but recall certain Dorothy Arzner poses. Foster was positioned between the giant shadow figures of motion-picture cameras, the actress now emblematically the director. Soon enough, though, *Time* magazine took over, splashing Foster on the cover under a banner headline that trumpeted: 'A Director is Born'. The article fell all over itself with superlatives, comparing Foster to Louis Malle and then quoting Malle's own praise of her as proof positive. What was notable in the article, above all, was the critic's clear confusion of Foster with her characters while a child actor and the projection of this fantasy displacement on to the woman director and her film product.

Jodie Foster, throughout her career, has been the repository of audience fantasies. The very nature of her persona has permitted

**Beyond sexuality: Jodie Foster turns the
tables in 'The Silence of the Lambs' (1991)**

the co-existence of contradictory projections on the part of her diverse publics. The adoration on the part of these publics, alternating recently between idolatry and demonisation, is itself a product of the unprecedented position which Foster occupies in the twin worlds of public and private discourse, pointing to the possible irreconcilability of these discourses.

Her mother traced Foster's early success to the rise of a women's liberation movement and the demand for a new kind of girl-child. What has happened, of course, is that the girl-child grew up. The sexuality that was such a frisson in the girl became a more threatening and potent quality in the woman. *The Accused* is a key moment in her career, then, not only for the reasons already cited, not only for the Oscar that crowned her comeback, but also for the break with sexuality that her character makes within the movie: kicking out her boyfriend, cutting her hair, cleaning up her act. Narratively, these acts are linked to her reaction to rape and the consequent need to testify.

In the larger narrative of the Foster career, however, what comes next is most relevant. What came next was *The Silence of the Lambs*, which, in desexualising violence for women, also desexualised the Foster character of Clarice Starling, removing even the vestiges of sexuality present in the novel. In the round of promotional pieces accompanying the release, director Demme could be heard to say that this was the first time that Jodie Foster had been allowed to show her intelligence on screen. A coincidence? Unlikely. Repetition proves the point. In *Little Man Tate*, Foster the director desexualises Foster the actress just as rigorously, this time in the service of motherhood rather than intelligence.

There's an inevitable rush to judgment. Has the tension that always existed in the Foster persona, that of sexuality combined with authority, reached its breaking point? In times of intense political repression such as now, perhaps sexuality loses its liberatory potential, perhaps women's sexuality does indeed carry as much danger as it does pleasure. Further, with a move into the directing chair, Jodie Foster the director may feel that the sexuality of her actress persona is a luxury she can no longer afford, as she begins to uncover the contradictions between these two cinematic roles of absolute authority and negotiated surrender. Finally, however, there's a different conclusion. Speaking at the Walker Art Center in 1991, Foster proclaimed herself ready to take on a new kind of role as an actress: 'I believe women should be sexual. And why not? What a great thing to be: a sexual woman, coming of age and discovering sensuality and the intoxication of it. I've seen so many movies about women who don't like sex and really don't want to have sex, or have that posey stuff in the Calvin Klein ads. Well, that's just not true and I'm sick of that myth being out there. What I'd like to do is develop movies that better reflect my generation of women.'

Foster's younger sexual personae were all about promise, potential, conflicted desire, or – most often – about being the locus of someone else's desire. It may be that the current desexualisation is a pause, not an end. It may be that Jodie Foster, whose position in the world owes so much to her perpetual willingness to take big risks, is preparing for the biggest risk of all: the gamble to fuse an active female sexuality with an equally active female authority. It may be that Foster the actor had to wait for Foster the director to emerge in order for this movie to be made. What it might look like is anybody's guess. Whether the public and private worlds of agency and fantasy can tolerate wholeness in one of the culture's most contested figures is equally the stuff of prophecy. The girl-child is a relatively unconflicting locus of desire. Grown up and suitably sexualised, she's a different story altogether. The wrath traditionally directed at the phallic mother is ever-present, as is the insatiable desire to consume entirely the adored object, while identification does its perpetual dance between self and other, seeking a stable position from which to gaze. It may well be that Jodie Foster, as director and actor, is facing a problem for which the culture that has produced and reproduced her as icon has found no solution.

First published in December 1991 (volume 1, number 8).

Andrea Stuart

The outsider: Whoopi Goldberg and shopping mall America

In an article in *Village Voice*, Marpessa Dawn Outlaw, outlining the many obstacles for black female film-makers in 'Gollywood', jokingly includes on her list the problem of how to make a movie without using Whoopi to play 'all the major roles'. It is an oblique acknowledgment of Goldberg's solitary supremacy in the curious history of the black female in Hollywood.

It is a position which is under even greater scrutiny with the release of Spike Lee's three-hour blockbuster, *Malcolm X*. For while the men-only club that is New Black Cinema (Lee, John Singleton, Mario Van Peebles, Matty Rich *et al*) finally got its first epic, black women directors such as Julie Dash lament that they can't even get themselves arrested in Hollywood, far less a five-picture, multimillion dollar deal like the one Spike has managed to pull off. But this is nothing new. Black women have always hovered like reticent servants on the edge of American cinema – eternal cyphers manipulated to reflect the ever-shifting state of play between the races. And whatever the seeming variety in black women's roles, there have only really been two types of cinematic coloured girl.

The first, of course, is Beulah, she of the brick bosom and bulging eyes, Hattie McDaniel pulling tight the stays on Miss Scarlett's corset, the woman whose heavenly charge was to keep those 'beautiful white babies' safe from harm. The other is Dorothy Dandridge, the tragic mulatto, a beautiful brown moth about to be singed in the dangerous fires of miscegenation. The legacy of this model's bright, light skin can be seen in the faces of Robin Givens, Whitney Houston, the carefully bleached Diana Ross and every one of Spike Lee's heroines – barring, of course, the appearances of his sister Joie Lee.

Goldberg's unique success is to have avoided both stereotypes. Indeed, cinematically she is not really constructed as a woman at all – neither nurturer nor siren, the faithful drudge of the ante-bellum South or the funky chick born to walk the wild side of the city's mean streets. Her movie persona is more in the tradition of asexual 'coon' entertainers such as Amos and Andy or Bill 'Bojangles' Robinson. The 'coon', a lovable black buffoon, the light-hearted cousin of the harassed but ever-faithful Uncle Tom, has roots as old as Hollywood itself. As far back as *The Ten Little Pickaninnies* (1904), black actors were cast as harmless, wacky, curiously pre-sexual characters who never seem to grow up.

But what about Whoopi? In 1986, in *Jumpin' Jack Flash*, she played Terry Doolittle, a computer programmer who accidentally receives a message from a British agent trapped behind the Iron Curtain. Infatuated, she determines to save him, and a series of comic events ensues, including one in which Goldberg is dragged through the streets of New York trapped inside a telephone booth. Her eyes 'a poppin', screaming madly, you can't help but be reminded of the comically fearful Butterfly McQueen in *Gone with the Wind*, the classic 'pickaninny' running down the drive at Tara screaming 'the yankees are coming, the yankees are coming'. According to black film critic Donald Bogle, the makers of *Jumpin' Jack Flash* saw Goldberg as 'an asexual creature from another universe' – and they weren't alone. When she took the role of Celie in Spielberg's version of Alice Walker's *The Color Purple* (1985), one critic went so far as to compare her to E.T.

But looks aside, part of Goldberg's other-worldliness stems from the fact that she rarely appears with other black people. Until her recent role in *Sarafina!* (1992), she has never had a black male love interest, and there are few indicators in her films of a cultural context – for example, a family. The black lieutenant in *Sister Act* (1992) may seem an exception, but even he is nothing to her – not a lover or friend, not blood, just a token black cop in a sea of white cameos.

The Color Purple, the only real exception, almost destroyed Goldberg's career. (Indeed, following the furore the film engendered, critics such as Bogle began to talk about her in the past tense.) The film's portrayal of violent black men and long-suffering black women provoked an Oscar nomination and a hailstorm of criticism, a disproportionate amount of which was directed at Goldberg personally. There were demonstrations outside cinemas at which the film was being shown, and a sanction was imposed by the National Association for the Advancement of Colored People (NAACP), which declared that the film 'misrepresented' black people.

And as if this were not bad enough, into the fray stepped Spike Lee, who called her a sell-out. But though Goldberg's remarks – 'I want to be considered an actress not a black actress'; 'I figure you look at me and you see I'm black, I don't have to say it' – were hardly designed to win friends among political black people, and indeed still enrage today, she managed to sink her teeth firmly into Lee's Achilles' heel by asking 'How many black women who look like me do you see in Spike's films?' Many applauded – Spike's bevy of brown babes and depiction of women in general have not made him popular with black women in the US. In fact, it is a criticism levelled at most of the new wave of black directors, who have done little to broaden the range of roles for black actresses, even as they have given a whole generation of black men – Denzel Washington, Wesley Snipes, even rap star Ice T – a grab-bag of new dramatic parts.

The battleground for *The Color Purple* may have seemed to be about politics, but in fact it was about class. And much of it was fought out on the symbolic landscape of Goldberg's clothes and appearance. The sartorial has been one of the few mechanisms for negotiating social hierarchies within black communities, so it is no surprise that the person who has appeared on the list of America's worst-dressed women more times than virtually any other actress should provoke her community's ire.

While many clearly felt that *The Color Purple* was a whitewash, the venom of the black media emerged fully only when Goldberg arrived at the Academy Awards dressed in trainers and yellow leggings. It was bad enough that in films such as *Jumpin' Jack Flash* and *Fatal Beauty* (1987), Goldberg – once described as looking like a 'covergirl for *Sharecropper's Monthly*' – should allow herself to be outfitted like a cross between a $10 Harlem hooker and a bag lady: all leopard-print shoes and sequined sunglasses. But to dress like that in public evoked a cringing embarrassment among sophisticated urban black America, which lamented not just her taste, but her lack of political commitment as well.

The curious thing is that in the street-cred stakes (if street cred has anything to do with black authenticity), Whoopi beats Spike

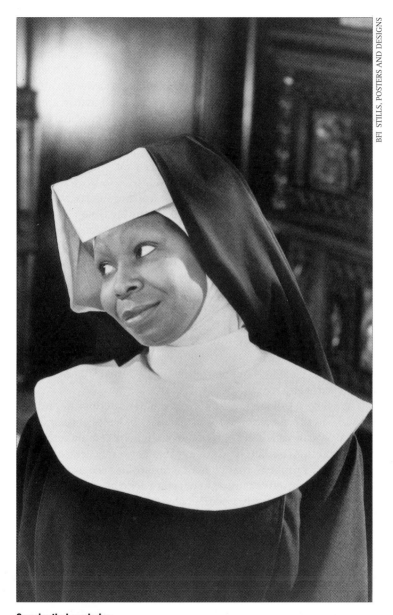

BFI STILLS, POSTERS AND DESIGNS

**Crossing the boundaries:
Whoopi Goldberg breaks the
mould in 'Sister Act' (1992)**

hands down. With his middle-class, college-educated background, Lee is more a child of the Cosbys than of the ghetto, whereas Goldberg is the second daughter of a single mother who was married and divorced before the age of 20, dropped out of high school because of a drug problem, and then spent almost a decade on welfare ($223 a month) in California bringing up her daughters on her own. Of course, being a welfare mother in San Francisco is a far cry from being one in Detroit or Dubuque, Iowa. In the thriving, striving alternative culture of San Francisco – a city in which everyone is chasing their own particular rainbow, is about to 'become somebody', 'do something', 'climb out of that closet' – to be on welfare is almost a career opportunity: at least for the drag artists, tattooists, film-makers and dreamers on the edge of the big time.

What emerged for Goldberg from these experiences was a stage act that eventually led to her much acclaimed one-woman Broadway show, *Whoopi Goldberg*, and to the attention of director Mike Nichols. What followed was a pair of stand-up films based on her character Fontaine, a drugged-out counter-culture hippy who finally kicks the habit in the early 80s and finds himself straight in the extremely bent world of Reagan's America. He is a treat: tough, slightly over-the-top, lost. Such comic characters are Goldberg's strength, and it is when she is allowed to develop this on film, as in *Ghost* or the glorious tampon routine in *The Player*, that her talent most clearly emerges.

At her best, Goldberg is the classic outsider. She appears entirely at home in the unorthodox social grouping of her television series *Bagdad Café*, in which she plays a non-malignant, female version of Jack Nicholson, but it is a side of her that has rarely been captured on film. It's a problem that Richard Pryor would recognise. Having established himself as the genius of razor-edge comedy, Pryor found movie executives clearly mystified about how to use him on celluloid. What resulted were films like *Silver Streak* (1976), and eventually a defunct film career. Removed from their very different constituencies, both Pryor and Goldberg became artists cinematically in search of an audience.

Nowhere has the removal of the Goldberg character from any meaningful context been more problematic than in the romantic arena. The same thing happened with Eddie Murphy in *Beverly Hills Cop*: you take the black star out of the black community to make him more palatable, but then who does he date? Studio fears that

America couldn't cope with Whoopi in the arms of a white lover were borne out by *Fatal Beauty*, where love scenes between Goldberg and co-star Sam Elliot ended up on the cutting-room floor after objections from preview audiences. But even when Goldberg has been allowed half-hearted romantic brushes with white male co-stars, as in *Sister Act*, her outlandish appearance effectively de-sexes her, and a taboo activity like interracial love loses its charge.

In order to cross over, it seems that Goldberg has had to jettison the loaded sexual exoticism usually associated with the black female performer, as well as any potential political disruptiveness. Despite the promise of her early stage persona, in her film career, the apolitical mode has stuck. Her involvement in *Sarafina!* may be an attempt to grasp some of the credibility that has eluded her, but even this is half-hearted, for despite some moving moments, *Sarafina!*, as a musical, has all the radical potential of *Yentl*.

Indeed, Goldberg's appeal, at least in film, lies perhaps in the fact that she is unthreatening, even relaxing. To many – black and white alike – her films are a delightful break from our society's endless negotiations on the subject of race, time out from which we can return refreshed for the next round. And perhaps, therefore, Goldberg is, in a strange way, a hope for the future: a black performer whose skin is an empty sign, like that of her white counterparts, that simply spells entertainment and does not carry with it the baggage of oppression or history.

But here in the present, many black people ask, 'How can you trust a woman who wears weave-on locks?', and it sometimes seems that Goldberg has found an audience only to lose her racial identity. But perhaps what Goldberg represents is the struggle between the popular and the populist. In contrast with the urbane and urban Spike Lee, she shares and reflects the mentality of shopping-mall America, whose black citizens, like its white, are not politicised or well dressed and whose only desire is to get on and get out, any which way they can.

First published in February 1993 (volume 3, number 2).

Michael O'Pray

A body of political work:
Tilda Swinton in interview

Tilda Swinton is an unusual actress. She is regarded as one of the finest acting talents of her generation in the UK, yet has achieved this position paradoxically through working totally outside and against the so-called mainstream. In film and theatre alike, her performances are notable for their commitment to work which is aesthetically risky (for example, the experimental films of Derek Jarman, Cordelia Swann, Klaus Wyborny), as well as politically provocative.

Tilda Swinton's idea of acting is one that runs against the present current. As a believer in Brechtian acting methods, she embraces a European tradition opposed to dominant Hollywood techniques. Her sympathies lie with a lineage stemming from the anti-naturalism of Meyerhold in pre-revolutionary Russia and passing through Eisenstein to Brecht before finding its cinematic proponents in Godard, Bresson and Straub/Huillet.

Central to the Brechtian method is a belief that drama has a social and political responsibility, not only to entertain an audience, but to educate it. But Swinton is critical of a political theatre that is purely what she calls 'site specific'. For her, the political or social point can be made better when the canvas is large, no matter what its historical context. She sees cinema and theatre as revealing a universal stance and not a local one: Benjamin Britten's *War Requiem*, Virginia Woolf's *Orlando*, Pushkin's *Mozart and Salieri*, Jarman's *The Last of England* can all connect creatively and intelligently with our lives. And certainly the Brechtian cinema promised by the British left in the late 70s and 80s has not been realised through political documentary, but through the exotic, wayward, angry and ultimately utopian films of Derek Jarman, in which Swinton's role has been crucial. As history should have told us, the radical edge has come from the most surprising direction – favouring, as always, the knight's move.

Born into an upper-class Scottish military family, Swinton spent a year working illegally in the South African townships before going to Cambridge University in 1980. When she met Jarman in 1985 to work on *Caravaggio*, he was receiving his first break from the film establishment since 1979, when he had made *The Tempest*. Swinton had never worked in film but had begun to establish a reputation in theatre – largely for a memorable performance at the Edinburgh Fringe in Peter Arnott's play *White Rose*. Her more recent work in theatre has also won her high praise, particularly her stage performances as a woman passing as a man in *Man to Man* by Manfred Karge (made into a film by John Maybury). Karge also directed her to great acclaim in another woman-playing-man role, as Mozart in *Mozart and Salieri*.

In Swinton's film work, the story has been rather different. Wyborny's film *The Open Universe* has not been seen in the UK, nor has her other German film work with Cynthia Beatt and Christoph Schlingensieff. And her excellent performance in Joan Jonas' video *The Laxdaela Saga* also awaits a screening. Her most visible work has been with Derek Jarman, and much of her reputation and image inevitably rests on his output.

To trace Swinton's career is to encounter many of the key political and social issues of the 80s – gender politics, militarism, Aids, the sexual repression of gays, class antagonism, the new rise of fascism in Europe, and the ancient problems of surviving any social system as a human being, especially as a woman. We have to go back to an older generation to find actresses of Swinton's quality who attempted to make links between their radical political engagement and their work – Vanessa Redgrave in Britain and Jane Fonda in the US are the most obvious examples, although both were markedly different from Swinton, most importantly in being 'stars'.

'If there was any model at all for me as an actress when I arrived at Cambridge, it was Brecht's actress, Helene Weigel. It's to do with having a sustained body of political work and the absolute importance of control. And Weigel ended up running a theatre company. I'll tell you a quick story about Brecht which is really important.

Helene Weigel cried on the opening night of one of Brecht's plays and a critic commented that she was identifying with the character, she has lost herself in the character. Brecht replied, and this is the last word on this, that Helene Weigel was crying for the character. There is always a commentary there. The performer is always there. It's rather like when you see those large-scale puppets and you see somebody in black is working them. It's the same sort of thing: as an actor, one is enabling, one is not the character. One is literally modelling the character's behaviour and commenting on it all the time.'

Swinton cites Bresson's use of actors and his renaming of them as 'models' as exemplary, too, of an approach which is essentially anti-naturalistic and anti-empathetic. Her performance as Isabella in Jarman's *Edward II* (1991), her famous dress-cutting scene in the final sequence of his *The Last of England* (1987) and the scene on the steps in his *War Requiem* (1989), where she steps out of the nurse role and utterly remodels the part, all show a use of excess and of pathos in which, as Roland Barthes remarks in relation to Eisenstein, the actor's 'expression... signifies an idea – which is why it is excessive – not some natural quality.' This aesthetic runs counter to the 'facial affectations of the Actors' Studio', as it does to the restraint of 'traditional' British acting.

'The great English acting tradition is very specific. It has never translated well over the Atlantic and I think this is because the English (although not the Celts) find it so difficult to discharge their emotions freely in their own lives that the concept of somebody doing it publicly is threatening and they have to believe that it's fake. People always say about Olivier that he had an enormous range and great technique, but I believe he just liked playing, liked showing-off. I liked the fact that he really enjoyed himself acting. But to say he was a terribly skilled craftsman distances it, makes it all very mysterious.'

Swinton's own commitment to Brechtian principles suggests ways of seeing Jarman's work in a neo-Brechtian fashion. There is no doubt that his characteristic use of the tableau has a Brechtian dimension. The implication of the tableau as an aesthetic strategy is that meaning is not the summation of a narrative, but is segmented by highly defined scenes in which the meaning is explicitly constructed and demonstrated. In Jarman's non-dialogue, anti-narrative films, the physical and visual setting-up of the scene in all its elements, including the actors, expresses the meaning as a gesture: what Brecht called the 'social gest'. Such films defy 'subject matter'; they are not about something, but rather are a series of images, each of which addresses the audience in the gesture of 'criticism, strategy, irony, propaganda, etc'. They have moral force, in that sense, as images.

Jarman's fondness for performers (poets, pop personalities) instead of actors similarly drives a wedge between actor and part: watching Toyah Willcox play Miranda in *The Tempest* we are constantly aware that it is Willcox playing Miranda, an effect strengthened by Jarman's *mise en scène* and liberal policy of actor interpretation. Naturalistic subsumption of the actor to the role is largely eschewed. Equally, Jarman's devices of excess, exaggeration and quotation, of interspersing song, music, dance in narrative (witness the anti-naturalistic device of Annie Lennox's appearance in *Edward II*) also create Brechtian distancing effects.

Jarman describes his films as 'collaborative ventures' with Swinton, and remarks that 'of all the people I've worked with, Tilda is the one who transforms the screen. I haven't found a male equivalent.' If we look at the female roles in Jarman's films prior to *Caravaggio*, there are only two major examples: the dispersed female images of *Jubilee* (1978) and the excellent use of Willcox as childlike innocent in *The Tempest*. In many ways, Jenny Runacre's two roles as Elizabeth I and the gang-leader Bod in *Jubilee* are recurring icons in his work – the 'good mother' or Madonna figure (a desexualised and idealised image of femininity) and the 'bad', sadistic female who is nevertheless a keen intelligence within the text.

Swinton has played both icons, although until Isabella the favoured role was the Madonna figure. What Swinton brought to these roles over and above a certain look or image was a centre of gravity, a sense of presence and personal disturbance within a more generalised, inevitably abstract chaos and turmoil. In films without dialogue, where expression is vital, Swinton was not simply iconic, but also a nexus of thoughts and feelings. For example, in *The Last of England* Swinton represents the loss and sacrifice of love within social and political repression. And in the end she also represents anger, rage and frustration in the face of that reality. As Swinton cuts up her wedding dress, swirling dervish-like in the night to a rising musical crescendo, the 'social gest' comes to the fore. The film's characteristic non-dialogue structure, referring back to silent cinema, underlines the gesture of the body in a chore-ography that is reminiscent of the scene on the steps in *War Requiem*.

'*War Requiem* is a piece of music which was a script for a film. Apart from the odd image, we did make up a lot as we went along. The only reason I'm on the screen at all is because of the soprano voice, which has a most extraordinary aria. What happened struc-turally was that Derek was not there when we shot it. He told me and the cinematographer to do what we wanted to this music. The film is a silent film, which interests me because I think that cinema has gone downhill since people started talking in it. One of the lux-uries of doing *War Requiem* was that we had a score we could play to, as they did in the silent cinema days. Not since the days of Lillian Gish has this happened.

'What I wanted to image in the film was something about the powerlessness of the position of women in war, the inability to express anger about it or to witness it on a frontline basis, at least in the First World War. What the frustration must have been of pick-ing up the pieces but not being there when the blood was spilt; the indignity of having silently to cope with what one might have wanted to stop happening in the first place. I wanted to cast a con-tentious image – the image of the weeping woman. If you notice I don't cry; it was very important not to weep.

'It is my method, and has been for a while, to creep up on the image and deconstruct it from within. The music was playing and I'm showing the awareness of that and also showing that there is both a pernicious and a celebratory aspect to war. One can be romantic about war and I wanted to look at that briefly – the pos-sibility of getting off on the romanticism. While this is perfor-mance, there is also the inevitability for me of the work being to some extent autobiographical. I've had discussions with feminists who have quibbled with the image of the weeping woman, but I had had a similar experience which made me know that this is not an unrealistic scene. A cliché is a cliché because it is often true. Women, and men too, weep about their sons, daughters and lovers being killed in war, so there was a point of reality within it for me.'

What has been described as Swinton's chameleon presence in films is none other than an ability and desire to range wide across roles. She remarks that she finds no difficulty playing a male role; in fact, if anything, playing women may be slightly more demand-ing. Her dedication to a behavioural-cum-Brechtian acting method

Questioning gender:
Tilda Swinton in 'Orlando' (1993)

makes such remarks and judgments utterly unremarkable. Certainly, her role in *Man to Man* is totally committed physically – the bad teeth, bare dirty face and exaggerated male stances. And typically, she found that one method of learning to play a man, or a woman passing as a man, was to strap on a penis-like object so that she could understand male sitting and stance in general. This refusal to identify so-called maleness with an essentialist psychological state reflects certain feminist positions on gender.

'Looking at the constraints of gender programming, not gender *per se*, is an abiding interest of mine. *Man to Man* is about a woman who dresses as a man; *Orlando* is about a youth who becomes a woman; Mozart was a genius and so was androgynous! Both *Man to Man* and *Orlando* are about being a realised human being. In *Man to Man*, a woman in order to survive cannot be a woman and so has to play out her life in the guise of a man by modelling male behaviour. She ends up thoroughly confused in old age. And *Orlando* is about the development of a human being. There is a fine tradition in the theatre of boys playing women, an original tradition. And a later tradition, when women were allowed on the stage, of women playing boys: as in the pantomime boy. The precedents are there. I don't feel it is any more difficult for me to behave as a man than as a woman. It is just as elusive a thing to find out the way of modelling female behaviour, possibly more so.

'What distinguishes working in theatre from film is energy, I think. You can learn and develop the technique for film. And you can fight it too. Concentration is of paramount importance. When you are looking into a camera you are actually looking at human beings, or at least at one human being at a time, which is how it is received. It is different from looking into a theatre audience and addressing that audience, which for me is a powerful and useful thing and for the audience an empowering thing. The contact is more intimate; they are aware of being looked at.'

Swinton is perhaps at the cusp of a change in her work, brought about by what she sees as a more optimistic funding situation for the kind of films she supports. The financing of *Orlando* in terms of millions and not thousands of pounds and the critical and commercial success of *Edward II* may signal a better clime for such work. Equally, that John Maybury's *Man to Man* is his first feature after years of work either in pop-promos or more marginal, 'art cinema' gives room for optimism about the future.

Swinton's perception of this work as mainstream and of the mainstream as marginal is characteristic. The commercial success of Greenaway's *Prospero's Books* (1991), Jarman's *Edward II*, and of work by 'experimental' directors like Gus Van Sant, David Lynch (of course), Martin Scorsese (forever experimental) and Paul Verhoeven bodes well. Whether the price to pay for 'buying in' to the industry will be too high in the end remains to be seen.

Swinton's vision of the marginal as mainstream is avant-gardism differently phrased. When art split from culture in the nineteenth century, the values, the critique, the political and social desires of a society were embodied in the work of a few, neglected until they could be repressively tolerated, as Marcuse claimed. For an actress who is continually offered mainstream roles and salaries, the refusal is made on a day-to-day basis. In a culture which at present offers hardly any political basis (the left almost dissolved by the 80s), decisions have to be made carefully and precisely about scripts, work situations, collaborations, issues.

'Actors are asked about their personal lives and the reason for this is the assumption that their personal lives are not in the films. My personal life is in the films. I also have no stories about how unbelievably difficult it is to play a certain role – I did not check into the Betty Ford clinic to research Isabella!'

First published in January 1992 (volume 1, number 9).

Carol J. Clover

High and low: the transformation of the rape-revenge movie

Rape, real or threatened, has been a staple of cinema more or less from the beginning. Until the early 70s, however, it was typically a side theme – a psychopathic flourish in a suspense plot, or one of several atrocities Indians might visit on whites in the Western. One 1972 film changed that: *Last House on the Left* (Wes Craven). It moved rape from the periphery to the centre – turned what had been a sideshow in any kind of movie to the main act, the central motivation, of that American favourite, the revenge plot.

The marriage of rape to revenge was made in movie heaven, to judge from the spate of films that followed. Ironically enough, it was a marriage for which the matchmaker was the women's movement, for in terms more or less explicitly feminist, rape became not only a deed deserving of brutal retribution, but a deed that women themselves (not cops, boyfriends, or fathers) undertook to redress. From low-budget, 'exploitation' products like *I Spit on Your Grave* (Meir Zarchi, 1977, aka *Day of the Woman*), *Ms .45* (Abel Ferrara, 1980, UK title: *Angel of Vengeance*), *The Ladies' Club* (A. K. Allen, 1986) and *Positive I.D.* (Andy Anderson, 1986) to glossy, mainstream examples like *Lipstick* (Lamont Johnson, 1976) and *Extremities* (Robert M. Young, 1986), women take knives and guns to their rapists, or their friends' or sisters' rapists, or just any man, on the grounds that all men are party to 'rape culture' and hence corporately liable and fair game.

Feminism has given many things to popular culture, some more savory than others. One of its main donations to horror cinema is the image of an angry woman – a woman so angry that she can be imagined as a credible perpetrator of the kind of violence on which, in the low-mythic universe, the status of full protagonist rests. Like slasher movies, rape-revenge movies pose problems for feminist critics; there is no doubt, however, that both genres were enabled by the women's movement and could only have emerged in its context. The rape-revenge film, at least in its grittier versions, is nothing more or less than the 'castrate rapists' slogan made flesh.

It's not just the sexual politics of the rape-revenge film that invites attention. It's also its cultural politics – the relation of the 'exploitation' versions to the mainstream ones – and its history. The issues raised by the genre emerge most clearly in a comparison between the 'worst' and 'best': the infamous *I Spit on Your Grave* and the Oscar-winning *The Accused*.

The plot of *I Spit on Your Grave* could hardly be simpler. A New York novelist named Jennifer who rents a summer house in Connecticut is first harassed by some young men in the neighbourhood and eventually raped by them in turn. The act begins in the meadow to which they have dragged her from the canoe in which she was sunning herself. After stripping her, the men first offer her to their virginal and retarded companion, Matthew, but when he runs away in fear, Johnny (the ringleader) falls on her and brutally rapes her. She rises and staggers from the meadow into a forest, only to be again captured and again raped, this time anally, by Andy (after again being offered first to Matthew). From the forest she staggers and crawls by turns back to her house, but they have preceded her.

This time, with the rest of them shouting him on, Matthew almost manages to penetrate her inert body, but his victory is short lived and he gives way to Stanley, who orders her to fellate him just before she falls into unconsciousness. They leave, but not until they have given Matthew a knife and instructed him to kill her. He goes in but is no more able to stab her than he was to rape her, so he wipes some blood on the knife to satisfy the others and they leave her for dead. So goes the first 40 minutes.

After a short transition (representing the passage of two weeks), during which Jennifer patches together herself and her manuscript (which they tore to shreds as they left), the revenge half of the film begins. Jennifer invites Matthew over and after some preliminaries, hangs him and rolls his body into the river. Johnny she invites for a ride, and only too ready to believe that she 'really liked it', he goes along. At a secluded spot she pulls a pistol on him and tells him to drop his pants; he talks fast and she seems to change her mind, tossing the gun aside and inviting him to her house for a hot bath. Cut to the bathroom, where the two of them are in the tub and she is fondling him with one hand and reaching for a knife with the other. 'God bless your hands,' he murmurs, 'that's so sweet – that's so sweet it's painful' – at which point he bellows and rises, covered with bubbles and blood gushing from his now genital-less crotch. Jennifer locks him in and coolly listens to opera downstairs as he bleeds to death. That body too goes into the river. There remain Andy and Stanley. They come to her place by boat with the intention of killing her, but after a struggle she pushes them into the river and takes over the boat. She puts an axe into one of them and dismembers the other with the propeller. With that the film ends, aftermathless.

The American reaction to *I Spit on Your Grave* was if anything more vitriolic than the British one. There is no doubt that the film is an extreme case, that it poses problems for the feminist critic, and that it is exceptionally hard to watch. The question is, why? Although there are a couple of men-only sequences, the film is framed from beginning to end as Jennifer's story. Most of the action is registered from her vantage point, and there is no doubt whatsoever that its sympathies lie with her. The film gives equal time, and in some sense equal terms, to the rapes and the revenge. The claim on the part of some reviewers that *I Spit on Your Grave* shows the woman enjoying the rape is flatly dishonest; not for a moment does she express anything but protest, fear and pain. The rapes are presented as almost sexless acts of cruelty that the men commit more for each other's edification than for physical pleasure. Nor is there any pleasure to speak of in the revenge half; Jennifer goes about the business of catching and murdering her assailants almost impassively. It is, in fact, an oddly external film.

One of the most disturbing things about *I Spit on Your Grave* may be its perverse simplicity. The men are not odd specimens, but in the normal range of variation; their brutality is not traced to dysfunctional upbringing (no Mother Bateses here). Jennifer takes the revenge she does, not for deep-seated psychological reasons, but because it is the punishment that fits the crime: there are no extenuating circumstances; the law is not involved, nor are legal questions raised; there is no concern whatsoever, not even at the level of lip service, with moral and ethical issues. If higher forms of the rape-revenge story involve us in a variety of ethical, psychological, legal and social matters, *I Spit on Your Grave* closes all such windows and leaves us staring at the *lex talionis*, or law of retribution, for what it is. The film shocks, finally, not because it is alien, but because it is too familiar, because we recognise that the emotions it engages are regularly engaged by the big screen but almost never bluntly acknowledged for what they are.

That is not to say that *I Spit on Your Grave* is entirely explanation-free. On the contrary, it has a thesis of sorts, a proposition about the group dynamic that drives men to deeds of which they might not be capable alone. It takes as its point of departure the retarded Matthew, whose status as a virgin seems to compromise the masculinity of the group. It is ostensibly to change that status, to bring Matthew into the family of man, that they capture Jennifer in the first place. The more he fails (three times he recoils and even runs away), the more they goad ('Here she is, Matthew. You want to be a man, don't you? Don't miss your chance, Matthew, you're going to die a virgin...') And the more they goad, the more they slip into the language of what we are to understand are the underlying issues of impotence, homosexuality and effeminacy.

To regard Matthew as a non-participant, as do the remarkable number of descriptions that speak of three rapists rather than four, misses an important point. For one thing, it is against his failed performance that the others can define their own as successful. They are what Matthew is not; Matthew is what they are better than. Once set in motion, the proposition that masculinity is little or nothing more than a function of comparison leads to another series of questions: how much better is Stanley than Matthew? Andy than Stanley? Johnny than Andy than Stanley? Matthew is not only the one they compare themselves with; he is the one they compare themselves through. If the fiction is that the assault on Jennifer is an act of generosity towards one of their members, the fact is that it is a sporting competition, the point of which is to test and confirm an existing hierarchy: Johnny the winner, Andy a strong second, Stanley the loser, Matthew on the bench. To all but Matthew, the woman is simply the playing field – and even Matthew is finally goaded into at least trying to join the game. The goading itself, particularly during the sequence in the house (when Matthew manages to effect penetration), echoes the crowd cheers of a football game: 'Hey Matthew! Come on, Tiger!' and then, in unison, faster and faster, 'Go! Go! Go! Go!'. Matthew, for his part, strips and imitates a victory trumpet as he falls on Jennifer. 'All right! Come on, killer!', the others shout. For *I Spit on Your Grave*, at least, gang rape has very much to do with male sport and pecking order and very little to do with sex, the idea being that team sport and gang rape are displaced versions of one another, male sorting devices both, and both driven by male spectatorship and misogyny.

Ironically, the men's individual protestations, when they find themselves at Jennifer's mercy, almost perversely acknowledge the force of the group dynamic. Stanley facing the boat propeller: 'I'm sorry, I really am. It was Johnny who talked me into it. It was Johnny made me do it. I didn't want to do it.' Or Johnny at gunpoint: 'Look, you've got the wrong man. Stanley, the guy with dark hair, the guy's a sex maniac.' Or Matthew: 'I hate you. I've had nothing but bad luck with you. I have no friends now because of you... I'm sorry for what I did to you with them, but it wasn't my idea. I have no friends.'

In a sense, each of the men is right to feel that he is not individually responsible, for the film keeps insisting that the dynamic of male groups is larger than the sum of its parts. But that does not mean, in this primitive universe of the *lex talionis*, that the individuals are therefore not responsible for the actions of the group. On the contrary, as under the bloodfeud, they are corporately liable; any of them – in this case all – are proper targets for retribution, regardless of their own degree of participation. For many viewers, the murder of Matthew is the film's most disturbing moment, for he is so clearly drawn as the others' victim. But *I Spit on Your Grave* gives no points for reluctance or action under pressure. That Matthew never quite made it off the bench is irrelevant: what matters is that he would have played if he could. Reviews may speak of 'three rapes' and 'three rapists', but, as the final body count of four shows, Jennifer knows better.

With *The Accused* (Jonathan Kaplan, 1988), the rape-revenge drama hits Oscar level. It is perhaps no coincidence that the most highly produced version of the story to date should also be the one not only most focused on third-party intervention, but also the one in which the third party succeeds in meting out justice, thereby proving the judicial system woman-friendly after all. This plot too is a simple one: a working-class woman named Sarah (Jodie Foster) – a little drunk, a little stoned, and very flirtatious – is gang-raped in a bar; she brings suit and is furious when her lawyer (the assistant district attorney, a woman) plea-bargains the case; she insists on another round, and that one she wins. It is, of course, true that the story is constrained by the facts of the real-life case on which it is based, but it is also true that there have been a number of cases in the last decade, some of them just as highly publicised, in which the outcome is less happy: cases in which men plead 'rough sex' and are acquitted, cases in which men are convicted and sentenced but come back to kill the woman who turned them in. But for reasons at which we can only guess, it is *The Accused*'s happy-ending, feel-good version of the rape-revenge story that made it through the Hollywood gauntlet and that proved one of the biggest box-office movies of the year.

The Accused has its considerable virtues, one of which is the broadside way it engages the issue of consent and another the way it highlights the legal difficulties of prosecution. And like other films of the tradition, it is informed by an analysis of sorts. Rape, in *The Accused*, is male sport. The college boys who turn up at the bar that night and end up party to the rape have just come from 'the game'; the television set blares out sports events; for her job waitressing at The Dugout, Sarah dresses as a baseball playerette; a framed newspaper on the wall in the DA's office bears the headline 'Plowing Match'; the rape takes place on a pinball machine featuring the game Slam Dunk; during the rape itself, the male spectators cheer and clap and chant in unison, 'One, two, three, four – poke that pussy till it's sore'; the rapists in turn undertake their task as if it were the World Series (one spits on his hands as he steps into the batter's box). The rape–sport analogy is hardly new – *I Spit on Your Grave* made the same point, right down to the recognition that they also serve who cheer from the sidelines – but with *The Accused* it enters the mainstream and the status of those who cheer from the sidelines is established as criminal.

But if something is gained in this most civilised version of the rape-revenge story, something is also lost. There is a sense in which the third party, the legal system, becomes the hero of the piece: focus has in any case shifted from the victim to her lawyer; from questions of why men rape and how victims feel to questions of what constitutes evidence; from bedroom (or wherever) as the site of confrontation to courthouse. (Compare the final shot of *I Spit on Your Grave*, which shows us a smiling Jennifer speeding along in a motorboat, to *The Accused*'s helicopter shot of the courthouse.) Sarah is vehement enough in her wish for revenge ('I want those motherfuckers put away forever!'), and when the law fails her on the first round she even engages in an act of vigilante justice (ramming her car into the pickup of one of the men who cheered her rapists on). But for the most part, the retaliatory urge is displaced on to the woman assistant DA who tries the case. And in our increasing engagement with her uphill struggle (to plea-bargain effectively in the first trial, to hit upon the right charge for the second, to gain the support of her cynical colleagues, to triumph over the warning that she'll ruin her career, to talk a reluctant witness into testifying, and so on), we lose sight of what the lower forms of the rape drama unfailingly keep at centre stage: the raped woman herself. Nor does the fact that justice is served not through the straightforward prosecution of rape but through the unorthodox deployment of a statute concerning criminal solicitation – presented, in the film, as a stroke of luck – do much to dispel suspicion about the law's efficacy in such cases.

No less undermining is the fact that the film ends where many women's fears begin, at the moment the jury delivers the 'guilty' verdict. Over and over, rape-revenge movies make the point that even when the law succeeds in the short run, it may fail in the long term. *Ladies Club* is a wall-to-wall indictment of the system that either fails to convict rapists or convicts and sentences them only to release them so they can rape (and/or murder) again: 'Where rape is concerned, the law stinks.' From the perspective of the rape-revenge tradition, and indeed from the perspective of those involved in real-life male-on-female violence, *The Accused*, in its implication that the story is over when the men are sentenced, is pure Pollyannaism.

Finally, there is the fact that although *The Accused* seems to bring male gazing to account (by bringing to bear on the cheering onlookers a charge of criminal solicitation), the authority for the conviction, and indeed for the status of the incident as a whole, rests solely with a male spectator: Ken, the college boy who witnesses the event, calls the police, and finally, after some equivocating, provides the testimony that convicts his fellows. The importance of Ken's vision is established in the first shots, and it is remarkable how often and at what length the film has us look at his eyes looking at something – or nothing, as in the case of two intercut shots of him staring pensively out of his fraternity-house window, shots whose only purpose can be to remind us that amid all the conflicting accounts there is a truth and this is where it resides. Likewise the rendition of the rape itself, during which the camera seems as interested in watching Ken's face watching Sarah being raped as it is in watching the rape itself. But the real giveaway is the fact that the rape can only be shown directly – the flashback can only happen – when Ken takes the stand and narrates his eye-witness account. Sarah testifies to precisely the same events shortly before, but whereas her testimony remains her own version, Ken's testimony becomes our version, the version. After a few sentences, his voiceover ceases and the rape unfolds before us as visible, omniscient history takes over.

Seldom has a set of male eyes been more privileged; without their witness, there would be no case – there would, for legal purposes, as the DA notes, be no rape. Those male eyes point up a fundamental difference between *The Accused* and the lower forms of the rape-revenge story, in which there is a rape because a woman knows she has been raped. The features of *The Accused* that make it such a welcome contribution to the ongoing consciousness-raising about the workings of rape law are the very features that make one understand why the self-help versions of the story not only exist, but flourish. Even respectable citizens can sink to the vigilante mentality when they feel inadequately acknowledged by the justice system. *The Accused* shows the system working, all right – but only barely (only by loophole), and only slowly, and only because a man of good will and a very smart, sympathetic and stubborn female lawyer happen to be in the right place at the right time.

Although *The Accused* may at first glance seem a world apart from *I Spit on Your Grave*, the two films are, in fact, pretty and ugly versions of the same story. And *The Accused* owes its very existence – its conception, its terms and much of its success – to a low-life ancestry that has been neatly erased in its migration from the category of horror to the category of courtroom drama. But take away *The Accused's* elaborate displacement machinery – its legal, psychological, ethical and social ruminations – and relocate it beyond the arm of the law ('out there where no one can hear you scream') and you have *I Spit on Your Grave*: the story of a gang-raped woman hellbent on revenge.

One can't quarrel with civilisation, but it's sometimes useful to look past its comforts to see the stories we tell ourselves, as a culture, for what they really are. I suggested earlier that what disturbs about *I Spit on Your Grave* is its perverse simplicity, the way it closes all the intellectual exits and leaves us staring at the *lex talionis* unadorned. Let me now be more explicit: what disturbs most about *I Spit on Your Grave* is the way it exposes the inner workings of *The Accused* and films like it – the way it reminds us that lots and lots of the movies and television dramas that we prefer to think of in higher terms are in fact similarly funded by impulses we would rather deny. *I Spit on Your Grave*, in short, is the repressed of *The Accused*, and it is probably for this reason as much as for any other that it has met with the punitive response it has.

The case could be made that horror movies in general are the repressed of a fair share of American mainstream cinema. Scratch the glossy surface of *The Silence of the Lambs* and you have a slasher film, complete with girl hero and effeminate psychokiller ('a *Nightmare on Elm Street* for grad students,' one reviewer called it). Scratch *Pacific Heights* and you are in an economy of bloodsucking that looks like nothing so much as a vampire film. Scratch any number of recent films – *Thelma & Louise* for one – and you are looking, once again, at rape, revenge, and the notion of corporate liability that makes every man pay. The similarities are not coincidental. Even a cursory glance at the chronology makes it clear that the direction of trickle here is up, not down. As any horror fan knows, much of what reviewers tout as mainstream innovation is not new at all, but has flourished for years, even decades, in the world of movies that lies beyond the world of reviews. No aficionado can see *The Silence of the Lambs* or *Mortal Thoughts* without thinking of all the low-budget, often harsh and awkward but sometimes deeply energetic films that preceded them by a decade or more – films that said it all, and in flatter terms, and on a shoestring.

One of many ironies in American film-making is that an entry-level position in the industry, and one of the few opportunities for something like genuine auteurship, has been provided by the low-budget horror and cult genres. 'Written and directed by' (not to speak of 'written, directed, and produced by') is a label more frequently encountered in the trashy underbush of American film-making than in the studio parks, and the story of the nickel-and-dime horror movie that catapults its maker into the Hollywood big time is something of a legend. Certainly the generation of film-makers that energised the low or border tradition in the 70s and 80s – conspicuously John Carpenter, George Romero, Wes Craven, Tobe Hooper, Larry Cohen, David Lynch, David Cronenberg and Jonathan Demme – have moved on to slicker things and often slicker studios as well. With them they have taken the themes and techniques of horror, as well as the lessons they have learned about young audiences (for horror audiences are young, and so prognosticate future trends). As with people, so with ideas; what critics avoid, scriptwriters follow and cannibalise, again on the presumption that, with the addition of some niceties (some fleshing out of character, motivation and political philosophy), today's 'meat movie' is tomorrow's blockbuster.

The most spectacular donation of yesterday's meat movie to today's blockbuster is the female victim-hero. In upscaling the tough-girl hero of the slasher movie, the Hollywood studios have made an honest woman of her, but they did not invent her from whole cloth. Nor did they invent the plot that devolves on a raped woman's angry pursuit of justice. That honour too belongs to the branch of film-making we call, ironically enough, exploitation.

First published in May 1992 (volume 2, number 1).

Manohla Dargis

'Thelma & Louise' and the tradition of the male road movie

'Whither goest thou, America, in thy shiny car in the night?'
Jack Kerouac, 'On the Road'
'I always wanted to travel, I just never got the opportunity.'
Thelma, 'Thelma & Louise'
Set in the late 40s, but not published until 1957, Jack Kerouac's *On the Road* is the beat generation's seminal celebration of the joys of roadside America. Fast cars, whisky, women, a few, last soiled dollars – the hipster's journey was the pleasure principle on wheels. His heyday was the 50s. Then the car transformed the American landscape and the population motored on in aerodynamically styled cars ready for lift off, as General Motors continued to displace public transport with its 'dynamic obsolescence'.

Years after Kerouac's death, the road remains a favourite idiom, whether of an ageing beat such as Robert Frank, a middle-aged *enfant* such as David Lynch or the scout Jim Jarmusch. And even if America's road network has been reduced to an endless tangle of freeways and concrete clovers – closer to J. G. Ballard's apocalyptic *Crash* than to Kerouac's literary joyride – the myth endures. It certainly fuels Ridley Scott's *Thelma & Louise*, the story of two women friends on the run for killing a rapist. But unlike its innumerable siblings, this film doesn't just recycle an idiom, it rewrites the road movie, custom-fitting it to female specifications.

The road defines the space between town and country. It is an empty expanse, a *tabula rasa*, the last true frontier. Its myth echoes down the history of US cinema, from films such as Nicholas Ray's *They Live by Night* (1948) to Robert Altman's remake, *Thieves Like Us*, shot nearly 30 years later. The road trip is always a male trip and the road movie makes literal the rite of passage that Oedipally-driven narratives demand of their male heroes. If a woman hops a ride with a man, the journey, perfumed with a female sexuality, breeds danger and violence rather than pleasure.

Motherhood tempers the *femme fatale*, as in *You Only Live Once*, but severed from the domestic sphere, as in *Bonnie and Clyde* or *Badlands*, women appear to provoke rituals of frenzied violence. For women who travel alone, the stakes are somewhat modified. They either end up victim to violence, as in *Psycho* – the ultimate bad trip – or land in a fringe subgenre, such as the women's prison film *Untamed Youth* or the biker film *She-Devils on Wheels*.

Veering off from the mainstream, *Thelma & Louise* has two women travelling the road together. But what explicitly separates this film from the generic chaff, making it more than a case of incidental cross-dressing, is the distinctive means by which the road to the self is travelled. In short, Thelma and Louise become outlaws the moment they seize control of their bodies. Theirs is a crime of self-defence, their bandit identities forced on them by a gendered lack of freedom, their journey grounded in the politics of the body. In a culture where the female body is traded, circulated in a perverse exchange, for a woman to seize power over her body is still a radical act.

The contrast with the sexual politics of three other road movies – Joseph H. Lewis' *Gun Crazy* (1949), Jonathan Demme's *Something Wild* (1986) and David Lynch's *Wild at Heart* (1990) – is revealing. In Lewis' peripatetic *amour fou*, the antihero, Bart Tare, is taken on a violent psychosexual spree through his dual obsession with guns and his lover, Annie Laurie Starr. In this *film noir*, the journey to manhood begins and ends in the pastoral milieu of youth, but is thrown off course by the relentlessly sexual woman. Brutal and explicitly non-maternal, Annie wilfully uses desire to pitch the couple into a fevered criminality that forces them on to the road. As in the earlier *The Postman Always Rings Twice* (a road movie with low mileage), the woman's body and the road are interchangeable, sites each man must travel to certain destruction.

In Jonathan Demme's *Something Wild*, a white yuppie's cross-country trip is the stuff of existential heroics, a search for self that pivots on his taming of a 'wild' white female body in soulful Africana drag. Over the course of the fugitive couple's journey,

Demme's heroine transforms from Lulu into Audrey, a metamorphosis that has her replace red lipstick, black wig and African accoutrements for blonde hair and a virginal white dress. It's a transformation that, as if to assuage the troubling teleology, Demme simultaneously parallels with a retinue of 'positive' blackness – homeboy, church-going folks, a singing cowboy.

If Demme's vision embraces a well-intentioned liberalism, David Lynch's *Wild at Heart* is its reactionary adjunct. A road film jerry-rigged as a post-modern *Wizard of Oz, Wild at Heart* is peopled with the director's routine obsessions – anomalies (physical and otherwise), sadistic cruelty, sex crimes. Lula Fortune and Sailor Ripley, young lovers on the run, are on the 'yellow brick road' of freedom and erotic escapade, trying to put distance between them and Lula's crazy mama, a woman obsessed with controlling her daughter and imagined as the Wicked Witch of the East incarnate.

Lula's body is already conquered before the film begins (she was raped as a teenager). It's a frontier that remains only to be explored, ravaged and eventually domesticated – by motherhood and marriage, no less. As in *Something Wild*, the woman's body is contested terrain, but the conflict here is more insidious. In *Wild at Heart* the struggle over Lula and the journey are launched by the death of a black man, whose brains are beaten out by Sailor within the film's first minutes. Later, in yet another grotesque tableau, a white woman screams 'fuck me' to a black man who pulls the trigger on a white man sandwiched between them.

Fear of miscegenation stalks this movie, from one death to another. This land is your land, this land is my land – but hands off the white women. Property is a constitutional right, and Sailor is a man whose sense of proprietary privilege is as baroque as his snake-skin jacket, which, as he reminds Lula, is 'a symbol of my individuality and my belief in personal freedom'.

As if in direct reply to this tradition, in which white supremacy is the unspoken subtext, a key scene in *Thelma & Louise* has a black Rastafarian cycle incongruously into the picture. Thelma and Louise have robbed a highway patrolman of his gun – a symbolic castration – and locked him in his car trunk. The stormtrooper-turned-crybaby wiggles a small, white, very wormy finger through an airhole after the women leave, only to have the Rasta blow back the exhaust of his spliff in reply. The American landscape has ceased to be the exclusive province of white masculinity.

While *Thelma & Louise* doesn't pretend to remedy a heritage of oppression, it does make tracks as a feminist road movie. And what sweetens the equation further is that it is also a Western, retooled with .45s not Winchesters, '66 T-Birds not pintos. Thelma and Louise embody classic Western archetypes, with a twist. Thelma is simple and sweet, childlike and unworldly. She's the woman John Wayne kisses goodbye in the *Red River* prologue, Marilyn Monroe in *River of No Return*, and again, later and sadder, in *The Misfits*. Louise is tough and knowing, a saloon gal like Dietrich's Frenchy in *Destry Rides Again* or Julie London in *Man of the West*. 'Not this weekend, sweetie,' jokes Louise to a male co-worker about Thelma, 'she's running away with me.' What begins as a retreat from masculinity, a weekend slumber party, ends up an adventure of girlfriends, guns and guts.

Thelma and Louise may drive out of town all smiles, Dolly Parton denim and lace, but their getaway turns ugly as soon as they leave home. At their first stop Thelma is assaulted in a parking lot by a man with whom she has casually danced and flirted. The film declares its intentions the moment Louise interrupts the rape, answering the order to 'suck my cock' with a bullet through his chest. Unlike *Wild at Heart*, this frontier isn't open to exploitation. When the women hit the road a second time, they're not on vacation from men, they're running from the law – not just the Pinkertons or J. Edgar Hoover, but the law of the father.

In contrast to *Bonnie and Clyde*, Thelma and Louise's crime isn't murder, it's subjectivity. What's at stake in *Thelma & Louise* is paternal authority, whether it's a rapist named Harlon, Thelma's noxious husband, or the father-like Hal. In *True Grit* and *The Silence of the Lambs*, strong female characters lean on, or learn from, men. In *Thelma & Louise* women look to each other to survive.

Within the usual terms of gender, it's a maxim that feminine desires are equated with passivity and masculine with action, a truism Scott's film upends. It's this familiar logic that frames the proverbial pioneer woman in the cabin doorway and fixes *Pretty Woman*'s Hollywood hooker for romantic conquest on her tenement fire escape. The same formula finds Thelma a dizzy housewife married to a domineering carpet salesman. 'He's your husband, not your father,' Louise reminds her friend. Down the road, Thelma repeats this homily to her husband in a telephoned declaration of independence and a life reborn.

Unlike films that submit women to a spurious transvestism

(such as Blake Edward's *Switch*), the changes in Thelma and Louise are more than merely cosmetic. As in *Something Wild*, clothing is saturated with meaning, but where Demme's Lulu strips away the 'exotic' to get at the essence, trading danger for gentility, black for white, Thelma and Louise are designing a different paradigm.

Louise swaps all her jewellery – including an engagement ring – for a white cowboy hat, while Thelma sports a black T-shirt that features a smiling skull and the legend 'Drivin' my life away'. But there's more to these outlaws than butch get-ups, more than whimsy at stake when Louise tosses her lipstick in the dirt. The physical transformations parallel the women's wild rush down the American road. At each state border they cross, another boundary – both ontological and literal – is transgressed. In *Thelma & Louise*, homicide and mayhem pale in comparison to the implications of the friendship of women.

In much the same way as Demme clutters his roadside America with white kitsch and negritude, Scott trots out a miscellany of masculinity. 'Fill her up', orders Louise to a gas-station attendant, ignoring the testosterone-swelled Michelin man who pumps iron nearby. Cowboy, outlaw, lawman: registers of masculine identity circulate in Scott's frame. There's Thelma's boorish husband, Daryl, who makes her a football widow; the women's cowboy lovers, J.D. and Jimmy; Hal, the friendly Arkansas chief of police and benign exception to unjust law – leading men relegated here to supporting roles.

A touring musician, Jimmy is the New Age cowboy with the seductive sulk of crooner Chris Isaak, while J.D., with his ten-gallon hat and twitching hips, is the sexual outlaw of *Giant* and *Badlands* – the film's lone camera movement across a human body is reserved for Thelma's gaze at the rippled muscles of his belly. Men are signposts along this freaky female trip – the good, the bad and the ugly, each suggesting a different heterosexual possibility, a potential refuge or threat.

From *Easy Rider* through *Butch Cassidy and the Sundance Kid* to *Midnight Run*, men in the buddy movie have a relationship in order to develop their individual autonomy. In contrast, Thelma and Louise forge an alliance that isn't based on joint narcissism and private prerogative – or the competing favours of men. It is most vividly realised in a scene in which the women rip through the night, dwarfed by a landscape of red buttes and mesas. Dramatic and imposing, this is the classic frontier tableau, the one eternally asso-

BFI STILLS, POSTERS AND DESIGNS

**Blocking the road: Susan Sarandon
and Geena Davis make their escape
in 'Thelma & Louise' (1991)**

ciated with John Ford's most memorable Westerns. It's the image that opens *Thelma & Louise*, when nostalgia – laden black and white – gives way to vivid colour, an iconic reference to a celluloid landscape as familiar as Lincoln's craggy profile on a nickel. It's the panorama that at a glance invokes the place where women are at once domesticated and uncivilised – as in *Stagecoach*, both the mother and the whore – and where the land, like women, is both good and bad, bountiful and punishing, wild and tame.

It's amid the buttes and mesas, a visual cue for Ford's Monument Valley, that Thelma and Louise mark one of the film's most intimate moments. As Marianne Faithfull's ravaged voice fills the air with 'The Ballad of Lucy Jordan', Thelma and Louise trade swigs of Wild Turkey: 'At the age of 37, she realised she'd never ride through Paris in a sportscar with the warm wind in her hair.' Later, parked at the side of the road, the women stand in silence to watch the dawn break, the fiery orange of the sun, the red ochre buttes and their matching scarlet hair in startling concert.

In clumsier hands the moment could sink into murky essentialism. But in *Thelma & Louise* the issue isn't woman as nature, but women in nature. Here, the female body is not a landscape to be mapped, a frontier under conquest. This is the liberated body, but, as well, the body of empathetic connection. In the absence of men, on the road Thelma and Louise create a paradigm of female friendship, produced out of their wilful refusal of the male world and its laws. No matter where their trip finally ends, Thelma and Louise have reinvented sisterhood for the American screen.

Bloated and alcoholic, Jack Kerouac died a recluse nearly 20 years after he wrote his most famous book. So much for the giddy masculine promise of *On the Road*. Route 66 has been closed, Detroit all but shuttered, and these days the US government wages war for the oil that feeds its automotive addiction.

In *Thelma & Louise* the history of the American road movie is filtered through a revisionist lens. It's as if step by step, Thelma and Louise retrace the familiar routes, but with the will to pleasure, not power. Tired scenarios and clichéd landscapes alike are reinvented, resuscitated with fresh perspective and never-before-told lives. On this trip, when women drive, Oedipus spins out of control.

First published in July 1991 (volume 1, number 3).

Amy Taubin

The 'Alien' trilogy:
from feminism to Aids

Situated in a mineral ore refinery and toxic waste dump cum max-
imum security prison on a planet at the 'rats' ass end of space',
Alien³, directed by David Fincher, mines an unconscious structured
by 100 years of cinema. It doesn't make allusions or tributes, neither is it a knock-off or a rip-off. It is, however, suffused with a particularly bleak and claustrophobic strain of imagery. It's every
prison, shiphold, sewer, grave-robbing, guillotine, morgue, con-
centration-camp, New York-subway, lunatic-asylum movie you've
ever seen. It's *Escape from Devil's Island* and *Island of Lost Souls*; *The Third
Man*, *The Trial, Othello* and (via Welles) *Apocalypse Now*; *Day of Wrath*,
Vampyr, Jeanne d'Arc and (via Dreyer) *The Seventh Seal*; *Dune* and *The
Shining, Bridge on the River Kwai* and you name it. It's whatever images
surface on your dream screen when what's really terrifying you is
Aids, or being pregnant with a monster, or being forced to carry a
foetus you don't want to term, or never being able to have a baby
though you desperately want one because this is the end of the
industrial age which is also the age of the movies, the end of pleasure and unpleasure, the end of the world as we know it.

Time stops dead at the 'rats' ass end of space'. If there's a future,
Alien³ can't imagine it. In that sense, it's the opposite of *T2*, another
end of the steel-age flick. *T2* sends the mixed message required of
blockbusters: on the one hand, it says if you think what's gone down
until now is bad (and that includes *Terminator* circa 1985), what
comes next – *T2* – is worse; on the other hand, the morphing of *T2*
is the biggest seduction in the movie.

In skeleton, *Alien* and *Aliens* are, respectively, a slasher flick and a war epic. *Alien³* treats these fossilised genres with blatant disrespect. Privileging the inchoate, it veers from the Hollywood straight and narrow towards what, for lack of a better term, is still referred to as avant-garde film.

Regarding the mysterious death of the protagonist of *Meshes of the Afternoon*, Maya Deren (its film-maker/actor, aka the mother of the American avant-garde) wrote: 'It would seem that the imagined achieved for her such force that it became a reality.' There is evidence to suggest that *Alien³* is, in its entirety, Ripley's nightmare – in the sense that *Meshes* was Deren's – a nightmare from which she never awakes. This is not merely to say that *Alien³* traffics in the fantastic; as sci-fi it obviously does. Rather, that the structure of this $50 million mega-sequel often seems like a secondary elaboration (in the Freudian dream work sense), a jagged and digressive cover to the anxiety churning beneath.

Released in 1979, Ridley Scott's *Alien* played on anxieties set loose by a decade of feminist and gay activism. Looking for a warm host for their eggs, the aliens didn't bother about the niceties of sexual difference. When the baby alien (or as one 42nd Street moviehouse denizen exclaimed, 'little-dick-with-teeth') burst from John Hurt's chest, it cancelled the distinction on which human culture is based.

Prehistoric in appearance, the alien embodied the return of repressed infantile fears and confusions about where babies come from and the anatomical differences between the sexes. Its toothy, dripping mouth was hermaphroditic: while the double jaws represented the inner and outer labia of the *vagina dentata*, the projectile movement of the inner jaw was a phallic threat. Granted that the terror of being raped and devoured by the monster loomed large for both sexes, *Alien* was a basically male anxiety fantasy: that a man could be impregnated was the ultimate outrage. But by making the hero a woman, however tomboyish, gender as well as sexual difference was destabilised.

A Pentagon-inspired family-values picture for the Reagan 80s, James Cameron's *Aliens* (1986) is the most politically conservative film of the series. A marine squadron does hand-to-claw combat with an alien army that has destroyed the inhabitants of a planetary outpost. New Age assault rifles and grenade launchers are fetishised, as is the nuclear family. 'Families', breathes Ripley in horror when she learns the identity of the victims.

During the 57-year ellipsis between *Alien* and *Aliens*, Ripley, deep in hyperspace with Jonesy the cat wrapped in her arms, drifted about in a time warp. In *Aliens*, Ripley's nurturing impulses are redirected from the cat to the girl child, Newt, the sole survivor of the alien attack. The director's cut of *Aliens* restores 20 minutes that were hacked from the theatrical version. Included is a moment in which the newly rescued Ripley breaks down when she's shown a photograph of an old woman – her daughter, who died at age 76.

The scene reinforces Cameron's preoccupation with back-to-the-future twists and tough mothers (Linda Hamilton in the *Terminator* films is a dumber, male-identified version of Ripley) but, in terms of Ripley's character, the trilogy works better when Ripley's maternal desire develops gradually on screen rather than being realised in the back story. In the first film, she's the career woman whose nurturing impulses are invested in her cat. In the second, she becomes the adoptive mother of Newt. In the third, having lost Newt, and with her biological clock running out, she discovers she's pregnant – with an alien. It's a betrayal of and by the body that many women of Ripley's generation (give or take a couple of centuries) understand too well.

Cameron's *Aliens* re-establishes sexual difference in both the human and alien spheres. Although the dialogue implies that the aliens are as indiscriminate as ever in their choice of hosts, on screen it's a female human who suffers the involuntary Caesarian birth. Similarly, it's the alien queen who, guarded by her warriors, lays the eggs.

Like *Alien*, *Aliens* climaxes with a one-on-one between Ripley and the alien. In the second film, however, the scene is structured as a cat fight between the good mother and the bad. (As in *Fatal Attraction*, or the more recent *The Hand that Rocks the Cradle*, the good mother is forced to defend her family against a crazy woman who invades her household and tries to usurp her position.)

However thrilling the entrance of Ripley in the power loader (she's transformed into a cyborg), the image is immediately tarnished by the obviousness of her line, 'Get away from her, you bitch', addressed to the alien who's about to do something terrible to the cowering Newt. The misogyny of the scene has often been analysed on a psychosexual level as the refusal of the 'monstrous feminine', of the archaic, devouring mother. But it also has a historically specific, political meaning. If Ripley is the prototypical, upper-middle-class WASP, the alien queen bears a suspicious resemblance to a favourite scapegoat of the Reagan/Bush era – the black welfare mother, that parasite on the economy whose uncurbed reproductive drive reduced hard-working taxpayers to bankruptcy.

'The bitch is back' is the tag line of the trailer for *Alien³*. Intoned above a two-shot of the alien pressing its drooling lips against Ripley's quivering cheek, it could refer to either of them, or both. Six years after *Aliens*, 'bitch' was a fundamental term in rap culture and it was the rap audience the trailer was addressing. No matter that it's out of synch with the elegiac tone of the film. No matter that viewers who expected a replay of Cameron's militaristic vision are bound to be disappointed. *Alien³* took a cool $27 million in its opening week, after which the box office dropped precipitously. The mainstream press was largely dismissive. Neither the gay nor feminist press realised immediately that the film is all about the Aids crisis and the threat to women's reproductive rights.

Alien³ picks up where *Aliens* leaves off, just after Ripley tucks her putative nuclear family – Newt, the husbandly Hicks, and the crippled android-nanny Bishop into their hyper-sleep pods before settling herself for the long night ahead. 'Can I dream?', asks Newt. 'I think we both can all the way home', Ripley assures her, as she, too, snuggles down.

Their dreams are anything but sweet. The shards of imagery that punctuate the opening credits of *Alien³* reveal that something is moving about the spacecraft, trying to crack open the sleep pods, starting fires. Ripley stirs in her sleep, but Newt and Hicks are oblivious and they are both DOA when the spacecraft crash lands on Fury 161. Ripley is alone – the sole woman in a prison labour camp with 25 YY chromosome lifers. In *Alien³*, the disgruntled workers of earlier films have become slaves of the military corporate state (The Company).

Although Ripley is the protagonist of *Alien* and *Aliens*, their narratives are not a function of her point of view. Often she seems as alienated (indeed!) from the story that's constructed around her as she is from her co-workers, or from The Company itself. *Alien³* is much more a first-person film (and one should not underestimate Sigourney Weaver's contribution to its authorship). The film charts Ripley's emotional course from despair to beyond despair to a brief moment of rebirth (in community) to a death that's no less bitter for all its principled defiance.

Former murderers, rapists and child molesters, the prisoners on

**Principled defiance: Sigourney Weaver
moves through and beyond despair
in 'Alien³' (1992)**

Fury 161 practise an 'apocalyptic millennarian, fundamentalist Christianity' of their own devising. 'We've taken a vow of celibacy and that also includes women,' one of them sneeringly tells Ripley. Their leader Dillon (Charles Dutton) is worried that Ripley's presence will cause 'a break in the spiritual unity' of his men. In their eyes, she's the alien.

Inadvertently, Ripley has brought two of the deadly creatures with her. One soon erupts from the belly of a pet dog and the other, 'a queen, an egg-layer', is growing inside Ripley herself. Ripley must persuade Dillon and his crew ('the YY chromo boys') to join forces with her to destroy the aliens, to sacrifice themselves to save humanity. Because, as usual, The Company wants an alien prototype brought back to earth 'for use in its biological warfare division'. In the language of US constitutional law, it has 'a compelling state interest' in the foetus Ripley is carrying. (In other words, no abortion rights for her.)

Unlike sci-fi creatures of the Cold War period, who took possession of souls and minds – even when they were called body snatchers – the alien is an invader and destroyer of the body. In *Alien³*, the body, which in retrospect seems to have been remarkably repressed in the first two films, becomes a landscape, obsessively probed and examined with fingers and eyes, penetrated in close-up with needles, knives and saws.

Early in the film, Ripley forms a blood bond with Clemens, the prison doctor (Charles Dance). He's a man with a tainted past: high on morphine, he once overdosed and killed a dozen or so of his patients. She's tainted too; although she doesn't realise it, she has an alien growing inside her. Clemens is off drugs now, but he still fetishises the ritual, as does *Alien³*'s director. Ripley and Clemens have perfunctory, mostly off-screen sex, but the truly erotic moments between them involve him shooting her up, not once but twice, in the space of 15 minutes, 'with his own special cocktail'. 'Do you trust me?', he asks, as Ripley stretches her opalescent-skinned arm across the screen. The sequences are achingly attenuated; each is about ten shots long. At the end of the second, the alien looms suddenly behind the translucent examining-room curtain and lops off Clemens' head.

Aids is everywhere in the film. It's in the danger surrounding sex and drugs. It's in the metaphor of a deadly organism attacking an all-male community. It's in the iconography of the shaven heads.

Exhorting the prisoners to defy The Company, Ripley shouts, 'They think we're scum and they don't give a fuck about one friend of yours who's died,' an Aids activism line if ever there was one. The alien's basement lair, with its dripping pipes and sewage tunnels, represents not only the fear of the monstrous-feminine, but homophobia as well. It's the uterine and the anal plumbing entwined. Which is why the alliance between Ripley and Dillon (the 'feminist' and the 'homosexual') is so moving.

More a possession film than its predecessors, *Alien*[3] has a look that's both claustrophobic and fluid. Fincher's predilection for extreme low angles emphasises the oppressively massive scale of the combination prison/hospital/blast furnace (Foucault in the twenty-sixth century) set. His refusal (whether intentional or not) of the conventions of continuity editing (most of the film is shot in close-up; what long shots there are could hardly be considered 'establishing') results in a space that's all the more confining for being without discernible boundaries.

The boundary that's most in question is between Ripley and the alien. 'You've been in my life for so long, I can't remember anything else,' she whispers. 'Don't be afraid, I'm one of the family now.' It's something more than her new haircut that suddenly makes Ripley's teeth the focus of attention, like the sharp little teeth of the possessed sister in *Vampyr*. The alien queen is inside Ripley, who's the mother in us all. It's the only baby she'll ever have.

Released 12 years after he directed *Alien*, Ridley Scott's *Thelma & Louise* prefigures the new *Alien*. By choosing to hurl herself over the brink rather than bend to the will of the state, the hero guarantees her transformation from woman to myth. More pessimistic and unsparing than *Thelma & Louise*, Fincher's *Alien*[3] suggests that Ripley knows that the odds are against there being anyone left in the world for whom her myth will have meaning.

Dillon is already dead when the representatives of The Company finally arrive. They try to trick Ripley into letting them have the alien foetus, into allowing them to take control: 'You could have a life, a child... trust us.' It's the climax of the allegory that *Alien*[3], like most blockbuster movies, has embedded within it – the allegory of its own making. When asked how Fincher, whose first feature this is, convinced Twentieth Century Fox to allow him such a grim ending, one Hollywood writer explained that 'having gotten the studio 90 per cent pregnant, it had no choice but to let him go all the way.'

All the way is Ripley, executing a backward swan dive into a fiery furnace. The sequence is strikingly similar to the earlier ones with the needle – the same sense of body stretched over space and time, the same fetishised close-ups, the same ecstatic abandonment to the inevitable. As she falls, the alien bursts out of her. She wraps her arms around it, pressing its hissing mouth to her breast – to prevent its escape, but also, to nurture it. A most complicated gesture, and quite unlike any other I've ever seen in movies.

R.I.P. Ripley

First published in July 1992 (volume 2, number 3).

Irene Kotlarz

Working against the grain: women in animation

When Walt Disney was expanding his workforce in the 30s to make the first animated feature film *Snow White and the Seven Dwarfs*, he advertised for young male art-school graduates to train as animators. The Hollywood animation industry set little store by the creativity of women. A public relations documentary made a few years later, *Inside the Disney Studio* (released as part of *The Reluctant Dragon* in 1941) shows many women working there – but in administrative or lower grades such as colour mixing or paint and trace.

Wayward Girls & Wicked Women is a collection on home video of mostly British, mostly recent films celebrating the impact of women on animation in the last 20 years. None of the films was commercially produced; some are student films, some made for Channel 4, the rest state- or grant-aided. Despite the lack of commercial financial backing, it appears that with the rise of feminism and the growth of independent film in Europe and North America, women animators have come into their own. A similar flourishing of creativity can also be seen in the eastern bloc, represented here by the work of Russian animator Nina Shorina, who provides a refreshingly different perspective on feminism, using an array of techniques from traditional puppetry to split-screen effects to explore themes from playful whimsy to social and political satire.

Of course, women have not been entirely absent from the world of animation, whether as characters – from Snow White to Jessica Rabbit – or as directors, from Joy Batchelor to Annabel Jankel and Diane Jackson. Female 'stars' of animation may be few and far between, but characters such as Olive Oyl and Betty Boop show that the image of women in animation has often been disruptive (Betty was an early victim of the Hollywood censors). Women animators today are well aware of the cartoon tradition – its techniques, generic conventions and stereotypes; most use it, send it up or react against it in one way or another.

Established in Hollywood and perfected by the Disney studio, cartoon production was via an assembly line. Production was rationalised into stages, the animation involving many levels of input from director to animators to painters and tracers who transferred the drawings to clear cels. The cels would be laid on backgrounds designed in one department while the characters, with their simplified forms, proportions and personality traits, would be created in another.

In the age of the classic cartoon, the 30s and 40s, production values (and costs) were high. The process of creating the illusion of movement from projecting thousands of separate still images was disguised, so that characters seemed to move smoothly as the camera zoomed and tracked apparently effortlessly through drawn forests, landscapes and animated interiors. Characters chased each other frenetically or bobbed along jauntily in a convention of exaggerated movement known as 'squash and stretch', which gave them a sense of weight, cuteness and believability. They were fixed in generic narrative traditions such as screwball comedy, fairy tales, violence and the chase.

One outcome was the appearance of what are by now familiar cultural stereotypes; otherness was represented in the form of physical and behavioural characteristics. The main movers in a story would usually be male, often animal, characters – from Mickey Mouse and Tom and Jerry to Roger Rabbit. Females, like Minnie Mouse, were often just a visual counterpart of the male with added eyelashes, bows and high heels. Teasing, flirtatious or winsome, they were also, occasionally, a cause of terror to the male, as in *Porky's Romance* (Frank Tashlin, 1937), where Porky Pig has premarital nightmares about Petunia's insatiable appetite and uncontrollable fecundity.

Human women, when they appeared, were usually a hybrid of signifiers of femininity comprising body parts like lips, hair, eyelashes, bosom and so on, and were sometimes derived in part from actual women film stars. From Betty Boop to Jessica Rabbit, the standard character was, and still is, that of a showgirl designed to be looked at. Animated with squash and stretch, the female body in action was offered as the object of pleasure or amusement; there's many a cartoon gag based on the bouncing-tit routine.

While I am not suggesting a male conspiracy – especially as many of the representations of women in cartoons suggest male anxiety as much as anything else – I am pointing out the process of signification with which animators engage. In animation there is no pointing the camera at a chosen subject and allowing 'reality' to speak for itself; everything you see has been put there by the animator. For animators who wish to present an alternative to the mainstream tradition and its political resonances, the question of image and the body, aesthetics and movement, as well as the techniques used, are crucial.

As the title *Wayward Girls & Wicked Women* suggests, either the films included in the collection or their makers are somehow going against the grain. Joanna Quinn, in her now classic *Girls' Night Out* (1987), turns the tables of the gaze on to a male stripper, complete with bouncing body parts. She lovingly sends up squash-and-stretch animation of the female body in her opening close-up shots of the huge, red, bouncing cherries being pressed on top of fairy cakes in the factory where the girls of the title work. Alison Snowden's *Second Class Mail* (1984), about a little old lady who sends away for an inflatable man, complete with flat cap, pipe and (when you pull the string) a rasping cough, questions the notion of desire being the preserve of the male through the simple expedient of reversing the stereotypical storyline. It is a pastiche of Bob Godfrey's *Dream Doll*, about a shy little man in love with a nubile inflatable. Both *Girls' Night Out* and *Second Class Mail* raise the question of female desire, the joke in both being the banality of the object choice.

The presentation of woman as desiring subject is the uniting concern of all the films, and animation allows the film-makers to express their concerns in ways which are unavailable to the live-action director. Within the family, desire is shown as repressed or distorted, as in Caroline Leaf's *Two Sisters* (1990), where the claustrophobic intensity of the relationship between two sisters who live together is probed using minimal animation to suggest the narrow, shuttered lives they lead. Karen Watson's autobiographical *Daddy's Little Bit of Dresden China* looks at the family as the site of incestuous desire. Watson draws on the common cartoon metaphor of the fairy-tale princess as the fantasy scenario used by the little girl in her struggle to come to terms with the reality of her father's abuse.

Two films by Emily Hubley, *Emergence of Eunice* (1980) and *Delivery Man* (1982) present a female subject trapped in her adolescent insecurities – anxieties about parental disapproval, sexuality, the death of her parents. Psychoanalytical, confessional and intimate in style, the films are reminiscent of aspects of the work of writers such as Sylvia Plath and Anne Sexton in their presentation of the intensity of a young girl's diary and dreams. But while Plath and Sexton were mature and accomplished writers, Hubley uses a scrawled felt-tip technique to represent rather than reflect on her subject's feelings. A similar presentation of a woman as she feels from the inside is offered by Candy Guard. The indignant little characters of *Alternative Fringe* – simply drawn in pencil – suffer anxieties with which many women are familiar: for example, failing to stand up to the hairdresser and ending up with a terrible haircut. *Fatty Issues* looks with brutal realism at the self-delusions of dieters – desire doomed to failure.

Erica Russell's semi-abstract *Feet of Song* shows a woman in control of her body and her desires as she revels in the physical pleasures of music and dance. And the final volume of *Wayward Girls & Wicked Women* is devoted to three longer films, all of which reject the cartoon tradition in favour of a more reflexive, ephemeral imagery of desire. In Suzan Pitt's *Asparagus* (1978), where the constantly transforming imagery has the heightened colour and clarity of hallucination, creativity is explored as a metaphor for desire. Vera Neubauer's *The Decision* (1981) slips in and out of animation and live action, the different strands of the film counterposing fantasy and desire, fairy tale and domestic reality, the flicker of the zoetrope reminding us of the process of animation itself. Desire is the ephemeral flicker, as Neubauer's little hand-drawn lovers boil and gyrate as they pass through the projector. In Joanna Woodward's *The Brooch Pin & the Sinful Clasp* (1989) images of desire are glimpsed by a tiny male voyeur through the windows of a rickety highrise building. One woman captures the moon and then irons it, another waits weeping by the telephone, and in the film's live-action epilogue, within which the opening animation shot is being projected on a screen, desire is animation itself.

First published in October 1992 (volume 2, number 6).

Linda Ruth Williams

Sisters under the skin: video and blockbuster erotic thrillers

Although Adrian Lyne's blockbuster *Indecent Proposal* – starring Demi Moore and Robert Redford – may look like the game of Scruples with a budget, its source is a maligned straight-to-video genre which is big business at many a local store. The film which launched a thousand dinner-party conversations has lower cultural roots than those who paid to see it – but wouldn't dream of renting an erotic-thriller video – imagine.

When Willem Dafoe posits the possibility that it's 'a crime to be a great lay,' he situates *Body of Evidence* also squarely in erotic thriller territory. High or low, blockbuster or denigrated sleaze video, the genre dominates the mainstream movie and video market – despite the fact that audiences and makers of films such as *Body of Evidence*, *Basic Instinct* and *Fatal Attraction* might dispute their connection with videos such as brand leader Alexander Gregory Hippolyte's *Night Rhythms*, *Carnal Crimes* and *Secret Games*.

On video, erotic thrillers are basic stories of sexual intrigue that use some form of criminality or duplicity as the framework to support on-screen sex which is as explicit as possible. Despite the popular image of the erotic thriller as a blanket term for unchallenging sleaze, as with any other genre there are good erotic thrillers and bad ones. Certainly some of these films are simply feebly acted 90s exploitation movies which fail to do anything interesting with the sex, but others are thematically, as well as sexually, provocative.

The classic opening narrative runs thus: a neglected wife, some years into her lousy marriage, is advised by her female friend to find satisfaction with some new blood. Early scenes in which wives fail to get their husbands to come to bed are legion: the resolutely downmarket *Carnal Crimes* and *Secret Games* both boast key scenes of pleading in underwear, while even the relatively chaste blockbuster *Indecent Proposal* demonstrates its kinship to the video genre when Demi Moore places the hand of her scribbling husband on her breast, only to have him remove it so he can get on with his work. Viewers in the know will spot this gesture as the first step on the slippery slope towards erotic thriller infidelity, and the perils as well as the pleasures of sex.

Without making radical claims for these movies, their primary brief generally ensures that there is something interesting to watch, since they explore danger and sex in a format which is both thriller and skin-flick, often figuring a female protagonist who herself combines the roles of sexual interest, enraged victim and vigilante survivor. The *film noir* seductress with a pearl-handled revolver is succeeded in the erotic thriller by the Beverly Hills housewife with an appetite for sexual danger or the 90s adventuress with a way with candlewax and a damn good lawyer. These are women who bring their handcuffs with them and use their charge cards only on designer lingerie – the low-budget daughters of Kathleen Turner in *Body Heat*, itself a reworking of *Double Indemnity*, perhaps the grandmother of all erotic thrillers.

While *Basic Instinct* was frequently compared to *Jagged Edge*, also written by Joe Eszterhas, an even less flattering parallel could be drawn with a number of more disreputable films. Sharon Stone as Catherine Tramell is only a more expensive version of erotic thriller video queen Delia Sheppard, who as Bridget the avenging lesbian of *Night Rhythms* at least sticks to her sexuality and refuses to be swayed by the charms of the first man to cross her path. *Basic Instinct* is surely Jag Mundhra's *The Other Woman* in reverse: instead of the cop falling for the wrong woman and in the process persuading her away from lesbianism, *The Other Woman* presents the more intriguing possibility of a heroine turning away from heterosexuality to another woman, challenging the notion that all she ever needed to put her on the right track was a good heterosexual seeing to (the message of *Basic Instinct*).

From their titles alone it would be hard to tell erotic thrillers apart, though this is as true of the blockbusters as of the straight-to-video releases. Almost all of them join two shocking words in a single come-on message, and there is a sense that any of these words could be remixed into a new combination. The erotic words tend to be adjectives, adding sexual emphasis to the nouns: instincts are basic, crimes are carnal, proposals are indecent, intent is sexual. But this can easily be reversed, for just as dark thoughts are sexy, so is sex deadly, attraction fatal.

Yet though both are animated by explicit sex and criminal thrills, the blockbuster erotic thriller, with its high production values, massive budget and stars who can open a movie, has a racy prestige which its video sister never gains, for all the desperately classy aspirations of its *mise en scène*. This perception of video erotic thrillers as the poor cousins of the films made for theatrical release is based partly on a general privileging of theatrically released films over straight-to-video works. Private viewing does of course change the nature of a film, and in that video erotic thrillers operate with a constant awareness of masturbation as a prime audience response and index of the film's success, they are able to flirt openly with pornography.

The Video Recordings Act of 1984, introduced during a wave of panic about 'private home viewing', was the first piece of British legislation to consider the criterion of 'suitability for viewing in the home' in its censoring and classifying of film. What this has meant is that video certification – because of the medium's capacity for repeated viewings and freeze-framing – tends to be more draconian than cinematic certification, a trend that runs contrary to the persistent notion that sex films made specifically for viewing within the home must be riskier, more offensive and more sexist than anything which could show at the cinema. Backing up this notion is one particular feminist line on pornography – that the further away from the mainstream (in cinema or magazines) sexually explicit material gets, the more pernicious to women it becomes. While it is true that many straight-to-video films have been released with their sexual riskiness intact, sexiness is not an index of sexism. Since their *raison d'être* is to be sexually stimulating, video erotic thrillers do of course sail closer to the wind of censorship than films such as *Indecent Proposal*, which was released in Britain with a 15 certificate (raising the question of what happens to a film which has its generic origins in pornography when you take the pornography out). If the video erotic thriller is 'harder', this is because it represents not only the passive women of 'softer', mainstream movies, but more explicit sex and male bodies in equal measure, as well as sexually aggressive women. Stealing the plots of their poor relations, cleansing them of any residual feminism and some of their raw, 'deviant' moments, what the blockbusters have done is to engage in a series of anodyne remakes, sanding down the revealing rough edges.

All of which suggests that there might be something interesting going on for women in a genre which seems marketed primarily for the male heterosexual eye. In a recent BBC Radio 5 interview, Dave Lewis of Medusa films called these 'good-quality B movies – B for beer, Biryani and bonking' which would appeal primarily to 'young guys aged between 18 and 30'. He added, however, that 'these are films that look at sex from a woman's angle,' and it is true that the pleasures for women here are substantial, and not simply because of the videos' willingness to represent in liberal doses good old-fashioned values such as strong female characters, female friendship and women being articulate about their desires and finding fulfilment without necessarily selling their sisters out.

The discourse of male ownership, for instance, permeates the fabric of both *Secret Games* and *Indecent Proposal*, but it is arguably only the former which challenges it. Where Julianne, heroine of *Secret Games*, independently capitalises on her role as her ghastly husband's prize possession by selling herself in a ritzy brothel (and enjoying it too), Demi Moore's Diana in *Indecent Proposal* is traded from husband to lover, protesting that she did it for her husband and that she could not make the decision alone. Women in both films might go back to where they 'belong' in the end, but only the video version presents the man who says 'You're for sale – and I'm going to buy you' as dangerously objectionable. 'You collect things, don't you?' asks Demi Moore of Robert Redford as she is herself acquired, but Redford emerges as a benign figure who, having 'collected' her, lets her go; *Secret Games*' Eric, on the other hand, is defeated by a group of women working together.

The men in the videos are generally unequivocally despicable, their threat to the heroines laying bare the oppositional nature of relations between the sexes and the danger as well as the desirability of men. Sex is both the answer to and the cause of women's problems, and in presenting sexual relations as a threat as well as an indulgence, erotic thrillers, for all their glossy post-feminism, are still dramatising a battle in the sex wars. There is little fudging the issue by presenting men – as do the blockbusters – who are nothing worse than likeably confused, misguided or blinded by desire (Michael Douglas in *Basic Instinct*, William Hurt in *Body Heat*, or Willem Dafoe in *Body of Evidence*). The husbands in the videos are at best unpleasantly indifferent to their women, at worse aggressive, while male lovers are frequently murderous. In *Carnal Crimes* the heroine's vile husband and feckless lover enter into a pact against her; in Kurt MacCarley's *Sexual Intent* the tale of a villain who systematically defrauds women is spliced with a series of candid straight-to-camera accounts by ordinary women elaborating with personal relish on the 'all men are bastards' theme (Madonna's line in *Body of Evidence*, 'I never know why men lie – they just do' is the faint, mainstream echo of many of the videos' angrier voices). It is easy to see the pleasures for women in *Sexual Intent*, not only from the vox pop testimonies, but as it turns from erotic thriller to rape-revenge narrative, when three of the women overcome their sexual rivalry to round up the villain and shoot him, only so a fourth can run him over. Even *Carnal Crimes* has its revengeful heroine redistribute her husband's money to the servants.

This is not to say that the simple presentation of men as villains constitutes a feminist move, even in tandem with a barrage of soft-feminist points. But neither could it be said that these are unambiguously misogynistic films; the suspenders may be manifold, the camera may frequently linger on the perfect Californian female body, but this is not the whole story. Indeed, in films which are so overtly directed towards male heterosexual desire, the narrative attack on masculinity presents something of a problem; the patterns of identification for male and female viewer are not simple.

The fact that erotic thrillers are so resoundingly ideologically confused, and that they wear this confusion on their sleeves in a way the blockbusters don't, facilitates other pleasures than those for which they were overtly designed. A scene in *Secret Games*, for instance, in which a group of women discuss the inadequacy of men ('Women are more considerate,' says one, while another protests that 'Men don't know what women want') takes place as the women lounge topless around a swimming pool: the sexualised bodies and women-only talk suggests male-fantasised lesbianism, but the talk itself takes the scene elsewhere. Earlier, three women offer a characteristically male-oriented voyeuristic spectacle by trying on their raunchiest underwear in front of each other – but on the whole, the scene combines the pleasures of shopping with those of sex in an atmosphere that is part Tupperware party, part orgy. Add to this confusion of signals a large helping of self-parody and something rather surprising is taking place. For example, Leon Ichaso's *Those Bedroom Eyes*, a non-explicit made-for-television film (the steamy saxophone apparently making up for the lack of steamy sex), cuts from the shooting of a man in a torrent of jacuzzi foam to a train going into a tunnel, in a film whose hero is a psychology lecturer with a cat called Freud.

If husbands are neglectful, best friends – in the video films at least – are indulgent. This is another key difference: in the 'lower' films women have buddies who look out for them, but not so in the blockbusters: Demi Moore in *Indecent Proposal* can share her moral dilemma with no one, while *Body of Evidence* pits all three women (Madonna, Dafoe's wife, and Anne Archer replaying her Fatal Attraction role as the now faithful secretary) completely against each other in a triangle of hate. In *Fatal Attraction* the solitary Glenn Close character is notoriously dispatched by Archer as righteous wife, and while in *Basic Instinct* Sharon Stone's Tramell is seen with a number of women of all ages, she hardly inspires affection. The videos tell a different story – loyalty and the benefits of sexual healing are central to the lore which circulates between female friends; here it is women's role to prescribe a sexual cure for the ills of marriage. Beyond the point that this is, of course, the justification for the heroine's subsequent strip and every sex scene in the film, the women are at least doing it for themselves rather than being swayed by sexual pressure from the first toy-boy who shows interest or kindness. Elise's best friend in *Carnal Crimes* encourages her affair and dismisses all guilt, while the distinctly unglamorous heroine of *Sexual Intent*, battered wife June, is told by her friend Kath, 'Sometimes you just have to go for it – listen to your gut for a change.' In the move from 'low' video to 'high' blockbuster, such female friends are lost.

The worst that can be said about this woman-to-woman remedy is that it ignores the post-*Female Eunuch* arguments against sexual liberation as a lifestyle, not to say political, cure-all. This is slick sex as therapy for social *ennui*, a silicone sexual revolution as prescribed by the Beverly Hills sisterhood in which you can have free love as well as face lifts. Most of the women do finally stick with their marriages: marriage does, after all, bring significant fringe benefits, in particular the pleasures of conspicuous consumption. In this, *Inde-*

cent Proposal is something of a departure, since Demi Moore opts for love's sake for husband and poverty rather than the paying stranger.

Compared to their low-budget, straight-to-video sisters, the women of the blockbusters have little obvious appeal for women in the audience, as the gut response of many women to *Basic Instinct* demonstrates. Here sex-as-crime enjoyed for its pervier pleasures is disavowed by a final message which condemns it – the return of family values, of wife to husband, the death of the harpy: in *Fatal Attraction*, *Body of Evidence*, *Indecent Proposal*, *Final Analysis*, you name it. The point isn't, as J. Hoberman has written in *Sight and Sound*, that the women-as-designer-sex-toys who populate the blockbusters have unexpectedly turned nasty: the shock of the ice-pick isn't the shock of a woman taking up arms, it's that someone has bothered to lay out their fantasy of female sadism made in the image of male masochism so explicitly and expensively while pretending it's something else. Women who kill in the blockbusters do so as part of the oiliest designer fantasy; men might die beyond the little death, but the women's powers are hardly self-appointed. It is left to the cheaper movies to explore more fully a woman's view of the kill, and her motives. At least the lower-budget women get good sex as well as the pleasures of the feminist vigilante. At least they can shoot the buggers honestly and for their own reasons, without finding that, after all, they were only playing out the active role in his last fantasy.

My objection to this streak in the glossies isn't that a particularly narrow mode of male sadism is having it out on the screen, but that it's pretending to be something smarter and less 'deviant'. Not so the low-budgets, which if they want to show forms of sado-masochism from one side or the other or indulge in any variety of gratuitous 'perversions' will do so. The ponderous sado-masochism of *Body of Evidence*, so desperate to shock, entirely lacks the routine nonchalance of the numerous scenes of three-way sex, voyeurism and domination to be found in the videos. The heroine of *Carnal Crimes* is initiated into infidelity as she drips blood from her wounded arm on to another woman, while a man – the film's 'purveyor of perversions' – takes pictures; the glamorous female shrink in *Sexual Intent* masturbates to the videos of testifying women. Before their own lesbian encounter in *The Other Woman*, Jessica watches a man pouring milk over Traci's breasts; the madame of the high-class brothel of *Secret Games* masturbates to the remote-camera images of her girls getting it on. The spectacle of female pleasure, particularly pleasure which excludes men, is central. There is little moral gloss, and women are seldom the villains, and even less often the villains by simple virtue of their sexuality.

Erotic thrillers may almost have done away with the *femme fatale*, but this doesn't stop their women from being unsettlingly exciting. However audacious they are, they don't get punished for it, and having enjoyed the sex they can then switch roles as the films slip genres and the women take their revenge. Compare this to the familiar track record of the blockbusters: Glenn Close in *Fatal Attraction* is dispatched in perhaps the most notorious female death in 80s cinema; in *Body of Evidence*, Madonna is put on trial, shot and then drowned. If *Fatal Attraction* had gone straight to video, avoiding the infamous preview screenings at which audiences, enraged by the original suicide ending, shouted 'Kill the bitch', the Close character might have escaped. Only the incredibly pernicious conclusion of *Night Rhythms* gets close to blockbuster punishment, as Bridget is carted off to prison with Nick accusing her not only of killing her lover Honey, but of being lousy in bed, a frustrated dyke and an ambitious career woman who has stolen his radio show.

Lesbianism is a central concern of these films, and its representation raises the question of female response both within the narrative and for women in the audience. Susie Bright, one-time editor of American lesbian porn magazine *On Our Backs*, has made the point that the sexual imagination is adept at appropriating material from a variety of sources, and that lesbians have long used male heterosexual porn, viewing against the grain of the text's heterosexual message to find other pleasures through it, including those provided by the stock images of lesbian sex that appear in these films. While none of them could unproblematically be called lesbian porn – even though at least one such sex scene seems obligatory in each – this is not to say that lesbians cannot enjoy watching them, or that the actresses involved did not enjoy what they were doing. But the values and images of the Hippolyte stable, not to say the 'higher' lesbianism of *Basic Instinct*, are nevertheless a far cry from the lesbian porn marketed specifically for women, using lesbian models, photographers and editorial staff, to be found in *On Our Backs* or the British magazine *Quim*.

Indeed Catherine Tramell and her video sisters, the designer dykes of the raunchier erotic thrillers, are not so much bisexual as hetero-lesbian, putting their lesbianism on show not, apparently, for their own pleasure but as a foreplay spectacle for the eyes of a man – or, in the case of *Basic Instinct*, as the primary weapon of heterosexual enticement. In this capacity, Tramell is fashioned by the sharpest misogynist knife (or ice-pick), as she manages to alienate other women not only by virtue of her indifference to them as sexual partners the minute Michael Douglas' cop waves his magic wand, but by her use of them to appear more alluring to him in the first place. In this light, the spectacle of Tramell and her psycho girlfriend becomes that of a pair of entwined Playmates of the month – maybe a bit murderous, but still looking fixedly into the male eye which is in the end more interesting.

If lesbianism, which ought to threaten and revolt men because it excludes them, is a come-on, then so is the possibility of murder, which ought to invoke an even stronger reaction in its threat to do away with them altogether. Yet here female murderousness is a partner in crime with hetero-lesbianism; male sexual exclusion and/or the risk of total annihilation become the most exciting things possible. In both cases the male sexual role is more central the greater the risk he takes, the more sexually and fatally threatened he is. The less a man seems to be needed in the sex scenes of these films, the more sure you can be that the whole thing is being played out for his benefit. When a character such as Stone's turns to women as she is turning on men, she may suggest the possibility of the man being done away with, but this is in fact a stylised ritual of taboo-breaking at which erotic thrillers are adept. Madonna's body-as-murder-weapon – 'no different from a gun or a knife' – is precisely what Willem Dafoe wants, even though, or perhaps because, he risks being its victim.

The rough incoherence of the videos – smoothed out to some extent in the blockbusters – facilitates a number of other readings. Susie Bright has written in celebration of dyke daddies, 'lesbian-identified men' who 'don't want to save the lesbians' (by giving them a bit of what they're really after), 'they want to *be* the lesbians'. Heterosexual response is obviously not as straightforward as some might like to think, with a range of subversive cross-identifications going on, for women as well as for men. It is this contradictory transgression of conventions that makes the video erotic thriller more engaging than its anodyne, high-budget counterpart.

'Today's "meat movie" is tomorrow's blockbuster', writes Carol

Clover in *Men, Women and Chain Saws*, which highlights a key relationship between low-budget, rough-edged 'nasties' and high-profile, high-budget glossy shocker-thrillers. Video erotic thrillers are equally the disavowed but influential underbelly of the current spate of sexy blockbusters. Scratch the surface of *Basic Instinct* and you have a straight-to-video erotic thriller with a bigger budget, while *Indecent Proposal* looks rather like *Secret Games* with most of the sex taken out. The soundtrack might tell us that this is 'no ordinary love' as Demi Moore and Woody Harrelson fuck on their bed of money, but it is the love that erotic thrillers are made of.

First published in July 1993 (volume 3, number 7).

Ginette Vincendeau

The beast's beauty: Jean Gabin, masculinity and the French hero

Why does *La Bête humaine* have such lasting power? To some, any Jean Renoir film must necessarily be a masterpiece. For others, the key lies in the subtle eroticism of the Jean Gabin–Simone Simon relationship. And train buffs rank it high as a train movie. Without denying any of these approaches, I want to focus on the film's special place in French culture, and on the figure of Jean Gabin, the French proletarian hero.

Since history likes great men, it is not surprising that *La Bête humaine*, in which three of the greatest names in French literature and cinema joined forces, has become emblematic. A life-size wooden replica of *La Lison*, Jacques Lantier's steam engine, was the final exhibit in the three-hour parade down the Champs-Elysées that marked the 200th anniversary of the French Revolution. Driven by a Gabin lookalike, the model was called upon to evoke an idea of the French proletariat visualised by Renoir in 1938, dramatically shaped by Zola in 1890, but clearly born on Bastille Day in 1789.

La Bête humaine has attracted a great deal of criticism. Renoir has been accused of taking the politics out of Zola, and of reducing the novel's social commentary on the corrupt *grand-bourgeoisie* of the Second Empire to a few glimpses of an elegant Parisian mansion and the office of a judge who claims that he 'knows' murderers by looking at their eyes. Above all, he replaced Zola's apocalyptic ending of a driverless train of soldiers speeding to inevitable disaster with Lantier's suicide, followed by a peaceful gathering of his SNCF mates around his corpse. So the film has been seen as a disappointing ideological turning point in Renoir's career. The Popular Front director who celebrated group solidarity and class struggle in *Le Crime de Monsieur Lange* (and *La Vie est à nous*) now appeared to regress politically, producing a story of individual doom in the tradition of the poetic realism of Carné and Prévert epitomised by *Quai des brumes*, which, incidentally, Renoir considered reactionary.

Another interpretation has it that *La Bête humaine* is simply symptomatic of the grim political climate of 1938, with the end of the Popular Front and the Spanish Civil War and the anticipated approach of the Second World War. In this version, Gabin's suicide at the end of the film comes to represent the lost hopes of the French proletariat.

How can a single film prompt such different readings? And, more surprisingly, how was it that this sombre story of murderous, suicidal, congenitally diseased workers was used as a symbol, in 1989, of the glory of the French Revolution?

In *La Bête humaine* Renoir drew on a tradition within nineteenth-century French literature and art of exploring the 'little people' of France. Zola, himself an accomplished photographer, saw his 'cinematic' writing as a means of documenting the lives of the French people. His *Rougon–Macquart* saga – of which *La Bête humaine* is a part – was a reply to Balzac's *Comédie humaine*, but equipped with the scientific baggage of the time, in particular ideas about heredity and the theory of evolution. But such novels shared more than a documentary impulse: they exhibited a positively voyeuristic fascination for the poor, the exploited, the criminal element. In these essentially bourgeois accounts, the labouring classes are also the dangerous classes – a cultural trope that found its way via Zola into the 'proletarian literature' of the 20s and was to be of great consequence for French cinema.

French cinema in the 30s has two major modes: light and dark. Partly because of its literary heritage, it is the dark tradition which has attracted cultural respectability and international fame for French cinema and through a number of mediations forms part of the archaeology of American *film noir*. (Lang's *Scarlet Street* was based on Renoir's *La Chienne* and *Human Desire* on *La Bête humaine*.) Photographed for the most part by the German émigré Kurt Courant, who also worked on *Le Jour se lève*, *La Bête humaine* displays many of the stylistic features of *film noir* – chiaroscuro and Expressionist lighting, Venetian-blind shadows – which are at their most powerful in the scene in which Séverine is murdered. Zola and German Expressionist cinema meet in these oppressive night scenes, as well as in the insistence on mirrors and reflections.

But Renoir's film is less relentlessly *noir* than *Quai des brumes, Le Jour se lève* or the works of Julien Duvivier and Pierre Chenal. The dark alleys, courtyards, hotel rooms and dingy hovels so characteristic of the dark tradition are relieved by light moments, both in mood and in the lighting of the film. There is the scene with Flore, with its emphasis on the bright sky; the meeting between Lantier and Séverine in the park; the workers' dance; several of the scenes connected with the train.

It is in the scenes centred around the railway that Renoir manages to be both faithful to Zola and historically located in the 30s. Echoing Zola's own methods, Renoir, Gabin, Carette and Ledoux all studied aspects of railway work so they could reproduce more accurately practices and gestures. Zola's elegiac description of the engine is transposed into the film's famous opening sequence, in which Gabin and Carette bring their train into Le Havre, communicating by looks and signals over the noise of the engine. This documentary impulse informs several other scenes between Gabin and Carette, especially their meals in the workers' canteen, where the recording of proletarian gestures and language gives banal moments a density far in excess of their narrative function.

The train in *La Bête humaine* is the embodiment of both the death drive and of social movement. Crime and suicide take place on it, and on a more abstract level it represents Lantier's murderous instinct. But Renoir is also careful to emphasise the solidarity of the railway workers and the function of the railway in the building of modern France. The newly created national company is prominently displayed in the word ETAT (state) on the side of engines and trains and is seen behind Roubaud and Séverine's heads as they are waiting to kill Grandmorin. After Lantier's death and Pecqueux's eulogy, a guard summons people to clear the tracks and get the train on its way – an image of professionalism and continuity. Rather than abiding by the *noir* tradition and ending the film with Gabin going off into the night, Renoir ends with a light moment. The tragic destinies of the characters are embedded in a more epic sense of workers' lives.

So *La Bête humaine* can be read both as the expression of failed hopes and as the symbol of workers' progress. Scholars may deplore what they see as the absence of social class in the film, but the railway workers' union, which awarded Gabin honorary membership in 1938, clearly approved of the portrayal of themselves. And when French railway workers went on strike in 1987, they invoked *La Bête humaine* as a nostalgic image of good working conditions.

But *La Bête humaine* also conjures up nostalgia for a time when cinema was a truly popular activity. The replica of *La Lison* on the Champs-Elysées evoked a memory of a form of community entertainment that has now more or less vanished. And central to this memory are the stars of the time – it was Gabin, as much as *La Lison*, who was on parade on 14 July 1989.

The often repeated anecdote that *La Bête humaine* was made because Jean Gabin wanted to drive a locomotive, true as it may be, masks the fact that without a star of his status, it would have been hard for Renoir to have raised the money to make the film at all. So in a basic economic sense, Gabin is as much the 'author' of the film as Renoir is. And the complete overlap between his star persona and the character of Jacques Lantier means that he shares the authorship of the film in other ways too.

Gabin was the perfect actor for the French *noir* tradition, combining a sense of working-class identity with crime. In most of his 30s classic films, his destiny is 'tragic' – as well as playing a murderer, he commits suicide (*Pépé-le-Moko*, *La Bête humaine*, *Le Jour se lève*), is killed or murdered (*La Bandera*, *Quai des brumes*), or morally destroyed (*La Belle Equipe*, *Gueule d'amour*). Yet he also played the regular guy who gets on well with his mates: 'Oedipus in a cloth cap,' as André Bazin put it. Gabin's ability to condense such contradictory values made him the perfect Jacques Lantier, the hero marked by the hereditary *fêlure* (flaw) but otherwise demonstrating health and solidity.

La Bête humaine confirmed Gabin as the top male star at the French box office. It was a popularity derived from a carefully judged style of performance – despite the impression he gave of always playing himself – and from his ability to present French audiences with an acceptable version of masculinity that nevertheless exposed some of its less acceptable aspects. Gabin came from the music hall, where as one of Mistinguett's 'toy boys' he sang witty ditties full of innuendo. Those familiar only with his 'classic' films might be surprised to see him with brilliantined hair and make-up in early features such as *Chacun sa chance* and *Paris-Béguin*.

**French proletarian hero: Jean Gabin
in 'La Bête humaine' (1938)**

La Bandera (Duvivier, 1935) signalled his entry into stardom, with a definitive switch to melodramatic roles and the adoption of a different style of performance. Gone was the exhibitionism of the music hall and in its place came an understated style of acting which worried some of his directors on the set until they saw the result on screen.

As Renoir put it, 'Gabin, with the slightest tremor in his face, could express the most violent feelings.' Many compared him with other French actors of the time who used a wide register of gesticulations retained from the stage (compare the performances of Gabin and Carette in *La Bête humaine*), and a rhetorical style of speech. Gabin bordered on the laconic, yet at the same time retained through his gestures a specific, class-inflected identity: the walk, the way the cigarette dangled from his mouth, the way he ate, not to mention his accent, which was to 'give him away' when he played *grand-bourgeois* parts in the 50s.

Another important feature of the Gabin persona was that he was equally appealing to men and women. As one writer put it: 'men want to slap him in the back, women to take him in their arms'. This status as a powerful figure of identification for both sexes is central to *La Bête humaine*: significantly it is Roubaud, not Séverine, who insists initially on inviting Lantier into their home; whatever happens in their triangle is not a question of male rivalry. Long before the 'new man' of the 80s, the Gabin persona included attributes traditionally considered feminine: gentleness and caring, but also weakness and passivity.

Masculinity is traditionally defined by action and power; in the Gabin persona it is characterised by immobility and failure. Though he is the main protagonist of *La Bête humaine*, Lantier is trapped and is 'objectified' by the camera, occupying the place traditionally assigned to women in classical cinema. *La Bête humaine* opens with Lantier on the train, but the narrative is really set in motion by the Roubauds' crime. His entrapment in their story determines his fate, which is sealed by Séverine's pleading look.

Lantier's ambiguous place in the narrative is paralleled by the camera work. It is hardly surprising that Gabin should receive star treatment, with many of the close-ups and camera movements ending on his face, but it is noticeable in *La Bête humaine* that his face is at least as glamorised as Simone Simon's. The lighting, with particular emphasis on his eyes, is not simply showcasing a handsome face, but is denoting a deeply disturbed mental state. This is made obvious in two shots in the scene after Séverine's murder: the tracking shot over her dead body ending on his face and the shot where he looks at himself in the mirror, connecting with the judge's earlier remark that he can recognise a murderer by looking at his eyes. The effect of entrapment is marked by repeated framings of Gabin in enclosed spaces, behind window panes, in bed.

So how could such a paralysed and disturbed hero come to epitomise the virile French worker? *La Bête humaine* is the perfect Gabin vehicle to work this out. His relationship to his community in all his films is ambivalent: he belongs and yet he doesn't. In *La Bête humaine* this is clearly shown in the dance scene, where the camera finds him on the edge, looking at his fellow workers dancing; he goes in very briefly, comes out again. His most antisocial act, the murder of Séverine, takes place during this community event, with Renoir linking the two together through the romantic song.

But the ambivalence of Gabin's position in *La Bête humaine* is on a wider scale. He is a passive 'object', trapped by the Roubauds' crime, itself determined by the wealthy Grandmorin and by a socially caused, inherited 'flaw': alcoholism. Yet he is also a subject, an agent with a social identity, competent at his job, liked and respected by his colleagues. Revered within his own group, Lantier is still nothing on the larger scale of a society ruled by the likes of Grandmorin. The fact that Séverine – the 'leftovers from an old man' – is passed from Grandmorin to Roubaud and then from Roubaud to Lantier highlights the doomed attempt by each man to take up symbolically the other's position higher up the scale. That the woman has to pay with her life for colluding in this male game is a story which deserves further analysis.

It is through this paradox of strong subject versus passive object that the Gabin persona defines working-class masculinity. And because he was able to smooth away many of the contradictions, Jean Gabin allowed his audience to empathise with his powerless position in French society while at the same time taking pleasure in his momentary triumphs. The fact that this 'human beast' was also beautiful, and beautifully shot, only added to the spectators' pleasure, then and now.

Gabin is certainly an icon of French cinema – scarcely a book on the subject is published without his face on its cover – but his place in French culture is more significant than that. The impact of his death in 1976 was rivalled in post-war France only by that of General de Gaulle. Both men incarnated a 'certain idea of France' – a consensual, populist dream of national unity in which the Popular Front of the mid-30s, the years of Gabin's greatest achievements, occupies a place second only to that of the French Revolution. The years 1935-38 saw not only the temporary unification of left and centre political parties, but also a cultural *rapprochement* between intellectuals and the working class. As the hero of *La Bête humaine* and *La Belle Equipe*, Gabin embodied this imaginary unity, bridging the divisions of a split society.

So powerful a symbol was Gabin that in the 60s, when he had become a rich landowner accused of excessive land accumulation, public opinion and the press (even on the left) sided with him against the legitimate demands of his neighbouring farmers. On Bastille Day 1989 the overlap between this mythical actor and a 'certain idea of France' was completed when Frédéric Mitterrand (film and television personality and nephew of the president) commented, as the parade was going by, that the best version of 'La Marseillaise' was that sung by Jean Gabin in *La Grande Illusion*.

First published in July 1991 (volume 1, number 3).

Amy Taubin

Grabbing the knife: 'The Silence of the Lambs' and the history of the serial killer movie

The serial killer has attained A-list status in several media in the 90s, and the press, spotting a trend, has geared itself up to dismember him and drink his blood. The noise around both Jonathan Demme's film *The Silence of the Lambs* and Bret Easton Ellis' yuppie splatter novel *American Psycho* began to build in autumn 1990 in New York. At around the same time Martin Scorsese announced himself as executive producer of the next film by John McNaughton, director of *Henry: Portrait of a Serial Killer*, and *Twin Peaks* came back on television with a second two-hour feature directed by David Lynch.

Ellis' book, an up-market *Texas Chain Saw Massacre* intended perhaps as escapist reading for recently unemployed business executives, was bound for the lit-crit hatchets from the moment its galleys were leaked. Demme's film, on the other hand, looked like the kind of artistic achievement that might seem too restrained to a mass audience accustomed to the high body count of cybergore and police action pictures. Yet *The Silence of the Lambs* broke through the $100 million mark, having raked in $71 million and held first place on the charts for the first five weeks of its run. Equally unexpectedly, the chill blue, cobra-hooded eyes of one of the film's serial killers, Hannibal Lecter (Anthony Hopkins), dominated the news-stands, peering insolently from the covers of *Newsweek,* the Arts and Leisure section of the *Sunday New York Times* and countless lesser journals – momentarily replacing Arnold-the-Terminator as reigning Ubermensch.

In the less respectable playgrounds of cyberpunk and splatter-punk, the serial killer is also the top dog. Fanzines publish profiles and memorabilia. Galleries such as AMOK in Los Angeles show jail-house paintings by Charles Manson (the first serial killer to become a household name) and John Gacy, the married Chicago business-man who was arrested for the murder of 33 boys and young men, some of whom he buried beneath his suburban home. Prior to 1950 new serial killers surfaced perhaps once a decade; today it's more like once a month. With just 5 per cent of the world's population, the US is believed to have 75 per cent of the world's serial killers.

Disturbing as these figures are, the fact is that the number of people who will die at the hands of serial killers doesn't even bear comparison with, for example, the number of women who will die because they don't have access to breast screening, or even know it exists. But institutionalised violence – the destruction of millions of lives through poverty and neglect, the abuse practised against women and children, the slaughter of 100,000 Iraqis – has no easy representation. The image of the serial killer acts as a substitute and a shield for a situation so incomprehensible and threatening it must be disavowed.

Unlike urban action pictures, which imply, with rare excep-tions, that the threat to America is ghettoised, that it can be policed and locked away (as long as the invading third world hordes are kept at bay), serial killer films are set in white neighbourhoods – suburbia, the farm belt, the backwoods. The serial killer is a marauder: he might turn up anywhere. And in fact, almost all ser-ial killers are white males who kill within their own racial group. Bred in the heartlands, he's the deformed version of the American dream of the individual. In *The Silence of the Lambs*, the second serial killer (Lecter's low-life counterpart) is named Buffalo Bill.

The Silence of the Lambs is not the first art/entertainment crossover to take on the subject of the serial killer. Classic examples include Fritz Lang's *M* (1931), Chaplin's *Monsieur Verdoux* (1947) and more peripherally, G. W. Pabst's *Pandora's Box* (1928). They depict, respec-tively, three pathological archetypes: the child murderer; the Blue-beard figure whose victims are wives (i.e. good girls); and Jack the Ripper who specialises in killing prostitutes (i.e. bad girls). But it was Hitchcock, who – by crossing the psychological thriller with the horror movie – established conventions that have governed the genre for the past 30 years.

Psycho was adapted from Robert Bloch's 50s bestseller of the same name, based on the truth-is-stranger-than-fiction case of Ed Gein, a small-town Wisconsin handyman. His necrophiliac compulsions escalated from digging up corpses (most of them buried in the immediate vicinity of his late mother) to murdering as many as ten women. He kept various trophies from his victims – their heads and pieces of their skin. In addition to *Psycho*, Gein partly inspired such films as Tobe Hooper's *Texas Chain Saw Massacre*, James Benning's *Murder/Suicide* and *The Silence of the Lambs*.

According to Stephen Rebello's study *Alfred Hitchcock and the Making of Psycho*, Hitchcock was anxious to make a picture that would not only prove more shocking than Henri Clouzot's *Diabolique* (1955), but would be perceived as the first 60s movie. While *Psycho*'s image of the knife-wielding maniac drove most of the slasher movies of the 60s and the teenie-kills of the 70s, the later films lacked the psychological dimension that distinguished Norman Bates (the pathological connections of sex and violence, voyeurism and sadism, castration fear and misogyny, and the confusion about gender played out in his transvestite splitting). Minimally drawn, the psychos of the slasher and teenie-kill films lack behavioural characteristics and developmental histories. The Freddys, the Michaels (*Halloween*) and the Jasons (*Friday the 13th*) correspond to the real thing only in that they find pleasure (ecstasy) in killing rather than in sex. The interesting exception is the original *Friday the 13th*, which intentionally reverses the *Psycho* syndrome by making the killer a woman – Jason's mother.

In such films serial killing is a function not of character, but of the internal narrative structure and motifs (the piling up of bodies one after another). Even more importantly, it is a function of the relationship of each film both to its sequels and to all the other serials in the genre. It is the killer's ability to rise from the dead in film after film – rather than his appearance, his physical strength or even the extreme sadism of his actions – that demonises him. Thirty years of these films have primed audiences to bind the words 'serial' and 'killer' into the image of a superhuman monster. 'He's back!' 'Coming again this summer!' But in fact, the serial killer is as mortal as his victims and his motives and feelings, while pathological, are not difficult to comprehend. It is the institutions and ideology which produce him that live on from generation to generation.

Just as the psychos of the teenie-kill films haunted the safe havens of middle-class suburbia, serial killers have now invaded primetime. Programmes such as *America's Most Wanted* and *Unsolved Mysteries* present mini-case histories (including teenie-kill style re-enactments of the crime) and invite viewers to assist in apprehending the criminal. John List (dubbed 'Murder Dad' by the *New York Daily News*) was found because of a tip from a viewer who recognised him from a photograph on *America's Most Wanted*. List was the model for the serial killer in *The Stepfather*, a sardonically witty attack on the patriarchal nuclear family directed by Joseph Ruben with a script by Donald Westlake. The stepfather marries into existing families (widows with children and well-kept suburban homes). When they fail to live up to his sit-com expectations, he slaughters them all and moves on. Dripping with references to television Dads *The Stepfather*, a failure in its cinema release, happily found a second life in the home-video market.

The most notorious of the television serial killers is, of course, Leland Palmer, father, murderer and rapist of Laura Palmer, the much fetishised 'dead girl' upon whose corpse the narrative of David Lynch and Mark Frost's *Twin Peaks* is hung. Of course, it should have been obvious from the start that the killer had to be a dad. Lynch's dads are always murderous. In *Blue Velvet*, it's not just Frank who is the threat. Take a good look at Laura Dern's police-chief father, who never takes off his gun, not even in his own home. It's the dads who pass on the lessons of misogyny and homophobia that they learned from their own fathers. So it makes sense that Bob is Leland's Mrs Bates, the projection of his own shattered psyche in the form of the person who had abused him when he was a child.

Television violence is almost always quick, disembodied and impersonal (during the Iraq war, the networks completely caved in to US censorship rules forbidding them to show 'pictures of soldiers with disfiguring or agonising wounds'). *Twin Peaks* is the first prime-time series to show bodies that bleed. Too bad that nearly all of them are female. Still, the scene in which Leland kills Maddie gives one a visceral sense of male sexual violence: what it's like when a middle-aged man beats a teenage girl to death. The legacy of male violence is what binds television's *Twin Peaks* to the cinema's latest incarnations of the serial killer – *The Silence of the Lambs* and *Henry: Portrait of a Serial Killer*, completed in 1987 but only in the 90s finding an audience on the art-film and midnight circuits. What cuts off

Henry from *Twin Peaks*, and even more from *The Silence*, is its point of view. The central character of Henry is a psychopathic ex-con who drifts through a killing spree that began when, at age 14, he murdered his mother. 'She was a prostitute. I don't hold that against her... but she made me watch her doing it... that wasn't right... sometimes she'd dress me up in girls' clothes to watch.'

In the first ten minutes, John McNaughton evokes an atmosphere of extreme disassociation which both suggests the pathological subjectivity of the killer and at the same time functions to put some distance between the viewer and the action. 'Distanciation', which in most current film theory is considered a positive condition, is creepily revealed as the emotional framework of murder.

Dazzlingly simple, McNaughton's method in these early scenes is basically to separate the sound from the picture and to ellide completely the visual image of the murderous moment. Four times in a row we see a woman's mutilated corpse, but it's not until the camera has retreated from the image that the sound begins: a woman screaming. The voice, crudely processed with echo effect, continues over a shot of the anonymous-looking killer walking across a street. Each time Henry describes how he killed his mother, the weapon changes.

Henry moves in with his prison buddy Otis and Otis' sister Luanne. She has run away from the violently abusive husband she married to get away from her sexually abusive father. Luanne is attracted to Henry, who talks soft and wears clean tank tops that show off his arms. Luanne thinks Henry is shy, but she's wrong. Henry is impotent; when he needs to prove he's a man he picks up a knife or an ice-pick or whatever's handy.

Then Henry decides to teach Otis about hunting humans. When the two of them start to work as a team, the sound and the picture in the film also get together. The kills, shown from beginning to end, follow one after another, and *Henry*, for all its dreamy camera moves and sly-eyed close-ups, begins to seem like just a regular exploitation flick, albeit an extremely sadistic one.

In the film's most ingenious sequence, Henry and Otis massacre a nice middle-class suburban family. The event is shot in real time, without cuts, from the point of view of a home-video camera. The premise is that Henry and Otis, having stolen the camera, take it with them on their adventure. They plug it into the family's living-room television set so they can watch themselves in live action. Less imaginative about technology than the serial killer in Michael Powell's *Peeping Tom* – another abused child – who turns his 16mm camera literally into a deadly weapon, Henry and Otis are at least up-to-date in their choice of equipment. In *Henry*, it is the home-video apparatus that is implicated in the repetition-compulsion of the serial killer and that demonstrates the connection between sadism and voyeurism.

Our view of the massacre is confined to the television (it fills the frame). On it we see and hear the following: Otis drags a screaming, struggling woman into the room and starts to tear off her clothes. The camera (presumably hand-held by Henry) pans down to the husband tied up on the floor, also struggling. A kid walks into the room unaware of what's happening. The image flops 45 degrees sideways (Henry has dropped the camera as he goes to grab the kid) and remains in this position for the rest of the scene. Henry throws the kid on the floor and breaks his neck. The wife is still struggling and screaming. Otis is laughing and groping under her pantyhose when suddenly he snaps her neck. Henry finishes off the husband and, noticing that Otis has started to get very familiar with the woman's corpse, says, with puritanical disgust, 'Otis don't do that.' Cut to Otis and Henry sitting side by side on the couch, relaxed and bonded like two regular guys watching football. 'I want to see it again,' whines the infantile Otis, hitting the slo-mo button on the remote.

The camera zooms languorously past their attentive faces towards the television screen. There is no doubt about whose eyes we're looking through, and as the scratchy theme music swells above the woman's screams, no doubt, either, about where the director's sympathies lie. A film that started off being about psychopathology and its relationship to misogyny has turned blatantly misogynist.

In his *Vanity Fair* review of *American Psycho*, Norman Mailer comes to the conclusion that the novel fails as a work of art because the central character, the killer Patrick Bateman, lacks an 'inner life', a subjectivity. The problem in *Henry* is that Henry is the only character who is allowed to be a subject. His victims certainly are not. For a while, McNaughton seems to toy with making Luanne into a second subject. Unfortunately, he cops out. When Henry kills Luanne, it happens off screen. McNaughton doesn't seem to consider that Luanne's reaction to Henry's attack might be worthy of attention. Nor does he show her corpse. Had he displayed the dead

Luanne in the same way as he did the anonymous mutilated bodies in the opening sequences, it would have been horrifying enough to transform retroactively the meaning of all the kill scenes in the film. But instead, McNaughton opts for a ghoulish joke – cutting from Henry and Luanne in a motel room, to Henry driving off alone, to Henry lifting an oozing suitcase from the trunk of the car and dropping it at the side of the highway.

What marks out *The Silence of the Lambs* is that it is a profoundly feminist movie. For women I know, most of whom have seen it more than once, the film is as exhilarating as it is harrowing. *The Silence of the Lambs* is to the psychological thriller-horror combo what the stories in Angela Carter's *The Bloody Chamber* are to gothic fairy tales such as 'Little Red Riding Hood' and 'Bluebeard'. It takes a familiar narrative and shakes up the gender and sexuality stuff. It's a slasher film in which the woman is hero rather than victim, the pursuer rather than the pursued.

Fledgling FBI trainee Clarice Starling (Jodie Foster) has been chosen by her boss Jack Crawford (Scott Glenn), head of Behavioral Science – the FBI unit that investigates serial killers – for a special task. A serial killer nicknamed Buffalo Bill is murdering women and doing something terrible with their skin. Tacked up on Crawford's wall is a tabloid clipping with the headline 'Bill Skins Fifth', and below it, polaroids of flayed female corpses. Clarice stares intently but she keeps her distance – as does Demme's camera. 'Do you spook easily Starling?', Crawford enquires.

Crawford believes that the brilliant psychiatrist and psychopath Hannibal Lecter, whose ferocious oral impulses find their release in language and, less acceptably, in human flesh, may know the killer's identity. Since Crawford has helped to confine Lecter for life in a hospital for the criminally insane, he doubts that the doctor will have much interest in helping him. He decides to use Clarice as a lure, sending her off to Lecter armed with a fake survey questionnaire. If Lecter is intrigued by Clarice, he won't be able to resist playing the omniscient analyst – leaking clues. And if Clarice is really lucky, Lecter might even tell her what to do. 'Whatever you do Clarice, don't tell him anything about yourself,' Crawford warns. It's a bit of paternalistic advice that demands to be ignored, especially by this hero, intent on finding her own way. Besides, time is running out. 'Anytime now, our Billy Boy is going to start looking for that next special lady,' Lecter taunts.

Faithful to the plot and incident of Thomas Harris' bestseller, Demme shifts its tone and meaning. The film makes Clarice even more central (and more isolated) than she was in the novel – a narrative fact that the mainstream media, infatuated with Hannibal the Cannibal, did its best to ignore. Harris' Clarice, for all her courage and desire for independence, was still the good daughter who needed to be valued by the men in her life. She was emotionally tied not only to her real father – the policeman who left her an orphan at age 11 – but to the substitute fathers: Lecter (the bad) and Crawford (the good). Harris' Clarice became romantically involved with Crawford, an unconsummated, guilty, Oedipal attachment, since he was married and his wife was dying.

Demme's and Foster's Clarice is remote in a way that signals something more complex than a novice's attempt at a professional attitude. Demme shoots the scenes between Lecter and Clarice in extreme close-up, shot-countershot, with the actors looking almost directly into the camera. You can see the tension in Clarice's face, her concentrated struggle not only to get the information she needs from Lecter, but also not to be overwhelmed by him – to maintain her separation from him.

And to get it right. And to do it all herself. When Lecter points out her limitations and her failures, there's no doubt she feels ashamed and angry. But it's because she hasn't lived up to her own expectations, not because he thinks less of her. Crawford gets in her way too and his paternalism annoys her. He never gets it more wrong than when he congratulates Clarice by saying, 'Your father would have been proud of you.' She doesn't care about that.

In terms of the frightening fairy-tale world that Demme's Grimm gothic imagery suggests and Lecter's locutions zing home, Clarice's mission is not to marry the prince but to rescue the maiden (the senator's daughter who has become Buffalo Bill's 'next special lady'). On that reversal her identity rests. It's also what fascinates Lecter and what wins him to her cause: unlike most heroes of either sex, she's more moved by vulnerability than she is attracted to power.

In its aching romanticism, Howard Shore's score is reminiscent of Bernard Herrmann's for *Psycho*. In the opening scene, where Clarice, alone in the woods, is running an FBI school obstacle course, it is tied to her yearning and terror and sense of loss. Demme punctuates it with sound effects that have enormous threatening presence. There are the piercing bird calls of the opening and the clanging gates as Clarice descends into the dungeons where Lecter is locked away. And there are the whirring deathhead moths that Buffalo Bill breeds in his oozing basement, the way the US, as Lecter puts it, breeds serial killers. ('Our Bill wasn't born like this. He was made to be this way through years of systematic abuse.')

Amazingly fluid, *The Silence of the Lambs* shifts back and forth from gothic fantasy to police procedural drama. Demme knows how to map psyche and history on to landscape and objects. The film is packed with 300 years of relics – of white America. Every time Lecter sends Clarice on a treasure hunt – to a storage warehouse, for example – she finds a flag or two tucked away with the rusty rifles, dressmakers' dummies and the odd severed head preserved in a jar. The flags look as if they've seen better days.

Detective stories and psychoanalysis both investigate traumas of the past. Here the two (Clarice's search for Buffalo Bill and Lecter's unorthodox analysis of Clarice) are mixed against a background of government buildings, chicken farms and lonely airports where everyone is walking around looking bewildered – as if they'd just noticed that they'd lost everything.

Near the end of the film, in the aftermath of Clarice's battle with Buffalo Bill, the camera lingers for a moment in a corner of the killer's lair, now lit with a shaft of light from a window broken in the struggle. First, there's a medium shot of a child's-size American flag leaning against a dusty army helmet and then a close-up of a sea-blue paper mobile with a butterfly design – a bit of Chinatown interior decoration or a trophy from Vietnam, Bill's inheritance and his legacy.

Which is why the final image of Lecter after his murderous escape, sauntering down a crowded main street in Haiti resplendent in his creamy tourist suit, is more disturbing than anything that has come before. The serial killer, an American gift to the third world, a fragmentation bomb, ready to explode.

First published in May 1991 (volume 1, number 1).

Pam Cook

'Cape Fear' and femininity as destructive power

A deafening silence surrounds the sexual politics of Scorsese's *Cape Fear*. 1992 has already seen two widely publicised rape trials in the US – and now we have a violent rape movie in which women apparently collude in their own punishment at the hands of a rapist. Yet for the most part critics, even when shocked by the film's brutality, prefer to discuss it in formal and/or moral terms – as 'cinema' or as a treatise on good and evil. Feminists too have been conspicuously quiet. This is not the first occasion on which Scorsese has thrown down a gauntlet to the women's movement. The challenge, it seems, has worn thin.

In the face of this general reticence, some male commentators have shown a willingness to speak up on behalf of oppressed womankind. For instance, Jeremy Campbell, the Washington correspondent of the *Evening Standard*, opened his vitriolic review with a poignant anecdote: 'At one particularly horrible moment in... *Cape Fear*, a woman in the audience put her hand to her face and half sobbed: "Oh, no!" I like to think the woman was protesting, not just at the scene, a sexual assault on a little girl, but at the appalling realisation that here were we, supposedly civilised adults, paying to see what the most debauched and degenerate Roman emperors might have gagged over.' Again in the *Standard*, in one of the few reviews to take account of sexual politics, Alexander Walker wrote: 'Feminists will squirm as, under the convict's smiling provocation, she [Lori Davis] proceeds to act out every seductive wile and wink that a promiscuous woman can invent. She certainly "asks for it" – though not, of course, in the form in which it soon comes.'

Such gallantry is surprising when it is considered that almost everybody is victimised in *Cape Fear*. A quick body count reveals that, of those who are assaulted, threatened, raped or killed, six (including Cady) are male, four female and one canine, while of the final survivors, two are female and one male. Yet, against all the evidence, this espousal of the female cause by the critics quoted above designates women as the natural and obvious victims of Scorsese's movie. These male writers seem to be motivated by a desire to exorcise their own feelings of victimisation, to put them where they belong, with the 'weaker sex'. That such defensive action should be necessary suggests that *Cape Fear* indulges in some disturbing gender bending.

It's no secret that, in a bid for commercial success, Scorsese decided to remake J. Lee Thompson's taut black and white thriller as a horror movie. The end result is no arty, upmarket revamp. For, despite its $30 million dollar budget, *Cape Fear* owes everything to low-budget horror movies – Abel Ferrara's 1987 *Ms .45* (*Angel of Vengeance*), for instance. It is a rape-revenge movie in reverse, with an avenging hero instead of heroine. This is a genre in which psycho-sexual anxieties, the coupling of sexual desire with aggression and the playing out of sado-masochistic power relationships are the narrative mainspring. A contract exists between film-makers and spectators in which the former undertake to 'do over' the latter; to frighten them, precisely, out of their wits. The audience for 'low' horror is one that pays to be hurt, to be assaulted in much the same way as the film's characters. This experience is about arousing the viewer's base instincts – it has nothing whatsoever to do with the 'uplifting' or purifying qualities of 'high' art.

Scorsese has taken this remit seriously. We cringe as the camera is used like a battering ram, lunging at the actors, glancing off De Niro's chin, or burying itself in Nick Nolte's abdomen, while the pounding soundtrack hammers away at the auditory nerves. We suffer exquisite torture as we wait with bated breath for Max Cady to penetrate the primitive defences of the Bowden house. We scream in terror when Cady leaps from the shadows to garotte private investigator Kersek, and our stomachs lurch in disgust at the sight of Sam Bowden slipping and sliding around in a pool of Kersek's thickening blood. Thus Scorsese makes masochists of us all.

Cinematic masochism offers a host of guilty pleasures, not confined to the terror tactics of the horror film, but nevertheless played out there in particularly blatant form. The suffering of the characters mirrors our own humiliation as we wait – literally 'held in suspense' – to discover their fate. We shift anxiously in our seats as we are drawn into games of disguise and pursuit which postpone the final resolution. And we revel squeamishly in scenes of ritualistic punishment and death. Scorsese, of course, has already proved himself a master of the masochistic aesthetic, in *Raging Bull*, for example, and most elaborately in *The Last Temptation of Christ*. In *Cape Fear* it is no longer subtext, but overt message.

It is well known that Freud thought that masochism was essentially 'feminine'. Fantasies of being beaten, violated and defiled, while common to both sexes, were 'natural' to women but signified 'perversion' (a receptive homosexuality) in men. Horror film-makers would seem to agree. Abject fear is coded as feminine as, in movie after movie, female victims with terrified expressions – wide eyes and gaping mouths – are stalked with evil intent by male aggressors. Yet, as Carol Clover argues in *Men, Women and Chain Saws*, this is certainly not the whole story. Horror movies can also be characterised by role reversals in which victims turn the tables on their aggressors. Here, the slasher/rapist, frequently a sexually impaired figure, usually ends up slashed, maimed or killed, often by an axe- or knife-wielding heroine. The female victim-turned-avenger takes on the aggressor role and is thereby 'masculinised', while the slasher/rapist becomes the victim and meets as nasty an end as any masochist could wish for. While victimisation is still regarded as an essentially 'feminine' state, men – at least as often as women – find themselves in it.

Horror's gender disturbances are given several more turns of the screw by Scorsese. From the beginning, his rapist is designated as a victim. Max Cady is victimised by a corrupt legal system which sends him to prison for 14 years on manipulated evidence. Not only is he sodomised in jail, but he loses his home and family as well. As he tells Sam Bowden, the lawyer whose actions put him away, he is now 'looking for his feminine side' – a bizarre assertion coming from a violent underclass ex-con, but entirely logical in the film's terms. Cady's sense of loss links him with the women characters, all of them 'done over' in some way by Bowden, whose resemblance to Cady the dialogue repeatedly stresses.

Cady's savage sexual (and vampiric) assault on Sam Bowden's mistress, Lori Davis, is both a mirror for Bowden's carelessly cruel

**Revenge is mine: Robert De Niro in
Martin Scorsese's 'Cape Fear' (1991)**

treatment of her and, as her refusal to testify makes explicit, an indictment of the legal system which would heap further humiliation on her – as, indeed, it does on Cady, who is subsequently arrested on a trumped-up charge and submitted to a full body search because Bowden suspects him of intending to rape his wife, Leigh. In the vertiginous final sequence, Cady does threaten to rape Leigh, but not before she has pleaded with him not to attack her daughter Danielle in a speech which emphasises their common experience of loss (his years in prison, her years of marriage). Cady's feminine side scandalously surfaces in the brief instant in which, dressed in the clothes of the Bowden family's maid, Graciella, he garottes Kersek in their kitchen. This scene has been much discussed as an obligatory, and therefore easily dismissable, reference to Hitchcock's *Psycho*. Yet De Niro's drag, in the class, ethnic and gender connections it makes between Cady and Graciella, is surely more than this.

Cape Fear's complex pattern of refracted images makes it plain that avenging angel Cady is acting on behalf of victimised women. In this light, the female characters' apparent collusion in their own humiliation – the fact that they are attracted to the rapist – takes on a different hue. They could be said to be drawn, not only to his violent sexuality, but to the distorted picture he reflects back at them of their own rage and pain, and of their desire for revenge. Scorsese's most controversial move in this respect is to bracket the main action with the narrative voice of Danielle telling the audience that the film is her reminiscence. This ruse shifts the bases considerably. If Cady is conjured up by Danielle, then the threat to the American family comes, not from an intruder, but from within. Problem child Danielle calls up Cady as a defence against her incestuous desire for Sam, and as a wish to find an escape route out of the claustrophobic confines of the Bowden family nexus.

Even more disquieting than the idea that the movie represents a teenage girl's fantasy is the notion that Scorsese, in the time-honoured tradition of storytelling, uses one of his characters as a mask for his own violent sexual fantasies, which include the seduction and rape of a 15-year-old girl. But what exactly is going on in this masquerade? Without speculating about his desire for a sexual awakening at the hands of De Niro's Cady, the director's delegation of the narrator's role to Danielle suggests at the very least strong feelings of affinity with this most receptive, most susceptible, of all the film's characters. An attempt by Scorsese to recover his lost innocence, perhaps?

Except that Danielle is far from innocent. She is the one who forms an alliance with Cady and, in a sense, 'employs' him to violate her mother and destroy her father. She is the one who sets fire to Cady in the final sequence and, as the narrator, sees to it that he is devoured by that familiar feminine trope, the swirling black vortex of Cape Fear river. (Indeed, the infamous scene in which Danielle and Cady meet in the school theatre, when he probes her mouth with his finger, can be read as a threat as much to him as to her – an intimation of his eventual 'swallowing up'.) And, of course, in the film's closing moments, it is Danielle's voice that reminds us that, through her dreams, she can raise Cady from the dead.

It would seem, then, that for Scorsese femininity is two-faced, embodying both suffering passivity and monstrous destructive power. Horror's bisexual games enable him to confront us with some unpalatable truths – that there is a victim, and aggressor, in all of us, for example. But in spite of all the gender juggling, Scorsese still adheres to a negative notion of the feminine. The real horror in *Cape Fear* is feminisation: the contamination of positive 'masculine' values (heroism, integrity, honour and so forth) by 'feminine' values of weakness, prevarication and moral laxity, typified by the ambivalent figure of anti-hero Sam Bowden. Scorsese has produced his most overtly feminophobic movie. We can hardly admire him for that. At the most, we can thank him for laying on the line with blistering clarity the way our culture devalues femininity as an alibi for male fears and desires.

First published in April 1992 (volume 1, number 12).

Carol J. Clover

'Falling Down' and the rise of the Average White Male

Falling Down tells the story of one day in the life of a laid-off defence worker (Michael Douglas). The eerie opening shots show him sitting in his car in a standstill traffic jam on a sweltering Los Angeles morning. Jaw set, face emotionless, forehead trickling with sweat, he takes in the sights and sounds around him – car stereos, a woman putting on lipstick, someone shouting into a cellular phone, a billboard, people arguing. Finally he moves: opens the door, gets out of his car, clambers over an embankment and sets off on foot across tracts of LA not usually seen by freeway commuters. Like Odysseus, he is heading home, except that instead of Scylla and Charybdis there are chicano gangs and homeless people, and instead of Penelope waiting patiently in Ithaca there is a former wife with a restraining order in Venice Beach. D-Fens, as he comes to be known after his license plate, always had a short fuse, and this is the morning he blew. 'This is not a bad guy,' director Joel Schumacher says, 'but he's had it.' He cuts a ragged swath through the urban wilderness, leaving behind him a trail of corpses and frightened witnesses. A cop named Prendergast (Robert Duvall), who has tracked his movements since morning, finally stops him on the Venice pier. Arms raised in surrender, D-Fens utters his final, incredulous question: 'I'm the bad guy?'

The critical reaction in the US to *Falling Down* is itself a study in confusion. A few reviewers praised the film. Most, however, dismissed it as yet another mean-spirited product of the Reagan-Bush backlash, underneath its glitz nothing more than a crude vigilante picture, appealing to the worst in us all.

The *New York Times* carried two reviews: an appreciative one by Vincent Canby, who thought the film smart satire, and a scathing one by Caryn James, who pronounced it irritating nonsense. The one thing that is clear is that audiences went to see it in large numbers and, once there, responded with shouts and applause. For better or for worse, *Falling Down* is one of those films (and Michael Douglas has acted in more than his fair share of them) that hit an American nerve. But which nerve was it?

There is an old joke about the Lone Ranger and Tonto atop a hill, surrounded on all sides by thousands of armed Indian warriors heading straight for them. 'What should we do now, Tonto?' the Lone Ranger asks. Tonto is silent for a moment, and then answers, grimly, 'What do you mean we, white man?' It is a joke that still resonates in American social discourse, haunting, among other things, the concern over the fracturing of the polity into identity-based groups – a concern summed up in the question 'how wide the circle of we?' That concern, and some form of that question, haunt *Falling Down*. D-Fens' 'I'm the bad guy?' is as packed with social meanings as his gym bag is with weapons. The question is: who is the 'I' in that sentence, and why is he so upset?

Midway into the picture, D-Fens goes into an army surplus store to buy a pair of boots. The owner scrutinises him as he enters and, taking off his dark glasses and earphones, follows him to the back of the store. 'I'm Nick,' he says, 'what can I do you for?' Moments later, a police car pulls up and an officer enters and asks the owner whether he has seen a white man wearing a white shirt and tie and carrying a gym bag. No, the owner says, as D-Fens lies low in a dressing room. When the officer is gone, D-Fens asks the owner why he lied. 'You're my friend,' the owner says, a little too intensely. The rest of the sequence will reveal the owner as a homophobic, racist, anti-environmental, misogynist neo-Nazi and will end with D-Fens calling him a 'sick asshole', shooting him, and going back out on to the street to continue his way home.

The police came because Prendergast, looking at his maps down at the station, figured something out. First there was a report that a Korean grocer's store had been smashed up – but not robbed – by a white man wearing a white shirt and tie. Prendergast is intrigued by the description and when a report of an equally odd incident in an adjacent neighbourhood comes in, he guesses immediately that its perpetrator too was a white man in a white shirt and tie. When his partner Sandra goes to investigate a hold-up at the Whammy-burger restaurant – where again nothing is stolen – Prendergast tells her to call him if it is a white man in a white shirt and tie.

Prendergast and the neo-Nazi have something in common: they both 'know' D-Fens even before they meet him. The fact that the neo-Nazi's knowledge is not quite right (for D-Fens is not a card-carrying Nazi) should not detract from the fact that he thinks he knows him. Prendergast, however, knows exactly, and is able to deduce not only D-Fens' direction and destination, but also what no one else can fathom from his unorthodox actions: his motivation. The set-up brings to mind a Dutch film of some years ago, *A Question of Silence* (directed by Marleen Gorris), in which some women browsing in a dress shop suddenly, on the slightest of provocations, join together and beat to death the male owner. The women have never met before; what joins them in common cause is their silent and sudden recognition of themselves as members of the category Woman, and therefore as angry victims of the category Man, of which the crowing shopkeeper seems an exemplary representative.

Falling Down has been widely reviewed as an Everyman tale and D-Fens characterised as 'Joe Normal', 'average citizen', 'universal hero', or simply 'all of us'. Many of the irritations and social ills in D-Fens' awful day are indeed things that can affect and offend anyone: the traffic jam, the annoying bumper stickers ('How Am I Driving? Call 1-800-EAT SHIT'), the ludicrous uniforms and protocol of the Whammyburger restaurant, the shopkeeper's refusal to give change, the general rudeness of all towards all. These are Everyone scenes, and they provide some of the film's most trenchant moments. But to let *Falling Down* go at that misses a crucial point – in much the way that the state authorities in *A Question of Silence* miss the point when they construe the shopkeeper's murder as motivated by insanity or class anger. Would the neo-Nazi and Prendergast have 'known' a woman who had done the same things, or a non-white man, or a disabled person, or whatever?

Three white men, three zones on a continuum. Reviewers have stumbled over the figure of the neo-Nazi, whose pathological hatreds seem so hyperbolically drawn. The excess comes into focus if we imagine the story without him. He secures a position we might otherwise be inclined to ascribe to D-Fens, whose words and deeds we might construe as too close to fascism for comfort. By locating genocidal viciousness and insanity in the neo-Nazi (and indeed hav-

WARNER BROS.

**Average White Male: Michael Douglas
in 'Falling Down' (1993)**

ing D-Fens kill him, moralising about freedom of speech as he does so), the film can define D-Fens as your average short-tempered neighbour who just happened to break one day. And what blows then is his self-control, not his sense of reality. No Travis Bickle, this. *Falling Down's* story is precisely not that of *Taxi Driver* (with which it has been widely compared): for better or worse, its whole effect depends on seeing D-Fens not as a vet descending into madness, but as a tax-paying citizen whose anger allows him to see, with preternatural clarity, the madness in the society around him. The neo-Nazi is established as a 'sick asshole' to make it clear that D-Fens is neither an asshole nor sick. He may be out of control, but he is 'not a bad guy' (again Schumacher), and he does see truly.

As with the neo-Nazi and D-Fens, so in muted form with D-Fens and Prendergast. D-Fens is extreme and dies and Prendergast is moderate and survives, but they are doubles in the same play, and it is D-Fens' ballistic reaction that enables Prendergast to let off a little steam. But Prendergast's relation to whiteness and maleness is no less decisive for being more gently drawn. The first time we lay eyes on him, he too is sitting in the same traffic jam staring fixedly through his windshield at a billboard. The left side is obscured by trees, but the exposed part features a tanned woman in a bikini next to the rubric 'White is for laundry'. Presumably some product like sun lotion or a Hawaiian vacation is on the hidden side of the billboard, but without that as a material anchor, the words drift into a bellicose racial register. If that were not enough, a graffiti artist has drawn on to the female figure's formidable cleavage, as if trapped there, a tiny cartoon man calling out 'Help me!' It is this billboard, much later in the film, that Prendergast will spot again and that will serve as the missing piece of the investigation, the key to the pattern of behaviour that to everyone else seems random or insane or both.

Along this double axis of race and sex, Prendergast's story too plays itself out. Certainly Prendergast's relation to his wife, a needy woman who has manipulated him into sacrificing his reputation at work and agreeing to a retirement he does not want, is neatly captured in the cartoon man's plight. And Prendergast's too is a day of racial encounters, starting with his being chided by an Asian colleague for asking him what the Korean grocer is saying ('I happen to be a Japanese, in case you didn't notice!'). Lest we miss the equation between him and D-Fens, it is spelled out for us in the scene in which the girl Angelina is being interrogated about the incident in which her chicano gangster friends are killed. None of her inter-locutors believes her when she says the man in question was a white guy with a baseball bat. Except for Prendergast. Moving in closer, he asks for a description. 'He was like you,' she replies, 'except taller and he had hair.' 'Did he have a white shirt and tie?' Prendergast asks. He is, at that moment and throughout most of a film in which 'white shirt and tie' has the status of a leitmotif, wearing a white shirt and tie.

Falling Down is hardly the first movie to feature a white man flail-ing self-righteously in a sea of people who are either not male or not white or neither and who are messing up his game. What dis-tinguishes it from the run-of-the-mill backlash fantasy is the demo-graphic precision with which it defines that man's consciousness.

It goes something like this. The Average White Male is the guy everybody is mad at and wants compensation from – the guy who pays the bills whether he personally deserves to or not and whether he can afford to or not. The Average White Male is surrounded by people who have claimed themselves as his social victims and clam-our for entitlement. By women who kick men out of the family and the home and expect child support (put aside for a moment the fact that D-Fens was evidently something of a problem husband and father), and by women who (like Prendergast's wife) play feminin-ity (and feminism) for all it is worth to keep their husbands in a state of guilt and control. By chicano gang members who demand a 'toll' from anyone who chances into those chunks of Los Angeles they have claimed as their own. By old people kept alive by the mir-acles of modern medicine, drawing Social Security all the way. (When D-Fens lets the elderly golfer die of a heart attack by keep-ing him from his pills, he pulls an imaginary plug on all old peo-ple living beyond their time and on the Average White Male's chit.) By Asian shopkeepers who self-righteously overcharge. By homeless people who bully and lie through their teeth. By gay men. (Lesbians and disabled people are oddly missing from D-Fens' hit list.) By blacks who shout racism whenever they don't get what they want. (The black man picketing the Savings and Loan believes that the phrase used on his loan denial, 'not economically viable', is code for racial discrimination, but it soon becomes clear that D-Fens qualifies for the same designation.) Indeed, if we are to trust the neo-Nazi's phantasmatic account, by 'black bucks' who pin the

Average White Male to the ground and shout 'Give it to me! Give it to me! Give it to me!' as they literally rape him.

Likewise property. The Average White Male is the guy who theoretically owns the world but in practice, in this account, not only has no turf of his own but has been closed out of the turf of others. D-Fens breaches two high walls in the course of his long walk home. One is the wall of a country club, where he meets with elderly golfers (arguably coded Jewish) who shout 'Get off my golf course! What am I paying my fucking dues for if guys can walk all over my golf course?' The other is the wall outside a plastic surgeon's mansion, where he encounters a caretaker he mistakes for the owner and who in turn mistakes him for the 'security man'. (Even Average White Males have trouble telling each other from the enemy, it seems. When D-Fens learns that the man he is facing is a trespasser like himself – the caretaker is using the plastic surgeon's barbecue on the sly for a picnic with his wife and child – his rage evaporates and he slips into confessional tone.)

But it's not only the rich who have walled him out; it's the poor as well. What he thought was graffiti art – on the rubble on which he is sitting to rest his feet – is in fact a sign, his chicano interlocutors inform him: 'Private fucking property, no fucking trespassing.' ('A pissing ground, is that what it is?' D-Fens responds.) Even the homeless man claims territory: 'What right do you have to walk through my park? I live here. This is my home, this is my park, what right do you have walking through it?' And, of course, the home towards which D-Fens is so single-mindedly making his way is also off limits: 'This is my house now,' his former wife tells him, buttressed by an order that stipulates that he may not come within 100 feet (or maybe yards – the wife can't remember). For this, the white male fought for his country? As D-Fens himself sums it up to the caretaker: 'I lost my job. Actually I didn't lose it; it lost me. I'm overeducated and underskilled – or maybe it's the other way around, I forget. I'm obsolete. I'm "not economically viable". I can't even support my own kid.' In the end, the Average White Male amounts to nothing more than a life-insurance policy, and in the film's climactic scene, as a last wretched act of support, he arranges for that to be liquidated too.

It's not hard to see what's wrong with this picture. Even Average White Males are better off than their Average White Wives or than Average Black Males or whatever; hold for class, in other words, and they still come out on top. But what interests me here is not the fairness or unfairness of the portrait. It is the simple fact that a portrait has been drawn and that the lines are where they are. For the group of which this group is construed as a part is not just any category. It is the great unmarked or default category of western culture, the one that never needed to define itself, the standard against which other categories have calculated their difference. In much the same way that Protestants of Anglo-Saxon stock were once synonymous with 'Americans' but came, at some point in this century, to be marked as one category among many, with its own peculiarities and eventually its own name (WASP), so now guys like D-Fens (and his worse version the neo-Nazi and his better version Prendergast) are being separated from the master category and outfitted with an identity and consciousness of their own. Not all white shirts are alike. Some are short-sleeved and have 'nerd packs' in the pocket. And if we are to take seriously D-Fens' change of clothing at the army surplus store, white shirts of this kind are just one temper tantrum away from becoming brown shirts.

How exactly does one go about carving an interest group out of the default category? The same way as other interest groups made themselves: by claiming oppression. Victim status is the coin of the realm as far as identity is concerned. The Average White Male claim is bankruptcy, both fiscal and spiritual. In the Whammyburger scene, D-Fens holds up the flaccid, colourless burger he has been handed and, gesturing to the juicy version on the sign, puts the question to his captive audience: 'What is wrong with this picture?' (After a long pause, a small black boy raises his hand.) So too the Average White Male: in the public imagination infinitely endowed with wealth and privilege, but in the real individual case, running on fumes: nerves fraying, guilt wearing thin, and down to an insurance policy.

To dismiss this as Reagan-Bush attitudinising, as most reviewers have done, does not do justice to the real sense of anger, grievance and pathos that attends the D-Fens story and that clearly affects audiences. There is, I think, something like Average White Male consciousness in the making out there. The men's movement is part of it (especially the throwing off the shackles of responsibility and guilt part), Joe Bob Briggs is part of it, and publications like *Heterodoxy* are part of it. An issue of this last speaks of the Clinton administration's mentality as one that 'is forgiving of America-bashing because it has been nurtured on a vision of the rampant white, heterosexual male – a synecdoche for America the bad – running roughshod over the country and the world'. It declares that a certain man was a 'walking bull's eye' for charges of child abuse 'because he was a white middle-aged male and a serviceman in addition to his other defects'. It fantasises a PBS series, hosted by Bill Moyers, entitled *Damn You White Man*, which iterates in 13 hours the annihilation of all the 'rich and varied cultures' of North America by white men ('guaranteed to induce intense guilt in anyone of Northern European ancestry'). *Heterodoxy* is not a neo-Nazi publication (though some readers may find it a short stretch). It is reasonably articulate (within the mode of heavy mockery) and sometimes trenchantly hits the point, though arguably it is just as self-righteous as the PCnesses it broadsides. 'The cultural equivalent of a drive-by shooting,' it calls itself. *Falling Down* is pretty much the cinematic equivalent of the same thing – and from the vantage point of pretty much the same constituency.

Canby regards *Falling Down* as quintessentially American, a film that 'couldn't possibly have been made anywhere else in the world today'. It is more particularly Californian – California being not only a traditional hotbed of identity politics, but an economy especially hard hit by unemployment (much of it related to defence cutbacks), and also, of course, a population in the process of dramatic 'colouring' (by 1999, whites will constitute less than half of its 32 million inhabitants). If ever a place were ripe for popular fantasies about Average White Males resigning from public responsibility, 90s California is it.

In his new book *Culture of Complaint: The Fraying of America*, Robert Hughes writes that 'Never before in human history were so many acronyms pursuing identity. It's as though all human encounter were one big sore spot, inflamed with opportunities to unwittingly give, and truculently receive, offence.' Contradictorily enough, however, the book goes on to enact the very process it decries, in claiming an identity and victim status for yet another group – the group that was supposed to be beyond the fray. Hughes ventures the possibility that 'By the time whites get guilty enough to call themselves "European-Americans," it will be time to junk the whole lingo of nervous divisionism; everyone, black, yellow, red and white, can revert to being plain "Americans" again, as well they might.' If *Falling Down* is any measure, the moment is upon us – but there is no discernible guilt here, only fury, and there is no sense whatsoever of reversal and regrouping in the offing. *Falling Down*'s answer to the question 'how wide the circle of we?' would seem to be both 'narrower than ever' and 'what do you mean, we?' – spoken by more and more people, in increasingly snarling tones, echoing into the future.

First published in May 1993 (volume 3, number 5).

Lizzie Francke

Men, women, children and the baby boom movies

'There never was a simpler, happier family until the coming of Peter Pan.'
J. M. Barrie, 'Peter Pan', 1911
In the late 80s, just as Wall Street crashed again and the recession began to take hold, Hollywood's biological clock exploded. In an economic climate reminiscent of the 30s, when Shirley Temple rose to fame, audiences could once more count their blessings by paying their dues to see the smiling faces of babies on screen. *Baby Boom*, *Three Men and a Baby*, *Look Who's Talking* and *Parenthood* were swiftly delivered and proud producers beamed as their films toddled to the top of the box-office charts.

This collection spawned two commercially successful sequels – *Look Who's Talking Too* and *Three Men and a Little Lady* – and marked the beginning of a new phase. With the John Hughes produced *Home Alone* – claimed to be the biggest grossing comedy ever – and the freak success of *Problem Child*, children moved with a vengeance into the big picture. Then came *Hook*, Spielberg's updating of *Peter Pan*, in which the perennial child had finally grown up, only to return to his youth. This long-gestating project had at last found its moment as, in this closing decade of the millennium, Hollywood seems determined to rediscover a lost innocence.

The subject of babyhood and childhood has become a major preoccupation of the current generation of film-makers. If the first wave of films, with their diaper do's and don'ts, came over as light-hearted parenting primers, it was because these Hollywood parents, the publicity machines assured us, do know how. In interviews Amy Heckerling, the director of *Look Who's Talking*, chats about her little girl; the *Baby Boom* production notes comment on writer/director/producer team Nancy Meyers and Charles Shyer's progeny; and the notes for *Parenthood* round up the number of children the crew has between them. At the same time, demographics pundits provide statistics for changing audience profiles which show that the baby-boom generation is putting cinema back in the family way. As innumerable Mr and Mrs Worthingtons groom junior for a star-spangled career, those 30s days, when movie moguls hired rosters of bright-eyed moppets to feature in wholesome and uplifting popular stories and Shirley Temple was Hollywood's top box-office attraction, seem to be with us once more.

These days, with the nuclear family in crisis and cases of child abuse regularly making the headlines, childhood cannot be so coyly romanticised. But infants are a sticky issue right from their inception. The uproar caused in 1991 by two images proved revealing. The clothing company Benetton, which has developed a flair for contentious advertising campaigns, hit the rawest nerve when it displayed a poster of a wrinkled and bloody newborn baby not yet severed from its umbilical cord. The picture provoked such outrage that it was withdrawn on the grounds that it was a contravention of 'good taste'. Only weeks before, *Vanity Fair* had attempted to boost its sales with an equally controversial cover photograph of the nude and heavily pregnant Demi Moore. That these images incited so many mailbags of passionately declared feelings shows how deeply uncomfortable our culture is with the bare and visceral facts of life, especially now that reproduction is complicated by the threat of Aids. The pictures may have been criticised for profaning the sacred experience of pregnancy and birth, but it seemed the protesters were wishing away the experience itself.

'*Wendy, I ran away the day I was born.*' Peter in 'Peter Pan'
The baby comedies certainly tidy away the embarrassing business of birth. Indeed, the era of the stork seems to have returned. In *Baby Boom* and *Three Men and a Baby*, the little bundles drop out of space like E.T. to precipitate change in the lives of their hosts. J.C. – the 'tiger lady' careerist in *Baby Boom* – inherits a 13-month-old girl whom she perceives initially as an appalling misfortune, while in *Three Men and a Baby* the female infant is deposited inconveniently at the door of three confirmed bachelors and mistaken initially for contraband goods.

This nervousness about baby matters can also be detected in the responses of 'grown-up' critics. It quickly became fashionable to gag on these movies, while the headline writers got back to basics with catchy titles. *Baby Boom* generated such sniggering phrases as 'Coochie-coochie goo' (the *Guardian*) and the more suggestive 'She Stoops to Caca' (*Village Voice*). Both babyhood and motherhood took on the associations of dirty and primeval, their otherness trivialised in a glib one-liner.

Baby Boom in particular was derided as facile and trite – *Variety* described it as 'transparent and one-dimensional' with 'the superficiality of a project inspired by a lame *New York* magazine cover story and sketched out on a cocktail napkin at Spago's'. But it tapped into a powerful and emotionally satisfying fantasy, in which women could 'have it all', in spite of a society that denies them this possibility in real life. For this to happen, J.C. and baby have to be banished from Manhattan's masculinised, strutting city culture to leafy Vermont. In this apple-filled Eden, J.C. meets and romances a softly spoken vet – a man who is kind to women and animals – as well as bringing up baby and running a successful food business.

Baby Boom is one of the few baby films to centre the predicament of parenthood on a woman – though of course in all these movies it is the value and status of motherhood and mothering which seem to be at stake. In *Three Men and a Baby*, the child arouses 'maternal' feelings in the macho trio. Their bachelor pad is transformed into a giant romper suite in which they can dress up and play at being mommies. They take up the challenge of Pampers and apron and prove that they too can nurture – a feminising experience which they are reluctant to give up when the baby's biological mother returns to the scene.

'I don't want to go to school and learn solemn things,' he told her passionately. 'I don't want to be a man. O Wendy's mother, if I was to wake up and feel there was a beard!' Peter in 'Peter Pan'

In *Baby Boom* the child precipitates a return to a forgotten pastoral idyll which comforts and nourishes the soul jaded by urban life. And the theme was taken up by another wave of films, in which adults resort to the childish as a sanctuary from the harshness of the city. Usually the change is provoked by a male identity crisis. In *Hook*, Peter Pan has grown up to be a workaholic corporate attorney who neglects his family. Instead of going to see his son play base-ball, he sends a flunky along to tape it, and he spends so much time on his portable telephone that he fails to hear his wife's complaints.

But when, on a visit to Granny Wendy in London, his children are kidnapped by a vengeful Captain Hook and whisked away to Neverland, Peter must return there to save them. As Spielberg expounded in an interview in the US magazine *Premiere*, Peter not only saves the family, but 'rescued the memory of himself as a child and carries this best friend with him for the rest of his life. It will never leave him again.' Adhering closely to the kind of male con-sciousness-raising manifesto expounded by Robert Bly in his best-selling book *Iron John*, this process involves much finger-painting and drum-beating as Peter gets back to nature, metamorphosing from yuppie lawyer into wild child. Only then has he the mettle to do battle with the steely Hook who has stolen his son's affections (his daughter drops out of the picture altogether).

With its quips about the Peter Pan complex, *Hook* indulges in a pseudo-psychoanalytical knowingness as good father confronts bad. As well as from *Iron John*, it seems to have culled its ideas from psycho-babble self-help books with titles like *The Child Within*. But what Spielberg leaves out in his affectionate re-reading of J. M. Bar-rie is the uncanny nature of the boy who refuses to mature. Described in the novel as a child with gnashing milk-white teeth, a greedy look in his eye and a detachable shadow, he seems to have an ominous connection with that other *fin-de-siècle* spectre, the vam-pire. He feeds on emotional sustenance from the countless Wendys he transports to Neverland, where they tell him 'stories about him-self, to which he listens eagerly'. This happy routine, the reader is told, will go on for as long as 'children are gay and innocent and heartless'. A problem child indeed.

Hook's Peter is not alone in his mid-life trauma. His journey back into childhood is shared by the protagonists of *Regarding Henry* and *The Fisher King* (which, like *Hook*, features the goblinish Robin Williams). Through some misfortune, the heroes of these films all regress to a helpless infantile state and, after being mothered back to health by an ever-patient wife or girlfriend, become kinder, nicer and more emotionally evolved individuals. The detestable Henry – an avaricious Manhattan lawyer who cheats on his wife and ignores his daughter – is shot in the head before he changes his ways. Once reborn, he has to learn to speak all over again and finds solace in painting flowers, baking cookies and being nice to animals. Both wife and daughter appear very proud of him.

Likewise, the rebirthing of *The Fisher King*'s heroes takes place in a Manhattan that is slowly being ground to dust. Lucas' career as a slick and mouthy radio DJ disintegrates after a massacre triggered by his goading one of his listeners too far. His salvation comes in the form of a babbling Holy Fool who sets him on a make-believe quest. As with *Hook* – and, indeed, the baby comedies – the restorative power of play and fantasy is crucial. In the film's final image, the two new-found buddies in their birthday suits sing under the stars in Central Park, which is about as close to mother nature as you can get in New York.

Mother nature is also all-embracing in the meandering *Grand Canyon*, Lawrence Kasdan's bigger chill for the fortysomethings. Here, the crisis of the central character Mack (another lawyer) is again precipitated by the collapse of a city culture – this time in a violent and ghettoised Los Angeles. As the City of Angels goes to the devil, Mack reaches out across social divides to other like-minded souls – Simon, for instance, a tow-truck driver whom Mack believes has saved his life.

Kasdan's pompous film expostulates feel-good sentiments about life-affirming friendships between black and white, rich and poor. That national monument, the Grand Canyon, provides a metaphor for these unions, representing a womb-like refuge for the disaffected. This return to a natural order allows men to bond with each other while the women trailing behind just to want to have babies.

The same notion of a healing return to nature is evident in *The Prince of Tides*, which opens with images of children playing like water babies in the briny waves – their sanctuary from a violent father. One of them, Tom, now grown up, estranged from his wife and creatively blocked, is the film's hero. In order to help cure his suicidal twin sister, he regresses to a childhood moment of horrific trauma, in which he, his mother and siblings were raped. Spellbound by his sister's therapist (played by the director and star, Barbra Streisand), whom he adopts as his own, he plumbs the depths of the past and eventually breaks the silence surrounding the event. This emotional journey is facilitated by his therapist's nurturing mother-love, which reunites him with his feminine side and enables him to return to the bosom of his family – again, women, like the sea, offer sanctuary.

'Families suck! I wish they would all disappear.' Kevin in 'Home Alone'
Is it a sense of disappointment in parental authority figures that
motivates Hollywood's regression to childhood? In *JFK*, baby-
boomer Oliver Stone looks back nostalgically to an era of political
innocence. Central to the 'grand conspiracy' idea explored in his
film is the beatification of Kennedy as a guiltless leader, with
Camelot displaced into a prelapsarian Neverland. Stone expands on
his thesis: 'And we, Kennedy's godchildren, the baby-boom generation that believed his stirring words and handsome image, are like
Hamlet in the first act, children of a slain leader, unaware of why
he was killed or even that a fake figure inherits the throne.' Stone's
stirring rhetoric portrays America as a dysfunctional family, with
a generation of betrayed children working through collective Oedipal neurosis in a mass psychotherapy session. *JFK*'s epilogue dedicates itself to 'the young in whose spirit the search for the truth
marches on,' while the valiant Jim Garrison looks to his son as the
future custodian of the gospel of history.

In Wes Craven's Grand Guignol pantomime *The People Under the
Stairs*, the hero is a 13-year-old boy named Fool whose task it is to
liberate a cellar full of blind, deaf and dumb lost boys from bogus
parents who bear a curious resemblance to Nancy and Ron. It tran-
spires that this sadistic couple have been stealing children in order
to find pure specimens. Any child who transgresses by hearing, seeing or speaking evil is punished according to its crime. Unsurprisingly, the one obedient child who has escaped their vicious abuse
is a girl – a fey Alice imprisoned in the attic of their rotting gothic
gingerbread house. In this grim fairytale, Craven, the creator of
child-killer Freddy, plays out fears about the warped values of
Republican America.

Billed as 'a family comedy without the family', *Home Alone* also
exploited cracks in the domestic framework and exhibited a lack of
confidence in parental figures. Wishing his family away and having
that wish granted when he is accidentally excluded from a Christmas trip, young Kevin must use his anarchic wits to keep at bay two
sinister but bungling intruders who attempt to violate the sacred
space of his suburban home. Kevin succeeds in repelling the invasion, unnerved only momentarily by the nightmarish jaws of the
basement furnace, and by his own reflection in the parental bedroom mirror, which sends him reeling away in an Edvard Munch-
style primal scream.

Though the family is reconstituted in a regular happy ending complete with sugary sub-plot, *Home Alone* does engage with the perils – and power – of being a child. And the film's success with adults suggests that what is going on is an identification with the young protagonist that answers a therapeutic need to return to the childhood sphere to work out some troubling unsettled score. Kevin's wishing his parents away proves in the end to be emancipating. He negotiates quite capably the absence he has created for himself.

'When ladies used to come to me in dreams, I said, "pretty mother, pretty mother". But when at last she really came, I shot her.' Tootles in 'Peter Pan' If films like *Home Alone*, *My Girl* and *Little Man Tate* could be said to resurrect buried memories of childhood for adults, they do so with all the ambivalence of a child's desire and demands. While problem parents can be wished away, they are also seen as necessary to the child's individuation and socialisation. And it is the mother in particular who is at the centre of these conflicts, shadowing these films with her absence as much as her presence.

Set in the early 70s, *My Girl* is unusual in that it features a young heroine. Veda grows up in a funeral home which lacks a maternal presence (her mother died in childbirth and she believes that she was responsible for killing her). Initially she resents the kindly, free-spirited woman who becomes consort to her father and friend to herself. But this female influence becomes an essential element in her progress to adult femininity through a world darkened by death – not only her mother's, but that of her best friend (a boy) as well.

In *Little Man Tate*, which chronicles one year in the life of a gifted child, the burden of motherhood is split between two women: Dede, Tate's biological mother, and Jane, his teacher. In a film where the male characters are conspicuously flimsy, both female figures are seen as essential to the well-being of the young boy and enjoy their relationship with him. *Little Man Tate* takes up the viewpoint of the intellectually precocious, emotionally needy son, but it also poignantly examines the women's perspectives as each in turn is rejected and then revalued by this 'little man'. Unlike many of these movies, this one allows considerable space to the frustrations of its mother figures.

These films attach positive values to motherhood – in *Little Man Tate*, to the exclusion of fatherhood. The horror comedy *Problem Child* is an exception. Here, the ghastly Junior messianically ditches his adoptive mom like a piece of unwanted baggage (she is trussed up in a suitcase and evacuated from the narrative) and gallivants off with dad in a celebration of male bonding. Generally, though, these Hollywood pictures gesture towards a re-evaluation of mothering as a regenerative force, giving it a surprisingly beneficent central role. But 'good' mother figures, of course, are those who stand by their little and big men, as do the stoical wives of *Hook*'s Peter and *JFK*'s Jim Garrison. Their own desires take second place.

Hollywood's wish to return to prelapsarian innocence is nothing if not ambivalent. The happy, smiling faces of its babies provoke intense anxiety, while existence in Neverland appears positively precarious. J. M. Barrie's own description says it all: 'The astonishing splashes of colour here and there, and coral reefs and rakish looking craft in the offing... It would be an easy map if that were all; but there is also the first day at school, religion, fathers, the round pond, needlework, murders, hangings, verbs that take the dative... and so on; and either they are part of the island or they are another map showing through, and it is all rather confusing, especially as nothing will stand still...' In such hazardous conditions, it is hardly surprising that the movies call up traditional images of maternal stability, or that they should reflect a conventional ambivalence towards maternal figures. For those who are asked to continue to rock the cradle, however, there is even less to celebrate. *First published in April 1992 (volume 1, number 12).*

Ginette Vincendeau

Fathers and daughters in French cinema: from the 20s to 'La Belle Noiseuse'

Jacques Rivette's *La Belle Noiseuse* and Luc Besson's *Nikita* are two French films that would appear to have little in common. The former is by a New Wave director and has all the hallmarks of a 'difficult' auteur film – four hours long, not much happening on the surface, but we read it as a profound reflection on artistic creation. One of its acknowledged sources is a short story by Balzac. *Nikita*, by contrast, is a popular, fast-paced 'post-modern' thriller, borrowing its aesthetics from music videos and advertisements. One of its acknowledged sources is an Elton John song. Yet these films share one important feature: the relationship between their beautiful young heroines and controlling father figures. This symbolic, or in some cases actual father-daughter axis constitutes a master-narrative which French cinema has repeatedly returned to, challenged or reworked.

La Belle Noiseuse and *Nikita* contain many of the elements that characterise this configuration. For example, each initially presents its heroine as rebellious: Marianne (Emmanuelle Béart) in *La Belle Noiseuse* refuses to pose for Frenhofer (Michel Piccoli), a famous painter whom her boyfriend wishes to please. Mysteriously, she then changes her mind, despite her valid objection that her boyfriend (and the movie?) has 'sold her arse'. Most of the rest of the film is taken up with Frenhofer forcing her naked body into increasingly uncomfortable poses. The eponymous Nikita (Anne Parillaud) is a criminal and drug addict, and the first scene shows her blowing out a policeman's brains with a gun. After her arrest she is offered freedom in exchange for selling her body and soul to the (futuristic) state; there follows a painful rehabilitation programme to turn her into a contract killer at the beck and call of her mentor, Bob (Tcheky Karyo). Both Piccoli and Karyo are clearly paternal authority figures at whose hands the young women undergo a humiliating and regressive process. (Nikita does much sobbing and snivelling and at one point cries for her mother.) *La Belle Noiseuse* is more subtle, but Frenhofer does subject Marianne to his will, in the name of his art, culminating in a pose with clear echoes of crucifixion. The painting we never see could be a record of this sadistic process.

The sadism with which the men treat the young women is in direct proportion to (and therefore a disavowal of) the sexual attraction they feel for them, heightened by the women's rebelliousness. Yet at the same time the men display a protective concern: in this Oedipal game, they are 'mothers' as well as 'fathers'. Bob slaps Nikita in the face and puts her through a brutal training programme; he also buys her cakes and gifts. After a day of gruelling posing, Marianne is offered bed and board by a kindly, non-threatening Frenhofer. But the films take the symbolic father-daughter relationship even further. When Bob visits Nikita and her young boyfriend, he pretends to be her uncle, and his nostalgic evocation of her imaginary childhood – when she used to have ribbons in her hair – is in excess of the requirements of narrative. Marianne in *La Belle Noiseuse* takes her place as the 'daughter' of the childless Frenhofer couple, replacing Frenhofer's wife, Liz (Jane Birkin), as muse and model. Liz is rubbed out of the painting to make way for Marianne in a bid by Frenhofer to renew his blocked creativity.

Liz's erasure from both the narrative and the work of art is indicative of the position to which the father-daughter axis relegates the mature woman: obsolete, or a token figure like the Jeanne Moreau character in *Nikita*. It is also typical of the master-narrative that in both films the young men (in each case the heroines' boyfriends) are displaced. Though Nicolas (David Bursztein) in *La Belle Noiseuse* is initially responsible for bringing Marianne and Frenhofer together, he subsequently disappears from the narrative. In both films, the young men are insubstantial, infantilised figures who play second fiddle to the older men, while the young lovers are depicted as 'children': Nikita and Marco (Jean-Hugues Anglade) 'play house'; we realise at the end that Nicolas' affair with Marianne took the place of his incestuous relationship with his sister.

A surprising number of French films in the 80s and 90s take up the father-daughter storyline, with seduction scenarios which sometimes go as far as incest. Serge Gainsbourg's *Charlotte For Ever* stars himself and his own daughter, whom he also celebrated in his song 'Lemon Incest'; Jacques Doillon's *La Puritaine* explores the semi-incestuous feelings between a father (Piccoli again) and his daughter (Sandrine Bonnaire); Bertrand Blier's *Beau-père* and Jacques Demy's *Trois places pour le 26* treat the same subject. Other films give centre stage to the relationship between a 'father' and his 'daughter' in a more symbolic fashion: Maurice Pialat's *A nos amours*; Claude Miller's *Mortelle randonnée* (in which Michel Serrault transfers on to Isabelle Adjani his obsessive feelings for his dead daughter); Jean Becker's *L'Eté meurtrier*; the Jean-Paul Belmondo comedy, *Joyeuses Pâques*, in which he pretends that his lover (Sophie Marceau) is his daughter in order to appease his wife. Even the long-running French soap *Chateauvallon* centres on the relationship between Antonin Berg (the head of the central 'dynasty') and his favourite child, Florence.

How can the preponderance of this pattern, which cuts across both popular and art movies of the 80s, be explained? Undoubtedly the fact that in French cinema it is generally men who hold power, while notions of feminine beauty are associated with youth, is a starting point, as is the fact that most films are now targeted at a youth audience. And certainly as the directors of the New Wave – Godard, Rivette, Rohmer – have got older, their heroines have become younger, a situation that reproduces the imbalanced gender power relation at the roots of the father-daughter narrative.

A classic reflectionist view would look at how these stories echo developments in contemporary French society: surely this obsession by male directors with the father, the exclusion of the mature woman and her replacement by a 'nymphet' has something to do with anxieties about female power? Though blatant sexism in both the media and everyday interaction persists in France, women have managed to enter the corridors of power in greater numbers than in most other western countries. And genetic engineering and changes in the inheritance laws have put the position of the father within the family in crisis, to the point where Fathers Associations have sprung up to fight women for child custody.

**Father-daughter axis: Emmanuelle Béart and
Michel Piccoli in 'La Belle Noiseuse' (1992)**

However tempting it might be to see the father-daughter scenario as a response to social changes, the theme in fact has a long history in French culture, going back to the eighteenth-century fairy tale 'La Belle et la Bête' and the great nineteenth-century realist-melodramatic novels of Balzac, Hugo and Zola. Some of Colette's novels (*Gigi*, *L'Ingénue libertine*) continued the tradition, with her gamines and their 'uncles' or mature 'cousins'.

The pattern began to appear in classical French cinema in the 20s – Abel Gance's *La Roue*; Jean Renoir's *La Fille de l'eau* – and was taken up with renewed enthusiasm in the 30s and 40s. Marc Allégret's *Gribouille*, Marcel Pagnol's *La Femme du boulanger*, Jeff Musso's *Dernière jeunesse* and Julien Duvivier's *Panique* (remade as *Monsieur Hire*) explicitly dramatise the conflict of the ageing man (played by Raimu in the first three of these examples) torn between his erotic and protective feelings towards a daughter, stepdaughter, adopted waif or very young wife. The influence of *Les Misérables* is clear, and indeed its hero Jean Valjean, embodied by Harry Baur, Jean Gabin, Lino Ventura *et al*, has haunted French cinema with his quest for his 'daughter' Cosette.

The risqué aspect of the story was exploited in comedies of the period, epitomised by the adapted boulevard play *Arlette et ses papas*, in which the hero (Jules Berry) marries a woman he believes to be his daughter (though the spectator knows she is not). This trend continued in the 50s, notably with a series of Jean Gabin films including *La Marie du port*, *Des Gens sans importance* and *Voici le temps des assassins*. The dialogue emphasises the point: 'We'll tell them I'm your father,' Gabin says to Nicole Courcel, whom he is about to marry at the end of *La Marie du port*; 'I could be your father' to Françoise Arnoul in *Des Gens sans importance*. The most famous in the series is *En cas de malheur*, in which his protective attitude towards his young lover (Brigitte Bardot) goes as far as spoon-feeding her and blowing her nose.

As the above examples, with the repeated appearance of actors such as Raimu and Gabin, make clear, casting is crucial to perpetuating the motif. And the creation of stars known for certain roles dictated the writing of new parts. Hence the reign of mature actors and young actresses. Following the success of films like *L'Effrontée*, *A nos amours* and *Betty Blue* in the 80s, directors seemed only to want very young women – Béart, Bonnaire, Sophie Marceau, Béatrice Dalle, Juliette Binoche – while older stars like Catherine Deneuve and Jeanne Moreau tended to be wheeled in for cameos, as was Moreau in *Nikita*. On the other hand, older male actors – Belmondo, Depardieu, Piccoli, Noiret, Rochefort, Delon, Montand – thrive. As the French magazine, *Première*, put it: 'Three leading parts in one year is almost unknown for an actress, but is common among actors.' Two of the most successful French films of the 80s, *Jean de Florette* and *Manon des Sources*, typify the trend. Yves Montand as Le Papet stepped into the shoes of Raimu and Gabin to play the troubled patriarch, while Depardieu and other mature male actors were played against the very young Manon (Béart).

Cultural sources, social climate and institutional forces thus conspire to perpetuate a pattern in which fathers dominate very young women (and in the process exclude mature women). Yet there have been moments of rebellion. The early films of the French New Wave – *A bout de souffle*, *Les 400 coups*, *Le Beau Serge* and so on – echoing the generational attack of their young male film-makers briefly displaced 'daddy' from the screen in favour of narratives that revolved around young men. Following May '68 and the rise of feminism, the more politically oriented cinema of the 70s produced some women-centred movies (*Céline et Julie vont en bateau*, *La Fiancée du pirate*, *Nathalie Granger*), while mainstream cinema and the classic stories provided 'strong', mature heroines, embodied by actresses such as Annie Girardot (*Mourir d'aimer*) and Miou-Miou (*La Femme flic*). The 80s, however, brought a noticeable return to the mature man/young girl pattern; director Aline Isserman in 1986 declared herself appalled by the 'infantilism' of the female characters in the scripts she was given to read.

Isserman is herself part of a contingent of women directors whose work represents a challenge to the master-narrative, in part through a shift in focus to the mother and mother-daughter relationship. In Diane Kurys' and Chantal Akerman's films, it is the father who is marginal or absent; if there is an authority figure for the young Mona (Bonnaire) in Agnès Varda's *Sans toit ni loi*, it is Mme Lantier (Macha Méril). Women directors have also worked towards breaking the mould of traditional casting by creating parts for mature actresses. Marie-Claude Treilhou's *Le Jour des rois* features Danielle Darrieux, Micheline Presle and Paulette Dubost; Nelly Kaplan's *Plaisir d'amour* has three generations of women.

Some women directors also tackle the father-daughter scenario from the daughter's point of view – for example, Catherine Breillat's *Virgin*, an exploration of the first sexual experiences of a 14-year-old girl and her ambivalent feelings about her attraction to a 40-year-old man. Bertrand Tavernier's *Daddy Nostalgie*, based on his ex-wife Colo Tavernier's semi-autobiographical text, explores the tragedy of the exclusion of the mother from the closeness of the bond between father (Dirk Bogarde) and daughter (Birkin), rather than presenting it as given.

Other 80s French films which challenge the reign of the father are the *cinéma beur* (*beur* is slang for Arab), made by second-generation North African emigrants. *Beur* films such as Mehdi Charef's *Le Thé au harem d'Archimède* and Abdelkrim Bahloul's *Le Thé à la menthe* document the demise of the father as a result of the culture shock and racism experienced by first-generation emigrants to France. The mothers here emerge as central figures, both in the social world and in the imaginary one which links the Arab motherland and the French *patrie*. But male *beur* directors tend to display little gender awareness in their representation of their young heroes. Strikingly different (though not strictly *beur*, since it was made by a Jewish North African emigrant) is Charlotte Silvera's *Louise l'insoumise*, the aptly titled depiction of a young girl's rebellion against the Jewish law of the father.

Beur women living in France have rarely had access to major film-making resources, so the merging of gender and post-colonial concerns tends to be found most strongly in films made by white French women. Though working for the most part in a classical idiom, these directors confront the gender and racial systems of mainstream French cinema. Claire Denis' *Chocolat*, Brigitte Rouan's *Outremer* and Marie-France Pisier's *Le Bal du gouverneur* take the spectator back to the directors' childhoods in the 40s and 50s, which coincided with the onset of decolonisation. In *Chocolat* and *Le Bal*, the figure of the mother is the crucial point of reference; in *Outremer* it is a community of sisters.

The challenges to the father-daughter master-narrative have come from avant-garde or politically committed film-makers, from women, or from second-generation immigrants – in other words, from those in marginal positions. In a truly 'post-modern' era, it is possible that mainstream French cinema will cease to exist and that these marginal positions will inhabit the central (albeit fragmented) arena. Even Rivette with *La Belle Noiseuse* and Besson with *Nikita* were not impervious to change. Whereas the rebellious daughters of the 'daddy's cinema' of the 30s, 40s and 50s had to return to the patriarchal fold (and bed), as in *La Femme du boulanger*, or come to a grim end, as in *Des Gens sans importance* and *En cas de malheur*, those of *La Belle Noiseuse* and *Nikita* escape and leave their 'fathers' behind.

Meanwhile, in classical mainstream French cinema the master-narrative persists, epitomised by one of Gérard Depardieu's latest popular comedies. The story of his ambivalent relationship with his teenage daughter, it is entitled *Mon père, ce héros*.

First published in March 1992 (volume 1, number 11).

B. Ruby Rich

Homo pomo:
the new queer cinema

1992 was a watershed year for independent gay and lesbian film and video. In the spring, on the very same day, Paul Verhoeven's *Basic Instinct* and Derek Jarman's *Edward II* opened in New York City. Within days, the prestigious New Directors/New Films Festival had premiered four new 'queer' films: Christopher Münch's *The Hours and Times*, Tom Kalin's *Swoon*, Gregg Araki's *The Living End* and Laurie Lynd's *R.S.V.P.* Had so much ink ever been spilled in the mainstream press for such a cause? *Basic Instinct* was picketed by the self-righteous wing of the queer community (until dykes began to discover how much fun it was), while mainstream critics were busily impressed by the 'queer new wave' and set to work making stars of the new boys on the block. Not that the moment wasn't contradictory: the summer's San Francisco Gay and Lesbian Film Festival had its most successful year in its 16-year history, doubling attendance from 1991, but the National Endowment for the Arts pulled its funding anyway.

The queer film phenomenon was introduced in 1991 at Toronto's Festival of Festivals, the best spot in North America for tracking cinematic trends. There, suddenly, was a flock of films that were doing something new, renegotiating subjectivities, annexing whole genres, revising histories in their image. All through the winter, spring, summer and autumn, the message was loud and clear: queer is hot. Check out the international circuit, from Park City to Berlin to London. Awards have been won, parties held. At Sundance, in the heart of Utah's Mormon country, there was even a panel dedicated to the queer subject, hosted by yours truly.

The Barbed Wire Kisses panel put eight panellists on stage, with so many queer film-makers in the audience that a roll call had to be read. Film-makers stood, one by one, to applause from the matinee crowd. 'Sundance is where you see what the industry can bear,' said panellist Todd Haynes, there to talk about *Poison*'s year on the firing line. He stayed to be impressed by earnest 18-year-old Wunderkind Sadie Benning, whose bargain-basement videos, shot with a Fisher-Price Pixelvision and produced for less than $20 apiece, have already received a retrospective at MoMA.

Isaac Julien was suddenly cast in the role of the older generation. Summarising the dilemmas of marketing queer product to general audiences, he described a Miramax Prestige advertising campaign for his *Young Soul Rebels* that used a bland image of guys and gals hanging out, like a Newport ad gone Benetton. Julien got them to change to an image of the black and white boyfriends, Caz and Billibud, kissing on a bed. The box office improved.

Tom Kalin struggled to reconcile his support for the disruptions of *Basic Instinct*'s shoot with his film *Swoon*'s choice of queer murderers as subjects. Australian film-makers Stephen Cummins and Simon Hunt related the censorship of an episode of *The Simpsons*, where a scene of Homer kissing a swish fellow at the plant was cut. The panel turned surprisingly participatory. One Disney executive excoriated the industry. Meanwhile, Derek Jarman, the grand old man in his fourth decade of queer activity, beamed. He'd never been on a panel of queers at a mainstream festival.

Try to imagine the scene in Park City. Robert Redford holds a press conference and is asked, on camera, why there are all these gay films at his festival. Redford finesses: it is all part of the spectrum of independent film that Sundance is meant to serve. He even allows that the awards in 1991 to *Poison* and Jennie Livingston's *Paris Is Burning* might have made the festival seem more welcoming to gays and lesbians. He could just as easily have said: these are simply the best films being made.

Of course, the new queer films and videos aren't all the same, and don't share a single aesthetic vocabulary or strategy or concern. Yet they are nonetheless united by a common style. Call it 'Homo Pomo': there are traces in all of them of appropriation and pastiche, irony, as well as a reworking of history with social constructionism very much in mind. Definitively breaking with older humanist approaches and the films and tapes that accompanied identity politics, these works are irreverent, energetic, alternately minimalist and excessive. Above all, they're full of pleasure.

All the same, success breeds discontent, and 1992 was no different from any other year. When the ghetto goes mainstream, malaise and paranoia set in. It can be ideological, or generational, or genderational. Consider the issues that might disturb the peace. What will happen to the lesbian and gay film-makers who have been making independent films, often in avant-garde traditions, for decades already? Surprise, all the new movies being snatched up by distributors, shown in mainstream festivals, booked into theatres, are by the boys. Surprise, the amazing new lesbian videos that are redefining the whole dyke relationship to popular culture remain hard to find.

Amsterdam's Gay and Lesbian Film Festival made these discrepancies plain as day. The festival was staged in November 1991, wedged between Toronto and Sundance. It should have been the most exciting place to be, but wasn't, not at all. And yet, that's where the girls were. Where the videos were. Where the films by people of colour and ex-Iron Curtain denizens were. But the power brokers were missing.

Christine Vachon, co-producer of *Swoon* and *Poison*, is sure that the heat was produced by money: 'Suddenly there's a spotlight that says these films can be commercially viable.' Still, everyone tries to guess how long this moment of fascination will last. After all, none of this is taking place in a vacuum: celebrated in the festivals, despised in the streets. Review the statistics on gay-bashing. Check out US immigration policy. Add the usual quota of internecine battles: girls against boys, narrative versus experimental work, white boys versus everyone else, elitism against populism, expansion of sights versus patrolling of borders. There's bound to be trouble in paradise, even when the party's just getting going.

Dateline: Toronto

Music was in the air in Toronto in September 1991, where the reputation of queer film and video started to build up. Or maybe I just loved Laurie Lynd's *R.S.V.P.* because it made my elevator ride with Jessye Norman possible. Lynd's film uses Norman's aria from Berlioz's *Les Nuits d'été* as its madeleine – supposedly Lynd sent Norman the finished film as a belated form of asking permission, and she loved it so much she agreed to attend the world premiere at

Queer new wave:
Tom Kalin's 'Swoon' (1992)

Toronto (with red carpet in place and a packed house going wild, she sat through the screening holding Lynd's hand). *R.S.V.P.* suggests that the tragedy and trauma of Aids have led to a new kind of film and video practice, one which takes up the aesthetic strategies that directors have already learned and applies them to a greater need than art for its own sake. This time, it's art for our sake, and it's powerful: no one can stay dry-eyed through this witty elegy.

Lynd was there as a producer, too, having worked on fellow-Canadian John Greyson's *The Making of 'Monsters'*. In it, George Lukács comes out of retirement to produce a television movie and hires Bertolt Brecht to direct it. Along with the comedy and boys in briefs, there's a restaging of the central aesthetic argument of the Frankfurt School as it might apply to the crises of representation engendered by today's anti-gay backlash, violence, and television treatments of the Aids era.

Both low-budget and high-end film-making showed up in Toronto. Not surprisingly, the guys were high end, the gals low. Not that I'd begrudge Gus Van Sant one penny or remove a single frame from *My Own Private Idaho* – a film that securely positions him as heir-apparent to Fassbinder. So what if it didn't get a single Oscar nomination?

At the other end of the spectrum was veteran avant-gardist Su Friedrich, whose latest film, *First Comes Love*, provoked catcalls from its largely queer audience. Was it because its subject was marriage, a topic on which the film is healthily ambivalent, mingling resentment with envy, anger with yearning? Or was it an aesthetic reaction, since Friedrich returns to a quasi-structuralist mode for her indictment of institutionalised heterosexuality and thus possibly alienates audiences accustomed to an easier queer fix? Was it because the director was a woman, since the only other lesbian on hand was Monika Treut, who by now should probably be classified as post-queer? Whatever the reason, Friedrich's elegant short stuck out, a barometer in a pack of audience-pleasers.

The epiphanic moment, if there was one, was the screening of Jarman's *Edward II*, which reinscribed the homosexuality so integral to its sixteenth-century source via a syncretic style that mixed past and present in a manner so arch that the film easily fits its tag, the 'QE2'. Think pastiche, as OutRage demos and gay-boy calisthenics mix with minimalist period drama. Homophobia is stripped bare as a timeless occupation, tracked across centuries but never lacking in historical specificity. Obsessive love, meanwhile, is enlarged to include queer desire as a legitimate source of tragedy.

For women, *Edward II* is a bit complicated. Since the heroes are men and the main villain is a woman, some critics have condemned it as misogynist. Indeed, Tilda Swinton's brilliance as an actor – and full co-creator of her role – invests her character with more weight, and thus more evil, than anyone else on screen. But the film is also a critique of heterosexuality and of a world ruled by royals and the Tory Party, and Isabella seems more inspired by Thatcher than woman-hating. Annie Lennox is clearly meant to be on the side of girls and angels. Her solo 'Every Time We Say Goodbye' accompanies Edward and Gaveston's last dance, bringing grandeur, modernity, even post-modernity, to their tragedy. The song comes from the Aids-benefit album, *Red Hot and Blue*, in which video Lennox inscribed images of Jarman's childhood in a tribute to his activism and HIV status. Thus does Jarman's time travel insist on carrying the court into today's gay world.

Dateline: Amsterdam

The official car showed up at the airport with the festival's own steamy poster of girls in heat and boys in lust plastered all over it. Amsterdam, city of lights for faggots and dykes, offered the promise of an event purely one's own in the city celebrated for queerness. Expectations were running high, but in fact the festival showed all the precious advantages and irritating problems that life in the ghetto entails. It was a crucible for queer work, all right, but some got burned. How does this event fit into the big picture set by the 'big' festivals? Well, it doesn't. The identity that elsewhere becomes a badge of honour here became a straitjacket. But would 'elsewhere' exist without the 'here'?

Amsterdam was an exercise in dialectics in action, with both pleasures and dangers. Film-maker Nick Deocampo from the Philippines was planning his country's first gay festival and hoping that the 'war of the widows' wouldn't forestall it. Race, status, romance, gender, even the necessity of the festival came up for attack and negotiation, on those few occasions when the public got to talk back. Pratibha Parmar affirmed the importance of a queer circuit – 'my lifeline' – sure that it's key to the work. Jarman disagreed: 'Perhaps their time is up,' maybe life in the ghetto now offers diminished returns. So though Jarman and Ulrike Ottinger got awards here, and though Jarman used the opening night to call for the decriminalisation of Oscar Wilde, the meaning of such an event remained contested.

Not that there weren't good films at Amsterdam. But the best work seemed to come from long ago or far away, like the great shows of German cross-dressing movies or the Mary Wings tribute to 'Greta Garbo's lesbian past' or the extraordinary 60s fantasy from Japan, *Funeral of Roses*. There were even two terrific new lesbian films, both deserving of instant cult status. Cleo Uebelmann's *Mano Destra* brought bondage and domination straight to the viewer, serving up knot fetishism and the thrills of specular anticipation with an uncanny understanding of cinema's own powers. From a trio of Viennese film-makers (Angela Hans Scheirl, Dietmar Schipek, Ursula Puerrer) came *Flaming Ears*, a surreal fable that draws on comics and sci-fi traditions for a near-human love story visualised in an atmosphere of cabaret, rubble and revenge. Its fresh 'cyberdyke' style reflects Austrian sources as diverse as Valie Export and Otto Muehle, but shot through with Super-8 visual rawness and a script that could have been written by J. G. Ballard.

It was a shame that the Dutch press marginalised the festival, because the kind of 'scoop' that the *New York Times* and *Newsweek* would later find in Utah could have been theirs right at home. A new kind of lesbian video surfaced here, and with it emerged a contemporary lesbian sensibility. Like the gay male films now in the limelight, this video has everything to do with a new historiography. But where the boys are archaeologists, the girls have to be alchemists. Their style is unlike almost anything that's come before. I would call it lesbian camp, but the species is, after all, better known for camping. And historical revisionism is not a catchy term. So just borrow from Hollywood, and think of it as the Great Dyke Rewrite.

Here's a taste of the new genre. In Cecilia Dougherty's *Grapefruit*, white San Francisco dykes unapologetically impersonate John, Yoko and the Beatles – proving that appropriation and gender-fuck make a great combination. Cecilia Barriga's *The Meeting of Two Queens* re-edits Dietrich and Garbo movies to construct the dyke fan's dream narrative: get the girls together, help them get it on. It's a form of idolatry that takes the feminist lit-crit practice of 'reading against the grain' into new image territory, blasting the results on to the screen (or monitor, to be exact). In one episode of Kaucylia Brooke and Jane Cottis' *Dry Kisses Only*, Anne Baxter's back-stage meeting with Bette Davis in *All About Eve* is altered, inserting instead of Baxter a dyke who speaks in direct address to the camera about her life working in a San Francisco lesbian bar, her love lost to Second World War combat. She's cross-cut with Bette's reaction shots, culminating with Davis taking her arm (and taking her home).

Apart from the videos, festival lesbians pinned all voyeuristic hopes on the 'Wet' Party, where they would finally get to the baths. Well, sort of. Everyone certainly tried. Outfits ranged from the campiness of childhood-at-the-beach to show-your-leather seriousness. Women bobbed in the pool, playing with rubber rafts and inflated black and white fuck-me dolls. (Parmar would later note that there were more inflatables of colour in attendance than actual women of colour.) San Francisco sex stars Shelly Mars and Susie Bright both performed, though the grand moment in which Bright seemed to be lecturing us on 'Oedipal underwear' turned out to be a cruel acoustical joke: she was actually extolling the virtue of edible underwear. But the back rooms were used for heart-to-hearts, not action. Caught between the states of dress-up and undress, everyone waited for someone else to do something.

Other parties offered other pleasures. At one, Jimmy Somerville, unscheduled, did a Sylvester homage. At another, Marilyn Monroe appeared, frosted on to a giant cake, clutching her skirt, only to be carved up by a gaggle of male chefs. In the end, somehow, Amsterdam was the festival you loved to hate, the place where everyone wanted the world and wouldn't settle for less, where dirty laundry could be washed in public and anyone in authority taken to task, where audiences were resistant to experimental and non-narrative work, and where criticisms were bestowed more bountifully than praise. Still, while the market place might be seductive, it's not yet democratic. Amsterdam was the place where a 'Wet' Party could at least be staged, where new works by women and people of colour were accorded pride of place, where video was fully integrated into the programming. Amsterdam was a ritual gathering of the tribe and, like a class reunion, filled with ambivalence.

Park City, Utah

Everything came together at the Sundance Film Festival in Park City. Christopher Münch's *The Hours and Times* is a good example. Audiences fell in love with this imaginary chronicle of Brian

Epstein and John Lennon's last tango in Barcelona. Münch's camera style and script are a reprise of *cinéma vérité*, as though some dusty reels had been found in a closet in Liverpool and expertly edited, as though Leacock or Pennebaker had turned gay-positive retroactively. Epstein tries to get Lennon into bed, using old-world angst, homo-alienation, Jewish charm. Lennon tries to sort out his life, balancing wife Cynthia against groupie against Epstein, trying to have it all and to figure out whatever will come next. Just a simple view of history with the veil of homophobia pulled back. It's rumoured that the dramatic jury at Sundance loved it so much, they wanted to give it the Grand Prize – but since it wasn't feature length they settled on a special jury award.

'Puts the Homo back in Homicide' is the teaser for Tom Kalin's first feature, *Swoon*, but it could easily apply to Gregg Araki's newest, *The Living End*, as well. Where Kalin's film is an interrogation of the past, Araki's is set resolutely in the present. Or is it? Cinematically, it restages the celluloid of the 60s and 70s: early Godard, *Bonnie and Clyde*, *Badlands*, *Butch Cassidy and the Sundance Kid*, every pair-on-the-run movie that ever penetrated Araki's consciousness. Here, though, the guys are HIV positive, one bored and one full of rage, both of them with nothing to lose. They could be characters out of a porn flick, the stud and the john, in a renegotiated terrain. Early Araki films are often too garage-band, too boychick, too far into visual noise, but this one is different. Camera style and palette update the New Wave. Araki's stylistic end runs have paid off, and this time he's got a queers-on-the-lam portrait that deserves a place in movie history – an existential film for a post-porn age, one that puts queers on the map as legitimate genre subjects. It's quintessentially a film of its time.

And so is *Swoon*, though it might seem otherwise, what with the mock-period settings, the footage purloined from the 20s, and the courtroom-accurate script, based on the 1924 Chicago trial of Leopold and Loeb, the pair of rich Jewish boys who bonded, planned capers, and finally killed a boy. In the wake of the Dahmer case, it would be easy to think of this as a film about horrific acts. *Swoon*, however, deals in different stakes: it's the history of discourses that's under Kalin's microscope, as he demonstrates how easily mainstream society of the 20s could unite discrete communities of outsiders (Jews, queers, blacks, murderers) into a commonality of perversion. The whole look of the film – director of photography

Ellen Kuras won the prize for cinematography in dramatic film in Park City – emphasises this view with the graphic quality of its anti-realism, showing how much Kalin, Kuras and co-producer Vachon tailored its look.

As part of a new generation of directors, Kalin isn't satisfied to live in the past, even a post-modern past. No, *Swoon* takes on the whole enterprise of 'positive images', definitively rejecting any such project and turning the thing on its head. I doubt that anyone who damned *The Silence of the Lambs* for toxic homophobia will swallow *Swoon* easily, but hopefully the film will force a rethinking of positions. Claim the heroes, claim the villains, and don't mistake any of it for realness.

Throughout Sundance, a comment Richard Dyer made in Amsterdam echoed in my memory. There are two ways to dismiss gay film: one is to say, 'Oh, it's just a gay film'; the other, to proclaim, 'Oh, it's a great film, it just happens to be gay.' Neither applied to the films in Park City, since they were great precisely because of the ways in which they were gay. Their queerness was no more arbitrary than their aesthetics, no more than their individual preoccupations with interrogating history. The queer present negotiates with the past, knowing full well that the future is at stake.

Like film, video is a harbinger of that future, even more so. Yet Sundance, like most film festivals, showed none. To make a point about the dearth of lesbian work in feature film and to confront the industry with its own exclusions, the Barbed Wire Kisses panel opened with a projected screening of Sadie Benning's videotape *Jollies* – and brought down the house. With an absolute economy of means, Benning constructed a *Portrait of the Artist as a Young Dyke* such as we've never seen before. 'I had a crush. It was 1978, and I was in kindergarten.' The lines are spoken facefront to the camera, black-and-white images floating into the frame alongside the words enlisted to spell out her emotions on screen, associative edits calling settled assumptions into question.

The festival ended, of course. Isaac Julien returned to London to finish *Black and White in Colour*, his documentary on the history of blacks in British television. High-school dropout Sadie Benning left to show her tapes at Princeton, and to make another one, *It Wasn't Love*, that proved she's no fluke. Derek Jarman and Jimmy Somerville were arrested for demonstrating outside London's Houses of Parliament. Christopher Münch and Tom Kalin picked up prizes in Berlin. Gregg Araki found himself a distributor. New work kept getting produced: the San Francisco festival found its submissions up by 50 per cent in June. The Queer New Wave has come full circle: the boys and their movies have arrived.

But will lesbians ever get the attention for their work that men get for theirs? Will queers of colour ever get equal time? Or video achieve the status reserved for film? Take, for example, Cheryl Dunye, a young video-maker whose *She Don't Fade* and *Vanilla Sex* put a sharp, satiric spin on black romance and cross-race illusions. Or Jean Carlomusto's *L is For the Way You Look*, a definitive portrait of dyke fandom and its importance for, uh, subject position.

For one magical Saturday afternoon in Park City, there was a panel that traced a history: Derek Jarman at one end on the eve of his 50th birthday, and Sadie Benning at the other, just joining the age of consent. The world had changed enough that both of them could be there, with a host of cohorts in between. All engaged in the beginnings of a new queer historiography, capable of transforming this decade, if only the door stays open long enough. For him, for her, for all of us.

Pratibha Parmar

Queer questions: a response to B. Ruby Rich

Queer cinema has been going on for decades, although not in its current manifestation – that is, a marketable, collective commodity produced by white gay men in the US. Jarman's work has always seemed queer to me, but now a collective confidence, taking queer as a given, is emerging. It's a point we've reached through years of political organising. In New York, for example, both Todd Haynes and Tom Kalin have been nurtured by queer activism such as ACT UP.

Elements of Rich's article seem somewhat misleading, in particular the marking out of Sundance as the beginning of a new queer historiography. I also felt perturbed by the obvious absence of a whole litany of lesbian film-makers who aren't referenced. The fact that a group of very talented white gay men are getting exposure and access to budgets is to be welcomed, but we also need to consider the difficulties, through gender inequality, of access to economic and marketing resources for lesbian film-makers.

I find the formal inventiveness of the recent films exhilarating. Queers have been marginalised to such an extent that we have felt compelled to subvert dominant genres. Now the question of pleasure is very high on the agenda, not surprisingly in the age of Aids. Cultural interventions can be pleasurable, too.

I am wary of talking about an overarching queer aesthetic, as my sensibility comes as much from my culture and race as from my queerness. In queer discourses generally there is a worrying tendency to create an essentialist, so called authentic, queer gaze. My personal style is determined by diverse aesthetic influences, from Indian cinema and cultural iconography to pop promos and 70s avant-garde films. My film *A Place of Rage*, which explores questions of sexuality but doesn't prioritise these, sold out in the LA and San Francisco lesbian and gay festivals, proving that audiences are hungry for queer visions painted on a broader canvas.

My work has much wider distribution and profile in North America. Racism and censorship exist on both sides of the Atlantic, but there is a sense in the US that recognition for my work is based on merit rather than personality or tokenism. Queer aesthetics has been developing in both places and there is an ongoing exchange. For instance, there is a filmic dialogue between *Looking for Langston* and *Swoon*, as there is between Marlon Riggs and Isaac Julien, even though their work is very different.

In Britain, there is clearly a gap in institutional support for most queer films. One of the only exciting developments in the recent past has been the pioneering *Out* television series, which has given many of us access to funding and to a much wider audience.

Rich's article suggests that there is an ongoing debate about the role and need for lesbian and gay film festivals. By arbitrarily putting Jarman and myself in opposite camps, Rich, I fear, is inventing a false debate. Queer festivals are essential for many film-makers, especially lesbians and people of colour, because it's often the only place we can get our work screened and affirmed. I know Jarman would agree with this. What's becoming clear, however, is that these festivals are programmed predominantly by white gay men and women who prioritise their own constituencies, further marginalising queers of colour. *First published in September 1992 (volume 2, number 5).*

Amy Taubin

Queer male cinema and feminism

Rooted in Cocteau and Warhol, Fassbinder and Kenneth Anger, Genet and Jack Smith, American queer cinema has achieved critical mass. Encouraged by 25 years of gay activism made urgent by the Aids crisis and a right-wing homophobic backlash, queer filmmakers have fought back through production of images.

Since 1989, gay-themed films have garnered the kind of attention that makes Hollywood want a slice of the action. Warners' follow-up to its *Malcolm X* biopic is a film about Harvey Milk, to be directed by Gus Van Sant. And TriStar has *People Like Us* (working title), a Jonathan Demme movie about a gay lawyer who is sacked when his firm discovers that he's HIV positive.

Demme and Van Sant are no strangers to the contradictions of gay cultural politics. Demme's *The Silence of the Lambs* was attacked as homophobic because its serial killer Buffalo Bill was read as a negative gay stereotype. And Van Sant's *My Own Private Idaho* was attacked by some of the same critics for its lack of positive images of gay life. But it's Van Sant's depiction of marginality – the teenage male hustler hopelessly in love with a slumming preppie prince in *Idaho*, the grocery clerk obsessed by an illegal Mexican migrant worker in *Mala Noche* (1985) – coupled with his non-linear, associative film-making strategies, that make him one of the leaders of American queer cinema.

Budgeted at $2 million, *Idaho* is the priciest queer movie to date. The $20,000 *Mala Noche* is a more pertinent model for a queer cinema that is subversive in content, form and methods of production, but maintains just enough of a narrative spine to win it theatrical or television primetime release. In 1991, the emblematic US queer films – Todd Haynes' *Poison*, Jennie Livingston's *Paris Is Burning* and Marlon Riggs' *Tongues Untied* – each cost less than $200,000. So did the most interesting and visible of 1992: Tom Kalin's *Swoon*, Christopher Münch's *The Hours and Times* and Gregg Araki's *The Living End*. These last three shared so many festival spotlights that it became impossible not to think of them as part of a single impulse. A quick look at their similarities and differences might provide some sense of the range and limitations of queer cinema.

A visually spare and emotionally intricate chamber film (60 minutes, black and white) about what might have happened between Brian Epstein and John Lennon during a weekend the two spent together in Barcelona in 1963, Münch's *The Hours and Times* is so far removed from biopic, docudrama or *cinéma vérité* as to seem *sui generis*. Münch is a pomo humanist – a rare combination – raiding the image bank for the purpose of constructing empathetic characters. He told me that what was missing from the material he researched was 'a sense of what it was like to be Epstein.'

Aided by David Angus' selfless performance, *The Hours and Times* shows precisely what it was like to be the intelligent, physically awkward, emotionally vulnerable, self-deprecating Epstein – the gay Jewish aesthete hopelessly in love with a working-class tough whose genius was his spontaneity and intuitive grasp of 'the hours and times' in which he came of age. The film flies in the face of the hetero culture of *Rolling Stone* by suggesting that Lennon was capable of a homoerotic involvement. And it defies simplistic gay identity politics by representing a deep affinity between two men that is not defined by the sexual act. That the film doesn't specify what, if anything, happens when Lennon and Epstein share a bed, is exactly the point. Because, either way, it didn't change the relationship.

Although *The Hours and Times* is about a relationship between two men, women figure prominently in its narrative. In addition to the off-screen presences of Epstein's mother and Lennon's wife, there's the stewardess who visits Lennon's hotel room. 'What would you do if I said I wanted to make love to you?', he asks. 'I might agree or I might not', is her self-possessed reply.

Like *The Hours and Times*, Kalin's *Swoon* uses black and white as a sign of history and memory. But unlike Münch, who evokes our identification with Epstein in terms of what Epstein says and does *vis-à-vis* his object of desire, Kalin wants us to admit the eroticism of protagonist Nathan Leopold's fantasies, which he suggests through fragmentary sounds and images and sliding camera moves. Tony Rayns nailed it when he wrote: 'the film uncovers an orgasmic truth between the flutter of bird wings and the sound of a whip lash.'

Kalin makes a pretty clear case for the process by which internalised homophobia and anti-semitism are transformed into sadomasochistic fantasies and a fascination with criminality. The first half of the film unabashedly identifies with Leopold, with his equation of glamour and deviance. If his homosexuality places him outside the law, it's also his connection to Chicago's underworld.

Swoon falters when it attempts the leap from erotic fantasy to the actuality of child murder. Abandoning Leopold's subjectivity, it perfunctorily filters the crime through various institutional perspectives – psychoanalytic, criminological, legalistic – all of them homophobic. At this point, I began to have the sense that Kalin was less interested in Leopold and Loeb than in the way their myth was formative in terms of his own sexuality. Failing to make that connection explicit and failing to illuminate the crime itself (in the way, for example, that Fassbinder illuminates the patricide in *Wild Game*), the film ends up as conceptually muddled as it's visually elegant. One should not underestimate, however, its importance in proclaiming a desire that is anything but 'politically correct'.

Gregg Araki's *The Living End* treats the queer-as-criminal theme from a contemporary perspective. An angry young drifter and an anxious young film critic, both HIV positive, fall in love, and, with nothing to lose, crash through to the other side of the law. The sex between the men is sweet, hot and extremely moving; *The Living End* is best when Araki sets aside his California cool and risks the aching romanticism of *Pierrot le fou* combined with the melodramatics of *Duel in the Sun*.

If one accepts these three films, along with *Poison*, *Paris Is Burning* and *Tongues Untied*, as the effective queer films of the 90s, then the limitation of that cinema is obvious: queer cinema is figured in terms of sexual desire and the desire it constructs is exclusively male. (Jennie Livingston is a lesbian director, but *Paris Is Burning* is about black and hispanic male transvestites.) Indeed women are even more marginalised in 'queer' than in heterosexual film; at least in the latter, they function as objects of desire. (Which is why the pre-feminist stewardess who comes between Epstein and Lennon is such a powerful figure.) Worse still, *Tongues Untied* and *The*

Living End are heedlessly misogynistic. Where does the politics of *Tongues Untied* – that 'black men loving black men is the revolutionary act' leave lesbians of any colour? I'd say high and dry. As for *The Living End*'s inept lesbian serial killers and the woman who kills her lover when she discovers he's bisexual, a case could be made that they are no more or less stereotypical than their nerdy hetero male counterparts: all of them function as comic relief. But then what is one to make of Araki's claim that the woman whose symbiotic attachment to the gay hero defines her entire emotional life is a feminist character?

In fact, this queer cinema has much more in common with male violence films (with Quentin Tarantino's *Reservoir Dogs* or Nick Gomez's *Laws of Gravity*, for example) than it does with any feminist cinema. Like Tarantino and Gomez, Araki and Kalin are also the sons of Scorsese, whose films define and critique masculinity through violence but also make Robert De Niro a homoerotic object of desire.

To find a cinema that is queer and feminist, one must look further into the margins, where Sadie Benning is using a toy Pixelvision video camera to monitor and exhibit her adolescent lesbian identity. Ten years younger than any of the queer male film-makers above (most of whom are under 30), Benning shares with them the pleasure of flaunting the fact that she's 'as queer as queer can be'. Unlike the women film-makers produced by the feminist film theory of the 70s, she doesn't have a problem about defining herself in terms of her sexuality.

Benning's work is easily as powerful as any of the queer films I've mentioned. In terms of form, however, she's making something radically different – a hybrid of video and solo performance in the tradition of gallery artists like Vito Acconci. Benning hasn't made the transition that Chantal Akerman made before our eyes in *Je tu il elle*, when she redirected her attention from the self to the other, acknowledging the narrative standard for theatrical release.

Like Akerman, Haynes, Kalin, Münch, Livingston, Riggs and Araki incorporate the formal and sexual transgressions of the avant-garde within a narrative of queer desire. As long as that desire remains exclusively male, however, it's only queer by half.

First published in September 1992 (volume 2, number 5).

Julia Knight

Female misbehaviour:
the cinema of Monika Treut

When Monika Treut's feature film *Virgin Machine*, a humorous les-bian coming-out story, was premiered at the Hof Film Festival in 1988, Helmut Schoedel, critic for *Die Zeit*, responded with a sting-ing pronouncement: 'Films like Monika Treut's are destroying the cinema.' Treut vividly recalls the occasion: 'They were walking out after ten minutes, and by the end there was only about one-third of the audience left; no one laughed throughout the film, nobody talked to me afterwards.' But Treut is no stranger to such reactions. Her debut feature, *Seduction: The Cruel Woman* (1985), was about sado-masochism. Co-directed with Elfi Mikesch, it was nearly banned in Canada and elicited a chorus of booing at its Berlin premiere.

Of course, Treut is not the first German director to have pro-voked such responses. If anything, this negative reception should have signalled her fitness to join the ranks of the New German Cin-ema's star auteurs, most of whom were repeatedly taken to task in their homeland for their supposed directorial failings. Like Fass-binder, Alexander Kluge, Herbert Achternbusch and others, Treut has also fallen foul of the country's film subsidy agencies. Yet while her work has quickly attracted champions abroad, in Britain, where the films of Fassbinder, Wenders and Herzog were readily picked up for theatrical distribution and were among the first European films to be given video releases, Treut has been largely ignored apart from a handful of festival screenings.

Germany is not short of female directors. But the plethora of lit-erature on the New German Cinema that began to emerge at the end of the 70s focuses almost exclusively on a small number of male

film-makers, completely marginalising established women directors such as Margarethe von Trotta, Helma Sanders-Brahms and
Ulrike Ottinger. The reasons for this neglect are complex, but a
major factor has been the narrow auteurist approach that dominated discussions of the New German Cinema at the peak of its popularity. For a number of years, Fassbinder, Wenders, Herzog and one
or two of the other male directors effectively came to constitute the
new cinema, marginalising others, including Germany's female
directors, who did not fit comfortably into the auteur mould.
Because of their subject matter – often autobiographical or based
on experiences of real-life women – women directors, despite enormous formal differences, tended to be treated as a homogeneous
group of 'documentarists and realists' at odds with the artistic
vision privileged by auteurism.

In such circumstances, it would have been remarkable if Monika
Treut had not encountered obstacles. And the challenging exploration of sexuality within her films has undoubtedly made it all the
more difficult for her to negotiate a foothold in the British market.
As Treut herself claims: 'It has to do with the Victorian thing... a
kind of fear English people have of relating to films and other works
with a strong sexual undertone.'

Virgin Machine is about a Hamburg journalist, Dorothee (Ina
Blum), who is researching a story on romantic love. Dorothee photographs couples, interviews experts, and pursues a relationship
with Hans. (The film also hints at a sexual relationship with her
brother.) Failing to find what she is looking for in Germany, she
departs for San Francisco, where she meets Susie Sexpert, who
introduces her to the city's lesbian sex industry. Fascinated by this
strange new world, Dorothee goes to all-women strip shows,
inspects Susie's dildo collection and tries a lesbian call-girl service.

Treut's documentary work deals with equally controversial
areas of sex and sexuality. In 1983 she made *Bondage*, an interview
with a lesbian SM devotee. *Annie* (1989) documents the career of
Annie Sprinkle, who made porn films in the 70s, has worked as a
prostitute, and now gives 'post porn modernist' performances for
the sexual 'underground'. In 1992, Treut completed *Max*, a story of
a female-to-male transsexual. The films were released, together
with a fourth about controversial US academic Camille Paglia, as a
feature-length programme under the somewhat tongue-in-cheek
title, *Female Misbehaviour*.

Treut has hardly been the only German director to confront questions of sexuality: although usually less direct in his approach, Fassbinder inevitably springs to mind. But entry into British cinema culture has been difficult for Treut not only as a woman director, but as a lesbian film-maker. Although lesbian films such as Alexandra von Grote's *November-moon* (1984) or Donna Deitch's *Desert Hearts* (1985) have been given UK cinema releases, lesbian work has not been accepted as part of British film culture to the same extent as films by gay male directors. For example, both Derek Jarman's *Edward II* and Isaac Julien's *Young Soul Rebels* warranted substantial coverage in *Sight and Sound*. This is obviously in part due to the relatively high profile achieved by gay men generally, whereas lesbians have remained largely invisible. And the virtual absence of women feature-film directors in the UK has meant that there are no lesbian directors in a position to speak out for their work. The result has been a lack of sustained engagement with and promotion of lesbian film-making within more mainstream film culture. Anything more challenging than the romantic love stories of Von Grote and Deitch has had difficulty finding an outlet other than at isolated screenings or lesbian and gay film festivals.

There are also important differences between the ways Treut and Fassbinder deal with 'deviant' sexuality. Whereas Fassbinder invariably constructed his protagonists as victims of an impersonal society, Treut represents her characters as having exercised a sexual choice and assumed control of their lives. Thus in *Virgin Machine*, she represents Dorothee as investigating and assessing various possibilities before finally opting for a lesbian sexuality. In contrast to other feminist and/or lesbian film-makers who have deconstructed mainstream cinema's representations of female sexuality or tried to construct 'positive' alternatives, the freedom to choose is the structuring principle of Treut's narratives. What her protagonists choose is almost incidental.

Sexual choice for women is still – despite feminist gains – often considered 'transgressive', something Treut acknowledges in the title of her documentary series, *Female Misbehaviour*. And the choices Treut explores are in themselves transgressive and controversial, if not taboo. *Virgin Machine*'s investigation of the lesbian sex industry flies in the face of the vociferous anti-pornography campaigns launched by feminist activists such as Andrea Dworkin and her German counterpart, Alice Schwarzer. According to Dworkin, pornog-

OUT ON A LIMB

**The pleasure principle: Susie Bright
(right) instructs Ina Blum in
Monika Treut's 'Virgin Machine' (1988)**

raphy 'requires the brutalisation of women' and there is no quali-
tative difference between straight and lesbian (or gay) porn.
Dworkin regards images such as photographer Della Grace's photographs of SM lesbians or Jill Posner's work for the US lesbian erotica magazine *On Our Backs* as 'self-hating' and denies any possibility
of consent by the women who have been photographed. To anyone
who shares Dworkin's views, *Virgin Machine*'s humorous approach
to its subject matter is entirely inappropriate and unpalatable.

Of course, not all women share these views, and campaigning
groups such as Feminists Against Censorship in the UK and the Feminist Anti-Censorship Task Force in the US are an important counter-
balance. But even awareness of the controversy can influence
acquisition decisions. For the small number of independent distributors – COW before its demise, Electric Pictures and Metro Pictures – which have in the past taken the work of European women
directors, sensitivity to the Dworkin argument can make Treut's
films problematic, while memories of feminist pickets outside porn
cinemas could make financial investment seem a risky venture.

Treut's film-making is transgressive not only in its subject matter, but at a formal level too. She does not so much bend or break
with cinematic conventions as mix them all up, using whatever
technique seems appropriate. This irreverent approach gives her
films an unplanned, meandering feel, leading some critics to liken
them (in no way disparagingly) to home movies. *Virgin Machine*, for
instance, is narrative-based, but the camerawork and editing during the first half have more in common with avant-garde cinema.
Filmed in black and white, there are moments where the lighting
and framing of Ina Blum's strong-featured face are reminiscent of
Weimar cinema. However, once the film moves to San Francisco,
Treut cuts joltingly from her fictional narrative to Susie Sexpert
talking direct to camera, as if being interviewed. Treut delights in
incorporating real-life women into her fictional stories, and the
character of Susie Sexpert is based on and played by Susie Bright,
safer-sex educator and editor of *On Our Backs*. Treut's *My Father Is Coming* (1991) features Annie Sprinkle as herself.

But perhaps Treut's most unforgiveable transgression is to
arouse expectations of sexual explicitness that are not fulfilled. The
titles of all her films are sexually suggestive, as are the posters that
advertise them. *My Father Is Coming* is a whimsical comedy about
Vicky, an aspiring actress working in New York who receives a visit

from her narrow-minded Bavarian father, Hans. Perfectly comple-
menting the *double-entendre* of the title, the poster is reminiscent of
a porn magazine cover – Annie Sprinkle is presented in close-up,
her pendulous breasts bared, leaning over the eager face of a pros-
trate Hans. A similar shot occurs in the film, but just as Annie is
about to satisfy Hans' desire, the camera pans away. Despite her preoccupation with sexuality, Treut rarely shows sex or nudity.

All this begs the question of who her films are aimed at and how
appropriate the 'lesbian film-maker' label is. Her choice of subject
matter and inclusion of cult figures such as Susie Bright and Annie
Sprinkle tend to suggest that her work is aimed at a lesbian sub-
culture. But Treut has angered some lesbians by her failure to
deliver the goods in terms of lesbian erotica, while others, looking
for romantic love stories, will be equally disappointed. Her films in
fact cover a range of sexualities (including both heterosexual and
female-to-male transsexual), though her association with porn and
SM may deter a wider audience.

Yet as the lesbian and gay distribution company, Out On A Limb,
has recognised, Treut's films do have the potential to appeal to a
wide audience. Unlike most 'heroines' in mainstream cinema,
Treut's protagonists openly enjoy their sexualities without fear of
punishment or the need for containment within marriage. This,
together with Treut's predilection for 'showing very outrageous
female characters', creates a strong sense of fun. As a female viewer,
irrespective of sexuality or politics, it is difficult to respond
unfavourably to images such as Susie Sexpert discussing her dildo
collection with Dorothee. As Treut recalls of *Virgin Machine*'s premiere: 'Some really hard-boiled feminists came to see the film,
ready to be angry; by the end, they were laughing and could not
hold an anti-porn stance with regard to the film.'

But Treut's most important transgression lies in the way she
challenges prejudices about sexuality. In direct contrast to mainstream films like *The Silence of the Lambs* or *Basic Instinct*, Treut represents as ordinary those people all too often constructed as deviant.
Her 'transgressive' brand of film-making is a much-needed intervention into the arena of sexual politics. If, as Susan Faludi asserts
in her book, *Backlash*, 'the last decade has seen a powerful counter-
assault on women's rights,' Treut's films and her 'misbehaving'
women are a vital form of resistance.

First published in June 1992 (volume 2, number 3).

Thomas Elsaesser

Leni Riefenstahl: the body beautiful, art cinema and fascist aesthetics

Leni Riefenstahl at 90: photographed by Helmut Newton in a pair of rainbow-coloured leggings, stiletto heels and a fur-trimmed coat, leaning against a sports car parked on a gravelled driveway. The clash of associations, the camp bad taste, the sheer improbability of this apparition (fronting an interview with Riefenstahl in *Vanity Fair*, September 1992) is suitably disconcerting. Is this nonagenarian *femme fatale* still worshipping at the fountain of youth, or is this a pose to make her part as the fluttering butterfly of the Third Reich more credible? Either way, the butterfly Riefenstahl is clearly made of steel: a specimen from a period that does not seem to diminish in scale as it recedes in time. For this incommensurability alone, *The Sieve of Time*, the 1993 autobiography of the director of *Triumph of the Will* (1935) and *Olympia* (1938) – two films that have come, rightly or wrongly, to epitomise Nazi narcissism – merits attention, even without the tediously irrelevant but apparently still lucrative frisson of how intimate she has been with the Führer.

From someone who has always professed her ignorance of the concentration camps, or of Gestapo terror acts, the title of *The Sieve of Time* is, to say the least, an odd choice. Self-critical irony or haughty defiance? The phrase seems to have been inspired by a line from Albert Einstein: 'One must take comfort in the fact that time has a sieve, through which most trivia run off into the sea of oblivion.' If media interest in Riefenstahl's autobiography has focused on her personal ties with Nazi leaders, the book seems to have been written partly to redress the balance, to give more space to her life after 1945 (the Nazi era takes up less than 200 pages), and to record her formative period in the 20s, as a dancer, briefly with Max Reinhardt, then as a movie star in Arnold Fanck's *The Holy Mountain* (1926) and her own *The Blue Light* (1932).

Riefenstahl is the first to admit that she is no great writer; but she has an acute mind, and always knew how to capitalise on her considerable charm. The films, on the other hand, have always been controversial. And a number of key points emerge from the decades of debate:

– In Riefenstahl's work we can see the continuity of Weimar cinema (especially Fritz Lang) with Nazi cinema. This thesis is based on the similarity of certain recurrent visual motifs (wild landscapes, dramatic skies, heroic bodies), shared genres such as the mountain film, to which Riefenstahl contributed as actor and director, and finally, a monumentalism which Siegfried Kracauer, apropos of *The Nibelungen* and *Metropolis*, has identified as the 'mass ornament': a dehumanising, quasi-military, strictly hierarchical and patterned representation of crowds (originally borrowed, as Lotte Eisner has shown, by Lubitsch, Lang and others from Reinhardt's theatre spectacles of the 1910s).

– Riefenstahl is responsible for two masterpieces, which, while politically abhorrent or at any rate highly suspect, continue to be aesthetically impressive, indeed brilliant textbook examples of how to make a stirring film out of a tedious event (a political party conference), and how to create a four-hour narrative of drama, human interest and suspense out of a two-week sports meeting.

– The reason we keep coming back to these films (and to their director) is because they have become prototypes of genres which to this day are central, if not to the cinema, then to the aesthetics of television. The coverage of presidential elections, political summits, the staging of the Olympic Games can all be traced back to Riefenstahl's invention of the 'photo-opportunity' which is *Triumph of the Will*. More critically, Riefenstahl's films are associated with the Nazi recognition that reality is an event which happens in order to be filmed.

– Taking these points together, it can be shown that Riefenstahl's career as an actor in the mountain films, as a film-maker of political documentaries, and as a photographer of vanishing African tribes is all of a piece, illustrating some of the quintessential features of fascist aesthetics and its visual imagination. This imagination continues to be fascinating to this day, because the kind of image-making it implies – which not only shows an abiding tendency to abstract the human figure from its historical and social inscription, but treats it as an empty sign or icon – means that the human figure can serve as a support for any kind of message, propaganda or advertising, all of which instrumentalise the body.

If this, broadly speaking, is the received wisdom on Riefenstahl the film-maker, does the autobiography contain anything which might help us settle the 'controversy'? The answer on the whole is: no. Riefenstahl once again defends herself vigorously against her critics, chronicling the innumerable law suits and libel cases she has fought since 1945, and citing testimonies, documents, affidavits in her favour. The most poignant case is perhaps that against Erwin Leiser's *Deutschland Erwache!*, for using footage from *Triumph of the Will* as if it were documentary, and intercutting it with shots of concentration camps. Since her reputation rests on the skilful juxtaposition of material, and since to this day she adamantly insists on her film of the Nazi party rally being 'a pure record of what happened', her position is doubly ironic: a fact that entirely escapes her. The most politically damaging allegation she got the courts to clear her from was that she had used as extras in *Tiefland* (finally released in 1954) a family of gypsies she knew was destined for a death camp.

While none of this may cut much ice in Riefenstahl's favour, more inadvertently and only obliquely, *The Sieve of Time* does shed some light on what made her 'tick', and to this reader at least suggests some thoughts which imply a slightly different interpretation of her career. First, there is the importance of dance to her world view. From her earliest, father-defying passion for the Laban school of modern dance to her conception of herself as a self-expressive film-artist, a consistent line runs through her life which seems to focus on the body as total expressive fact. This needs to be seen historically. Not only was *Ausdruckstanz* something of an upper-middle-class craze in the 1910s and 20s (the Isadora Duncan phenomenon), but Riefenstahl also shared in its wider cultural significance as part of a German youth movement (the *Wandervögel*) which was progressive in inspiration, libertarian, and whose *Freikörperkultur* (free body culture) has to be seen in the context of Wilhelmine collars, corsets and covered piano legs. As was the case with so many other movements to do with the body and sport in the 20s, the Nazis were able to co-opt some of the dance movement's adherents during the 30s, until 'self-discipline and ecstasy' (as one critic called it) became one of the central attractions of Nazi aesthetics.

It seems clear that Riefenstahl remained faithful to her early ideals in this respect, and not only as far as the outdoor life of skiing, hiking, swimming and diving was concerned. For instance, the autobiography leaves no doubt that she enjoyed sex, and liked talking about it – at a time when this was unfashionable. Not only did she have many affairs – with her cameraman, her fellow-actors, men she met almost anywhere and fancied – but film-making was evidently for her a very erotic and sexualised activity. On the set of *The Holy Mountain*, for instance, she played off Fanck against star Luis Trenker, keenly aware of the older man's sexual torment when she favoured Trenker.

Another telling episode occurs in 1932, when Riefenstahl starred in Fanck's *S.O.S. Iceberg*, produced by Paul Kohner. A dual-language, German-American co-production (the American version was directed by Tay Garnett and produced by Carl Laemmle at Universal), it was shot in Greenland by a team made up of a film crew and a scientific expedition (the latter, one gathers was necessary in order to get permission to film among the Eskimos, whom the Danish government wanted to protect from disease). Sandwiched between her first meeting with Hitler at Wilhelmshaven and his visit to her Berlin studio to look at photographs (and disapprove of some Käthe Kollwitz charcoal drawings on her wall), the Greenland trip takes in an escaped polar bear, a switch of lovers (from Hans Scheeberger to Hans Ertl), and a rescue by Ernst Udet, the stunt pilot in Fanck's films, of one of the scientists, Dr Sorge, whose boat smashed when a huge iceberg began to 'calve'. There exists an account by Sorge himself (*Mit Flugzeug, Faltboot und Filmkamera in den Eisfjorden Grönlands*, Berlin 1933), which focuses on the research part of the expedition. Where Sorge mentions Riefenstahl, he complements her story, down to the details of her urinary problems and the fact that she not only kept a portrait of Hitler in a sealskin frame by her bed, but kept quoting – to jibes from the scientists – from her bedtime reading, *Mein Kampf*.

What I think is significant about this episode is that Riefenstahl's pan-eroticism and nature worship was matched by a very down-to-earth, 'modern' appreciation of her own sexuality, which had little of the repressive, prudish atmosphere that surrounded Hitler. But it also tells something about the film-making milieu to which she belonged. It was Fanck, himself a curious mixture of the Arctic explorer-scientist and autodidact film-technology freak, who taught Riefenstahl film directing. The glimpses one gets of the milieu of mountaineering and movie-making are as intriguing as they are brief: Fanck, an independent producer, funded by UFA's American rival, Universal, with a crew partly on loan from UFA's prestigious but maverick Kulturfilm production unit, and made up partly of Fanck's First World War airforce cronies, with the troublesome Luis Trenker itching to make his own films; and Riefenstahl taking out a rowing boat to sunbathe on an iceberg with one of the cameramen.

Fanck was at heart a still photographer, forever experimenting with different lenses, exposure times and developing baths. Influenced by the Renger-Patsch tradition of the New Realism, he wanted to bring to his movies of mountain, ice and snow the textures and tonalities of the photographic print: using slow motion, back lighting, contrasts in scale and strong separation of background and foreground. None of this was lost on Riefenstahl when she came to shoot *Triumph of the Will*, and it may have some bearing on the argument of how 'inept' it is as a piece of film-making. Rather, I would argue that it strikes one as a camera(wo)man's film, introducing a certain photographic aesthetic into the hitherto shunned areas of crowds, power and politics. If *Triumph of the Will* is the triumph of form over substance, this is partly because it is a box of photographer's tricks, blended with point-of-view editing techniques picked from feature film-makers, squirrelled away like a film-school graduate, and then flamboyantly, impetuously shown off on a commission (affidavits to the contrary notwithstanding) she could not refuse. It is this 'experimental' dimension which to this day makes some documentary film-makers her most ardent fans, professing to have 'learnt from her'. But these film-makers also know that when helping themselves from *Triumph of the Will*, a little goes a long way, for part of the potency of the film is that, in its genre, it goes too far – but on a road television documentary has often travelled since.

Fanck also put Riefenstahl in touch with Harry Sokal, the Jewish producer who backed her financially and logistically for *The Blue Light*, giving her the opportunity to found her own production com-

**In the open: Leni Riefenstahl filming
for 'Olympia' (1938)**

pany, a fact which was very important to her not only after 1945, when she argued in her defence that neither *Triumph of the Will* nor *Olympia* were 'official' Nazi films, commissioned and financed by the party.

The salient question, in a way, is not the extent to which *Triumph of the Will* has or has not influenced documentary film-makers (there are tributes not only from Grierson but also from Paul Rotha), but what kind of causal link – and therefore responsibility – can be established from this film to the Nazi newsreel tradition, and the countless documentaries and propaganda films made in the 30s and 40s. From a film-historical point of view, the malleability of the material through editing is less remarkable than the contribution made to the editing by the sound montage and Herbert Windt's score, sound obviously being the technology in which to be experimental in the 30s. It is here that Riefenstahl did something original: putting staged tableaux to movement, music and vocals. Hence the point Riefenstahl expends many pages refuting – that there was re-staging and re-shooting on *Triumph of the Will*, as mentioned in Albert Speer's *Inside the Third Reich* – is something of a red herring. Speer, who acknowledges the difficulties Riefenstahl had, as an independent-minded woman, with the party hierarchy, confesses, somewhat disingenuously, to being shocked when Streicher, Rosenberg and Frank agree to re-takes in the studio. Hess, 'with his special brand of ardour, turned precisely to the spot where Hitler would have been sitting, snapped to attention and cried: "Mein Führer, I welcome you in the name of the Party Congress." He did it all so convincingly that from that point on I was no longer sure of the genuineness of his feelings.' Riefenstahl herself mentions the many re-shoots necessary for *Olympia*, mainly in connection with the stormy love affair she had with the American decathlon winner, Glenn Morris, which apparently made her miss some crucial heats in the competition.

Since *Triumph of the Will* and *Olympia* have to this day remained, for an international public at least, the best-known films the Nazi cinema produced, the fact that Riefenstahl directed both of them weighs against her when she protests her lack of interest in politics or propaganda. However, from a film-historical perspective, the films may not belong together as logically as is usually asserted. *Olympia* is stylistically quite different from *Triumph of the Will*. Yet even if one emphasises stylistic similarities (low-angle shots of erect bodies against an empty sky, and so on) there remain substantial differences in terms of function. While *Triumph of the Will* was made mainly in order to bind the leaderless SA to the Party, after the Röhm putsch and the 'night of the long knives', *Olympia* was a compromise project, negotiated between the regime and the Olympic Committee, which aimed to give to the world an image of the games as supra-individual and supra-national, a celebration of youth in communal competition. That these representations are carefully 'constructed' is evident, but this in itself hardly differs from the construction of the nation on the *Nine-o'-Clock News*.

What is more indicative is the use the games, and Riefenstahl's film-making, seem to have been put to – namely to front another enterprise altogether, that of allowing the Nazis their first experiments with television, and the live transmission of events. The new technology and its potential preoccupied the various ministries involved much more than the ideological content of *Olympia*.

Two issues come into play here – one is that the Nazis, while keeping a tight rein on film production, did not consider film to be their main propaganda medium. As far as the audio-visual media were concerned, it was radio that interested them, and its penetration into the home and potential as a public address and alarm system were as significant as what was broadcast. During the war, simultaneous broadcasting and the emphasis on 'live-ness' became a crucial part of the morale-boosting, mass-mobilising function of the media. For these objectives, film was too slow a medium. One might even argue that the Nazi film industry was developed as an entertainment industry, for the films and stars acted as inducements to bring spectators to the newsreels. None of the technological or media-political considerations seems to have occurred to Riefenstahl: the memoirs make no mention of the presence of television cameras at the games.

There is perhaps a more important reason why it did not strike her. The way the cinema developed in Germany was not at all in the direction of Riefenstahl's own idea of cinema. In the 30s and 40s, UFA, Terra and Tobis – the three major production companies – were run by and large as studios churning out films designed to make money. While they were broadly in line with the regime, they continued a genre cinema already well established in the 20s whose mainstays were melodramas and comedies, musicals and biopics – genres whose formulas were often copied directly from Warner

Bros or MGM prototypes. Where politics massively operated in the Nazi cinema was in the realm of personnel politics (the compliance of UFA in Hitler's racial policy is well documented) and in the style and content of the newsreel.

Not only was Riefenstahl an 'independent' producer/film-maker in a film business increasingly centralised and industrialised, but – as already indicated – hers was in inspiration an art and experimental cinema. While her films, as well as Fanck's, were released through UFA, UFA was not their production company: on the contrary, Fanck refers to himself as the 'Freiburg School', and had little but contempt for studio-bound film-making as practised in Neu-Babelsberg or Munich. Riefenstahl was less radical, but she too was committed to the outdoor view of cinema. Riefenstahl's aversion to being identified with propaganda, newsreel and commissioned films has, it seems to me, more to do with her self-image as a film-artist than with any attempt at political whitewash.

The question the memoirs prompt, then, when viewed from the point of view of film industry and film politics, is how did Riefenstahl fit into the Nazi cinema, as opposed to echoing motifs or tendencies of other Nazi films? The answer seems to be, not very well. For one of the puzzling aspects of her career is why she made only these two films, if she was so important to the regime. The one other film she worked on throughout the 30s and 40s was *Tiefland*, and what she documents about this project is a tale of failures and disappointments, of outright official betrayal.

It is here that Riefenstahl's paranoia is most noticeable. Perhaps in order to explain to herself the lack of support she received as a film-maker, she builds up Goebbels as her arch foe, though whether this tortured and highly eroticised relationship explains anything about her film-making career is less clear. It does demonstrate the fact that Riefenstahl was not very adept either tactically or analytically, revealing once again her tendency to personalise and sexualise whatever happened to her. In fact, Goebbels brings out the melodramatist and pulp novelist in her: 'He said, looking round the dark, deserted street: "We can't stay here, you'll be drenched." I glanced at my small Mercedes parked in front of the building... There was only one thing on my mind: nobody must see us... As we turned into the forest I saw him produce a gun from his raincoat pocket and thrust it into the glove compartment. Noticing my alarm, he smiled. "I never go anywhere without a weapon"... He grabbed my breast and tried to force himself on me. I had to wrestle my way out of his arms... Besides himself with rage, he held me against the wall and tried to kiss me. His eyes were wide open, and his face completely distorted.'

To be fair, Riefenstahl knew there was a thin line between being the Führer's favourite film-maker and ending in disgrace, so there may have been a grain of truth in the paranoia, a sense of real terror, when trying to dodge not only Goebbels' grasping hands, but film commissions from the Party. Riefenstahl knew that these things could go horribly wrong, as they did in the case of her friend and cameraman, Willy Zielke. Zielke was commissioned by the Reichsbahn to make a film celebrating the German railway's centenary, giving the story of the inventors and developments from the steam engine to the diesel locomotive. In *The Steel Animal*, 'Zielke had turned this difficult material into a thrilling picture. His locomotive looked like a living monster. The headlights were its eyes, the instruments its brain, the piston its joints, and the oil dripping from the moving pistons looked like blood... When the officials saw the movie, they were so horrified – according to Zielke – that they left the room speechless.' The film was not only not shown, the railway board had the prints destroyed. Riefenstahl tried to intercede, and arranged for Goebbels to see a print. He thought it showed talent, but found it too abstract for the public: 'It could be a Bolshevist film.' 'But that's no reason to destroy the film,' replied Riefenstahl. 'I'm sorry, but the decision is entirely up to the Reichsbahn, which has financed the film.' More than the film was destroyed: Zielke's sanity suffered, and he was interned in a mental hospital, apparently blaming Riefenstahl for his committal.

Beyond the human element, the episode also shows that there were a number of non-fiction film-makers who tried to continue the more experimental and formal film-making of the 20s, like Walter Ruttmann's, influenced by Eisenstein and Russian film – an art cinema, in other words, with which Riefenstahl had a great affinity. With the beginning of the war, and the gearing of the industry into a more overt propaganda and morale-boosting machine, directors like Riefenstahl saw their opportunities for making films dwindle, and Riefenstahl herself became more and more marginalised compared to directors who, like top managers or the captains of industry, put themselves in the service of the regime. Directors like Veit Harlan and Wolfgang Liebeneiner, Karl Ritter, Gustav Ucicky and

Josef von Baky fitted this industrial strategy completely, and had the same cynical attitude to keeping production going at any price (as with Harlan's *Kolberg*) as Speer had in the armament industries. It may be Riefenstahl's vague knowledge of this that made her so sensitive about the accusation of using gypsies from the concentration camp, for while the use of forced labour might have been possible for a major production, it adds insult to injury where the mostly aborted *Tiefland* project was concerned. However, she never seemed to realise that her cult of the body beautiful had become a blasphemy in a Germany where bodies were labour power to be worked to death in munitions factories or rocket test sites; this in turn made her incapable of seeing those who could not forgive her as anything other than personal enemies, motivated by spite and 'human nastiness'.

Although it would be plainly absurd to suggest that Riefenstahl was a pawn of the Nazi regime, there is a sense in which she had little control over what became of her career, which was effectively finished before the outbreak of the war. The memoirs both know this and disavow this knowledge. How, then, can one understand Riefenstahl's 'I only live for what is beautiful' other than as the desperate plea of someone who could never see herself in relation to any kind of history, or in any kind of social or political context, and who was therefore incapable of humour, wit or irony, but also incapable of recognition, reflection, remorse? The world view that inspired all her actions is certainly older than Nazism and goes deeper: the contrasts between nature and civilisation, between the simplicity of physical strength and the complications of social existence. Even the basic untruth of her position, namely that in order to glorify and romanticise unspoilt nature and simplicity, she had to deploy all the technological acquisition of civilisation, as well as participate in a state apparatus of Byzantine deviousness, is not of itself what makes her a Nazi: to that extent, Riefenstahl may have been a fellow-traveller and a beneficiary, but nothing like as brazenly as many a Party-member (which she was not) officially rehabilitated during the 50s and allowed to enjoy top positions in West German government, industry and the judiciary. Having survived so long would appear to have been a mixed blessing for her, since it traps her into perpetually having to downplay the brief period in her long life which alone still makes her news; yet the limelight also blocks her life from being looked at more kindly or more dispassionately. It is because she is still around that fingers will be pointed at her and, in turn, fans or ardent admirers will step into the breach.

Does it mean there is necessarily a tragic dimension to Riefenstahl's life? Perhaps not, but there are none the less ironies that make one pause, for she seems to have borne the brunt of public shame more openly and more frequently than the real culprits of the regime, most of whom, as far as film-making goes, were quite happily reintegrated into the industry. After 1945, the vast majority of them found work, even Veit Harlan, whose *Kolberg* and *Jud Süss* did not even split opinion between admirers and detractors the way Riefenstahl's films had always done. No, it was not the exposed nature of her films that put paid to her film-making career, but the fact that she was not 'one of us', that she had never really belonged in the first place. She was, it seems, as much an outsider to the film industry during the Third Reich as she was to be in the Federal Republic.

It is doubtful whether Riefenstahl fully understood even the film-historical side of the history in which she briefly played such a prominent part, for the memoirs give no clue to it. Yet it is difficult to take such a balanced view of Riefenstahl's memoirs or too charitable a view of her historical role. Compared to the aristocratic unrepentance displayed by another *vieille dame indigne* from Hitler's entourage, in Syberberg's *Confessions of Winifred Wagner*, the irritation provoked by *The Sieve of Time* comes less from Riefenstahl's apolitical aestheticism than from her sympathy-seeking. Shocked by the Holocaust as she now seems, and no doubt also aware of some dimensions of this story she does not touch on, she constantly buttonholes the reader, as if to absolve herself from a knowledge for which there could be no forgiveness, while evidently preferring the verdict of irredeemable naivety to that of culpable ignorance. Film history may not be able to help her out of this impasse, even where it can recognise that such an impasse exists.

First published in February 1993 (volume 3, number 2).

Angela McRobbie

Chantal Akerman and feminist film-making

Chantal Akerman was only 23 when *Je tu il elle* was first shown. It marked the start of an interest in sex and sexuality which has stayed with her, and which is taken up again directly in her 1991 film, *Nuit et jour*. Akerman's films have been linked with feminism ever since the early 70s, when *Je tu il elle* (1974), followed by *Jeanne Dielman, 23 Quai de Commerce, 1080 Bruxelles* (1975), were taken up by theorists and film critics as reflective of the new feminist politics. Her work was also seen as pioneering in that it seemed to herald the development of a distinctively feminist aesthetic.

Je tu il elle featured Akerman herself in three set pieces and was shot within a week on a tiny budget. The speed and intensity of its production work their way right through the film, from the first section where Akerman is seen obsessively eating from a bag of white sugar while contemplating the end of a relationship, to the second where she is sitting in the noisy front seat of a lorry, masturbating the driver, and finally in a scene of prolonged, convulsive love-making with a woman. It was indeed a spectacular debut.

Akerman's own relationship with feminism at that time, and particularly with feminist theory, was tinged with ambivalence. *Jeanne Dielman* was seen by several critics, including those from *Screen*, as visualising, in its use of 'real time', Julia Kristeva's idea of 'women's time'. Akerman disputed this, as she did the suggestion that the low level of the camera subverted conventional ways of looking. It was, she replied, much more to do with the fact that she is a very small woman.

It is difficult to locate the nature of these tensions with femi-

**Feminist ambiguity: Chantal Akerman's
'Je tu il elle' (1974)**

nism outside the specific context of French feminism in the 70s and 80s. Akerman certainly resisted, perhaps rightly, the pressure to conform to the high political expectations that would be made of her were she wholeheartedly to represent herself as part of the women's movement. Of course it's all different in the 90s: as the movement has fragmented and diversified in terms of who it represents, where and how, there is not the same intense relationship between film and politics. That Akerman's path, from *Jeanne Dielman* onwards, has been singularly removed from the requirements of theory might have been a source of disappointment to her feminist audience. In particular, the recurrent references to lesbianism which find a focus in *Les Rendez-vous d'Anna* (1978), where the filmmaker at the centre of the narrative tells her mother of an affair with a woman one night when they share a bed and hotel room, were not developed.

Interviewing Chantal Akerman in London, she told us that feminism had not successfully entered the political agenda in French culture. 'In France now,' she said with a hint of resignation and frustration, 'we don't speak a lot about women. Not since 1981. It's out of fashion.' According to Akerman, political disillusionment has immobilised both the left and the women's movement. It is only around issues of race that there is any sense of political energy, with little sign of involvement from the older 'new left' or the women's movement of the 70s. In this environment, Akerman seems to be working in the same kind of chosen isolation as she has always done, with the help of a few collaborators and her long-term producer, Martine Marignac.

Looking back on her career, Akerman points out the continual disparity between the generous press coverage she has had from papers such as *Libération* and the small audiences her films have attracted. To raise money to fund her films has always been a struggle, though she acknowledges that one of the advantages of working in France is that she usually 'has a home' for her work once it reaches the initial stages. *Nuit et jour* cost £1 million to make – not a large budget, and with fewer people going to see films, and particularly independent films, she does not expect to make much from it. But in comparison with independent film-makers working elsewhere in Europe, and in particular in the UK, she is aware that she is 'well protected'. 'Even those of us not working in the mainstream still have room to work. *Un Jour Pina a demandé* [1983] was commissioned by French television. There is also INA [L'Institut National de l'Audiovisuel] and the state television network is obliged to give space to what INA produces. So *Pina* came out of that space, and they also allowed me to do a piece about my grandmother.'

How is the work of an independent French film-maker who produces films in a wilfully self-styled feminist aesthetic to be understood in the 90s? Cultural politics has moved on to more global terrain; the European avant-garde, which some might claim remains the home of a director like Akerman, is seen as representing a particular historical moment that has been thoroughly challenged and superseded; the debates of post-modernism have unsettled, if not undermined, the project of 'theoretical' film-making. Both the theorists of the 70s and the post-modernists of the 80s encountered obstacles in their desire to bring together politics and art. The search for good theory in film practice narrowed the focus of film scholarship, since so few films measured up to the expectations of theory, and in any case there was less and less money around to fund independent film. At its worst, the shift a few years later to endorsing a post-modern practice led to a neglect of all the feminist art, feminist film-making and other examples of 'serious' cultural production that did not fit that mould. More recently, artists and photographers such as Cindy Sherman, Barbara Kruger and Sherry Levine in the US, and in the UK painters like Therese Oulton and Rosa Lee as well as the photographer Mitra Tabrizian, have been applauded for successfully bringing together feminism and post-modernism.

But rather than explore the possible crisis in feminist cultural practice, or else the extent to which it does not fit with the overarching concerns of post-modern theory, there has been a move instead on the part of feminist film scholars to a fashionable preference for reading the popular (the Madonna phenomenon) in terms of its account of gender relationships in the new climate of sexual politics. What this shows is the narrowness of the world of feminist film-making, and the close relationship between practitioners, feminist academics, and the university departments which act as cultural legislators. While Akerman's early work fitted exactly with the requirements of the new feminist film scholarship that took root in the 70s in educational establishments in the US and Europe, it is more difficult now to place her concerns within broader debates. This alone is evidence of many of the weaknesses in current theory. But it also raises usefully awkward questions for critics who have avoided the question of style and aesthetics and the autonomy of vision in feminist art practice: precisely the space Akerman occupies.

Despite dropping out of film school early on, Akerman remains the product of a certain kind of art-school education. Her films are adamantly 'hers', and what characterises them is a continuity and development of style and imagination, within a distinctively French tradition (with Godard and Marguerite Duras as long-term influences). One of the difficulties of looking at Akerman's career is that she has been over-appropriated by so many different 'interest groups'. In France, her films attract the critical attention of psychoanalysts, who see in them the repeated expression of a kind of pre-Oedipal femininity (lesbianism in this context is a retreat to a state of being close to the female, and hence to the mother). Feminists not working in the field of film theory emphasise her overriding concern with mother-daughter relationships, something which Akerman says she has now worked through and left to one side, while at the same time feeling forever indebted to her own mother for encouraging her to have a career at a time when young girls in France were still being brought up to be housewives. Akerman is also looked to by lesbian-feminists, who trace in her films a turning away from heterosexuality and a continued concern with female sexual pleasure. And finally there is the Akerman whom the quality press in both Britain and France would interpret as the archetypal auteur.

Not surprisingly, Akerman has been seen as letting down some of these groups, some of the time. Perhaps now it can be recognised as a strength that her films sidestepped theory and, in a moment of didactic film-making, resisted the pressure to pontificate or indeed to be certain. The thread of uncertainty and ambivalence that winds its way through all her work, together with a kind of daydreaming, introspective femininity occasionally bursting through into passion or violence, are what characterise her vision of what it is to be a woman. For example, the underrated *Golden Eighties* (1983), about the very female experience of working in the fashion and beauty business, is concerned not with the more politically fashionable pleasures of shopping, but with the fantasies, stories and gossip that shop workers and beauticians indulge in to pass the long hours of work. Although the film possesses a whimsical, humorous edge, Akerman sees it as harshly critical of a world where work is repetitive and unrewarding, one which she experienced at second hand through her mother, who worked in a boutique and who, according to Akerman, described it as a form of prostitution, of having to sell yourself in order to sell the clothes.

If fashion and the body play a key role in *Golden Eighties*, it is sex and love which Akerman returns to in *Nuit et jour*. It is a film which seems on first impression to be almost perversely conventional in its replaying of the heterosexual love triangle from which the female protagonist, Julie, eventually walks away. At points, the love-making is claustrophobic and familiar in its tracking of the young and flawless female body. The narrative is precious and yet familiar; the protestations of both men are too ardent, too much the traditional and perhaps outmoded 'language of love'. And even Julie's pleasure in both men is unsurprising.

From any other female director working in the 90s, it would be tempting to regard *Nuit et jour* as a post-modernist pastiche, an ironic idyll of love and romance viewed from a post-Aids, post-feminist perspective. But no, it doesn't quite work like this. Instead, it is a profoundly French film, paying tribute perhaps to Godard, and in its lyricism evoking a history of French cinema from *Jules et Jim* to *Celine et Julie vont en bateau* to *Une femme est une femme*.

Akerman has worked, at her best, with questions of female (and Jewish) identity. She is also, like Godard, a profoundly urban filmmaker. If in her most recent work she is overwhelmed by a weak narrative (never her strongest point) and by the force of a national film culture to which she seems to be paying tribute, then, having paid her respects, perhaps we can assume that Akerman will in future return to a film-making practice that more successfully develops the personalised, semi-documentary style and urban images which she so wonderfully captured in her New York film, *News from Home* (1977).

First published in September 1992 (volume 2, number 5.)

Carole Angier

Monitoring conformity: the career of Doris Dörrie

Men was a shock. A low-budget ($400,000) comedy on the frailty of men made by a German woman, it was an unexpected hit not only in Germany, but also in the US. Suddenly Doris Dörrie was a name, and Hollywood studios showered her with offers of screenplays. In the way of Hollywood studios, they were all comedies about men. She turned them down.

That was in 1985, when she was 30. She'd already made several shorts and documentaries, and one feature: *Straight Through the Heart* (*Mitten ins Herz*, 1983). *Straight Through the Heart* set the pattern for all Dörrie's films. It was adapted, by her, from one of her own short stories. It was about an outsider: a girl, Anna, who drops out from conventional consumer society, only to fall hard for a rich, cold, arch-consumer man, Armin. It was itself an outsider's film, off-centre, even bizarre – and 'bizarre' is one of Doris Dörrie's favourite words of praise.

Anna dyes her hair blue; she writes letters to herself, which we hear in voiceover; in a last bid to get Armin she steals a baby, and when this fails she murders him. It's a deeply disturbing story, told coolly and brilliantly, in a pared-down, understated, witty and laconic way. Anna and Armin coldly destroy each other, but the only thing that shocks him is the way she decapitates her egg.

Straight Through the Heart was a success at Venice and other festivals, and gave Dörrie her chance to carry on. Since then she's made almost a film a year: all (except one) from her own stories; all 'bizarre', in her own words, or 'radical', in the critics'; all extremely well made; almost all successful. *Money* (*Geld*, 1989), for instance –

in which a dull provincial couple take off on a *Bonnie and Clyde*-like binge of bank robberies – did well in Germany, as did *Paradise* (*Paradies*, 1986), a dark tale about the hell (hence the title, as Dörrie explains) of dependent love.

In between came *Men* (*Männer*, 1985) – the mega-success, with over 6 million attendances worldwide. Yet *Men* too is pure Dörrie: off-beat and downbeat, about the collapse of social roles and existential certainties. Julius is a rich and successful conformist (like Armin), Stefan an artistic dropout (like Anna). In the course of this crazy but utterly convincing story they change places. But the great difference from *Straight Through the Heart* is the humour. *Straight Through the Heart* is witty and ironic, and the irony keeps us, and Doris Dörrie, at a distance from her characters. *Men* is gloomily, warmly hilarious.

Interestingly, *Men* is not Dörrie's favourite film. It's too easy to digest, she says; she's suspicious of its success. I suspect she's more comfortable keeping her distance, not only from her characters, but also from us. This was certainly the case with her next venture, *Paradise*, which she calls her 'weirdest' film; and then with *Me and Him* (1987), an adaptation of an Alberto Moravia story and a dialogue between a man and what Dörrie calls, in broad American, 'his dick'. That she managed to make this movie at all, in Hollywood, was a typically eccentric achievement; but it was also a nightmare. The backers, Columbia, fought and changed everything she did. And *Me and Him* is Doris Dörrie's only bad movie.

My impression at times is that she has tried to forget all about it – and succeeded. She says things like, '*Men* is the only straightforward comedy I've made,' and when I respond with, 'But what about *Me and Him*?', she gives a startled laugh and replies: 'Oh yes – that's right... I keep forgetting about *Me and Him*, because it really isn't my kind of movie.' And I suspect that she's right. It isn't.

Which brings us to *Happy Birthday*. This is, triumphantly, her kind of movie. Like *Men*, *Paradise* and *Me and Him*, it's about a man; like *Straight Through the Heart*, it's about sex and violence; like all Dörrie's films, it's about outsiders and insiders, loneliness and love. It has quite a few laughs, but *Happy Birthday* is not a comedy. Dörrie's irony has not moved closer to us, as in the ruefulness of *Men*, but still further away, into angry satire.

The film's German title is *Happy Birthday, Türke!* and it is Dörrie's adaptation of a detective novel starring a Turkish private eye. Turks, of course, constitute the largest group of *Gastarbeiter* and are seen as a major 'social problem' in Germany. They are not German citizens, and have limited civil rights. They collect in visible groups in the big cities. Racism and xenophobia have looked in danger of reaching monstrous proportions in Germany of the 90s for the second time this century, in response to the influx of huge numbers of asylum-seekers and ethnic Germans from Eastern Europe and elsewhere. The Turks are a different case, but neo-Nazi thugs do not distinguish.

By choosing a Turkish hero and setting her film in Frankfurt, Dörrie has moved her concern from the inner, existential outsider to the outsider as a current and urgent social problem. And by choosing the particular circumstances of Kayankaya, she has touched on a long-term problem as well, because like thousands of second-generation Turks in Germany, he is caught between the two communities. Kayankaya is something of an extreme case, because, orphaned as a baby and brought up by German parents, he speaks perfect educated German and no Turkish. He is the complete Dörrie hero: an all-round dissident, a belonger to no group. As played by Hansa Czypionka, he is a battered, decent, mess.

One day, in classic Sam Spade tradition (the film is full of nods to the genre) Kayankaya is approached by a Turkish woman, Ilter (Özay Fecht). Her husband, Ahmed, has disappeared, and she wants him found. Things turn nasty almost immediately. When Kayankaya questions Ahmed's workmates he gets viciously punched; when he visits Ilter he finds a hostile brother, a psychotic sister, and a wall of silence. Then he discovers Ahmed with a knife in his back – and is instantly jumped by a sadistic young cop.

Dörrie is appallingly convincing at violence, and everybody in the film commits it, including Kayankaya himself. When Hanna, a pathetic young addict and prostitute, refuses to answer his questions, he silently destroys her filthy flat. When he gets too close to the truth about Ahmed and his father-in-law, Wassif, he is brutally beaten in his bath. When he finally discovers the truth, he and Hanna force a confession out of the young cop, Eiler, in a scene of such graphic torture that I defy anyone to watch it without gagging.

This is, then, a tough, big city, modern movie, about underclass crime and police corruption, in the new Kathryn Bigelow mould: another female film-maker outmachoing the men. But it is also classic Doris Dörrie. There is the abiding theme of outsiders, and the cruelty with which insiders treat them. This is worse the further inside you go: vicious treatment is meted out to Kayankaya by the rich and powerful, while the poor – his janitor, a station barmaid – though they begin in prejudice are capable of kindness by the end.

Connected to this is the theme of the coldness and corruption of the consumerist bourgeoisie: Dörrie's old enemy since Armin of *Straight Through the Heart*. There she explored the fascination of cruelty and power; now she explores its depravity and self-loathing. The streets of Frankfurt are lined with sex shops; the fat and ugly bourgeoisie keep whips and chains in their bedside cupboards, they stuff themselves with *Wurst* and *Kraut*, they have no children, only dogs. Contrasted with them are the Turks, with Ilter at the bottom of the heap. Not sentimentally – Ilter is no more interested in truth, or even justice, than the corrupt policeman, Futt. But all Futt wants is money and power for himself; what she desperately seeks is survival for her family.

That, it seems to me, is Doris Dörrie's underlying value, for which the Turkish community in Germany has stood since *Straight Through the Heart*. The only decent person in that film was Armin's Turkish housekeeper; the film ended with Anna fleeing towards Turkey with her stolen Turkish child. And the main humanity in *Happy Birthday* is in Ilter's family, despite its failures and crimes: in the loyalty of the adults, in the sweetness of the children. Ilter and Kayankaya become, briefly, lovers, and after they make love, Ilter says: 'This is the only thing that helps against death.' But it is not sexual love that is the central value in this film. Ilter disappears back into her family and even with Kayankaya is more like a lost mother than a lover; Hanna, we learn, loved not Ahmed but Wassif, who was old enough to be her grandfather. It is families that Futt and the other moral bankrupts lack, families that she and Kayankaya both need – just as Anna did, and tried to steal, in *Straight Through the Heart*.

Happy Birthday, then, is no mere *Krimi*, no mere genre movie. It continues Doris Dörrie's explorations of her main subject, the problems of conformity, and sets them firmly in the particular and important context of present-day Germany. And it continues, too, her experiments with style. Her films have always been bold, but since her collaboration with her husband, Helge Weindler, as cinematographer (which began on *Men*), they have become even bolder. *Paradise*, for instance, experimented with different camera languages – handheld for the tormented hero Victor, rigid and still for his women – and with a vocabulary of colours, starting with the stale white rooms of Victor's dying marriage and growing steadily redder as he pursues his obsession of love.

Happy Birthday continues both forms of experimentation. Outside, the camera and its objects keep restlessly on the move, on roads, bridges, underpasses. Inside, we are always in medium or close shot, so that people crowd us and each other, their violence and suffering huge and inescapable.

And once again Dörrie and Weindler concentrate on the colour red – this time by eliminating it almost entirely. 'Everybody is dressed in blue, grey or purple clothes; we painted every wall, every detail, every prop in special colours, we created lipsticks in special colours,' says Dörrie. She gives a technical reason: in order not to look like every other television detective story set in a big city, to escape a 'TV realism' so clichéd that it looks artificial. But also, she adds, 'to shock': to make sure that whenever red flares out, we notice. And we do.

It's not too much to say, I think, that in *Happy Birthday* red is love, and as rare as love. One scene alone is shot entirely in red: Kayankaya's and Ilter's faces after they make love. We also see them upside down, and this too, I think, is deliberate. For red, of course, is the colour of the 'red light district'. And it is typical of Dörrie that she reverses the respectable view, and puts the possibility of real love for Kayankaya here (just as she did for Victor in *Paradise*). For red also glows in the bar where Kayankaya meets Margarit – who says 'Happy Birthday, Turk', who helps him, and whom he rushes off to find at the end. And red bursts out too, perhaps brightest of all, when he goes to Ahmed's rubbish depot and meets a group of dustmen, all in bright orange. The film draws a constant line – as Kayankaya's janitor does physically in the opening frames – between Turks and garbage: in Ahmed's job as a dustman (one of the jobs in Germany most frequently done by Turks); in Ilter's picking up the rubbish in Kayankaya's room; in the janitor blaming him for all the detritus dumped in the corridor. This is what Germans think, Dörrie is saying: Turks are garbage. And when the dustmen blaze out in red, we see her dissenting view: Turks are love.

Apart from the violence, my only reservation about *Happy Birthday* is its end. Dörrie often seems to have trouble with her endings: for example, both *Men* and *Me and Him* change gear suddenly and sign off with post-modern self-mockery. In these two it works – in *Men* because this is close to its overall style, in *Me and Him* because the final song and dance is the best thing in the movie. But in *Happy Birthday* it doesn't work.

This is a serious film, in the best sense of the word 'serious', and it feels like a failure of nerve for our last glimpse of Kayankaya to be purely comic – his bouquet of daisies sticking up behind his head and out of the boot of his car, like the daffodil hat stuck up out of the bum at the end of *Carry On Nurse*. It struck me as yet another retreat by Dörrie from engagement with her characters. She is – in both her films and her stories – a brilliant storyteller, but a cold one. What *Happy Birthday* expresses most clearly is hatred for the corrupt and cruel (for Armin, for Futt and Eiler) rather than compassion for their victims.

Indeed, though the main victims are the Turks, I didn't feel much pity for them: Ilter was so obviously strong, and Kayankaya, as the private eye, was always going to win. The character who really moved me was Hanna (Meret Becker): the hopeless, corrupted, childish German prostitute. This is a superb portrait: completely rounded, completely understood. It made me brood about the fact that this film about Turks in Germany wasn't made by Turks: the novelist Jakob Arjouni a pen name) is a German; the star, Hansa Czypionka, is a German; Doris Dörrie, of course, is a German. It's not fair to blame her for that. But her camera dwells on Hanna just as it did on Anna in *Straight Through the Heart*, suggesting a hidden emotional truth about her film.

Nonetheless, *Happy Birthday* is Doris Dörrie's best combination of social criticism and technical skill since *Men*. And like *Men*, it is a bold and completely successful intrusion by a female film-maker into a male subject, and by a subversive film-maker into a mainstream genre and style. Doris Dörrie, with her distrust of success, probably doesn't want another hit. But if this is really the case, she should stop making such damn good movies.

First published in October 1991 (volume 1, number 6).

Andrea Stuart

Mira Nair: a new hybrid cinema

Shot on two continents with 79 speaking parts on a $6 million budget, *Mississippi Masala* is what director Mira Nair fondly describes as 'an epic on a peanut'. The story of a love affair between a young Asian woman and an African-American man, the film is an altogether more ambitious offering than her first feature, the 1988 Cannes Caméra d'Or winner, *Salaam Bombay!*. 'When we made *Salaam!* it was a source of great pride that we could show the same film in Leicester Square and in a small town in India. But *Mississippi Masala* was made with a more international audience in mind.'

Mississippi Masala is a film that anticipates the social conditions of the next century. Until now, most films featuring the 'race thing' – be they love stories like Spike Lee's *Jungle Fever* or socio-documentary dramas like Alan Parker's *Mississippi Burning* – have focused upon black–white relations. But in *Mississippi Masala*, the Indian-born Nair shifts the spotlight to debates and conflicts between 'minority' communities.

The first of the director's films to be set largely in the US, *Mississippi Masala* could not be more historically resonant. In New York, where until recently Nair had her home, more than half the population is now from non-white ethnic groups, while 15 other major American cities have more people from so-called minorities than those of European descent. By the middle of the next century, white Americans are expected to be in a minority right across the continent. Relationships within the 'colour hierarchy' have never been so crucial.

For some, these statistics provide confirmation of their worst nightmares. Remember Tom Wolfe's beleaguered mayor in *Bonfire of the Vanities*. 'Do you really think this is your city any longer? Open your eyes!... Come down from your swell co-ops, you general partners and merger lawyers. It's the third world down there!' For others like Bharati Mukherjee, chronicler of America's Asian immigrants, the figures represent a glimpse of the promised land. 'When I sit on the subway, I look around and most of the faces that I see are brown and black. I feel good – these faces are like mine.'

Courted energetically after the success of *Salaam Bombay!*, Nair rejected the Hollywood offerings ('you wouldn't believe the inanities I was sent') in favour of developing *Mississippi Masala*, an idea which had been preying on her mind since 1983. But the Hollywood executives were almost as dismayed as Wolfe's city official when she presented the proposal. 'They asked me if I could make room for at least one white protagonist. I assured them,' she giggles, 'that all the waiters would be white.'

Nair was convinced that theirs was a singularly short-sighted response, and the subsequent commercial success of films like *Boyz N the Hood* and *New Jack City* has proved her right. Whether the studios' dismay was prompted by box-office anxiety or pique at the usual colour not being the centre of attention, Nair took the reluctance as a good sign. She has, she says, grown comfortable with resistance. 'It makes me feel that I must be doing something right.'

Inspired by the mass expulsions of Asians from East Africa in the 70s, Nair's idea for the film was developed into a script by her long-time collaborator, writer Sooni Taraporevala. The film traces the story of the Loha family, who were forced to leave Uganda in 1972. Eighteen years later, mother, father and daughter find themselves relegated to the position of poor relations of an affluent Indian family which owns a motel in Greenwood, Mississippi.

A progressive lawyer during his time in Uganda, patriarch Jaymini Loha (Roshan Seth) spends his days dreaming of Africa and trying to sue the Ugandan government for the loss of his property and the violation of his human rights. Disappointed and disillusioned, he transfers his ambitions to his daughter, Mina, who works at the local motel. But she meets and falls for Demetrius (Denzel Washington), an African-American carpet cleaner. When the relationship is discovered, the reverberations are substantial. Jaymini is prompted to return home in order to deal with the wounds of the past; Mina is forced to make painful decisions for the future.

'It seemed that this point in history was one where these notions of colour – conflict between black and brown – really came together,' says Nair, referring to hostilities that emerged in the early

70s between Asians and Africans over what some Africans regarded as the separatist inclinations of the Asians, whom they felt were trying to make a little India in Africa. 'You have profited from us... but you will not let your daughters marry our sons,' says the Idi Amin figure as he announces the expulsion order.

Nair was also eager to document the influx into the US of Asians, who have taken over the motel business in much of the Deep South. 'It's history repeating itself, with the Asians coming between black and white people, but in a different context. I wanted to explore what would happen if a member of one community crossed the border of colour into another. So I came to the film from an intellectual starting point, but one which had the potential to explore exile, memory, nostalgia, dislocation: this thing we call home.'

The experience of migration has been a dominant cultural concern for most of this century. But – as in the Oscar-winning film, *Journey of Hope* – the migrant is usually depicted as victim and his contribution is all too often seen as negative by the community he enters; a source of anxiety rather than positive renewal. Increasingly, this is a position that feels outmoded, particularly for migrants themselves. As Salman Rushdie declares in defence of *The Satanic Verses*: 'It celebrates hybridity, impurity, intermingling, the transformation that comes of new and unexpected combinations of human beings, cultures, ideas, politics, movies, songs. It rejoices in mongrelisation and fears the absolutism of the Pure. *Mélange*, the hotch-potch, a bit of this and that is how newness enters the world. This is the great possibility that migration gives the world and I have tried to embrace it.'

For 'New World Upstarts' like Nair, migration is not necessarily a tragedy leading to irrecoverable loss. In *Mississippi Masala*, the victim has turned protagonist. Instead of anguish, Nair revels in the *mélange* migration creates; instead of sinking into nostalgia, her characters move forward to embrace their hard-won new place.

'I believe strongly that to be a Masala, to be mixed, is the new world order. So many of us think in one language and are forced to speak in another... The alliance of the future is that between black and brown. Look at South Africa, where Indians have joined in the political struggle at the expense of their in-between status of being Coloured.'

Watching *Mississippi Masala*, one is struck not only by how much the two communities have in common, but also by the director's

**Mixing it: Sarita Choudhury in
Mira Nair's 'Mississippi Masala' (1991)**

obvious affection for both groups. 'I have a tendency to be irreverent, but to be irreverent without affection is empty. I didn't want anyone or any community to be the bad guys.' The only characters that seem peripheral are white, which Nair describes as a conscious decision. 'I wanted the white characters to be absent. There are other stories to tell.'

Yet *Mississippi Masala* is no rainbow coalition tract. Culture clashes abound, and Nair is aware that this particular brown-on-black combination might make critics angry. Despite the advice and input of Denzel Washington, she knows that as an Asian woman she is vulnerable to criticism for her depiction of African-American life. The separatist/nationalist imperative of the work of directors such as Spike Lee seems incompatible with Nair's positive attitude to intermingling and cross-fertilisation.

The strongly cosmopolitan quality of Nair's work and the confidence with which she moves from space to space is something she explains by quoting Nehru: 'You have to be terribly local in order to be global. And I'm terribly grounded, rooted, in my background.' Born in 'the original hick town', in the remote Indian state of Orissa, she went to Harvard at the age of 18 because it was the only university which offered her a full scholarship. Initially interested in drama, she dropped out when confronted with 'yet another production of *Oklahoma*' and then dropped in again to take a film-making course, which at Harvard meant documentaries.

She proceeded to make a series of highly acclaimed films, including the story of a subway news-stand worker in Manhattan waiting to be reunited with his pregnant wife in India, and *India Cabaret*, a look at the lives of Bombay strippers which, like *Mississippi Masala*, emerged out of an existing social problem. She eventually got bored with what she describes as the 'waiting' of a documentary. 'I wanted more control.' And, as before, she found the inspiration for her first feature on India's streets.

The result was *Salaam Bombay!*, a film about the disordered lives of Bombay street kids. As well as the Caméra d'Or, it won an Oscar nomination for Best Foreign Film, but still failed to provide Nair with the financial security that she had expected. 'After the success of *Salaam!* I almost went broke,' she laughs ruefully. 'They just didn't know what to do with me; I got offered everything about children you could imagine. South African kids, European kids...'

Somewhere *en route* from Bombay to Mississippi, Nair did gain the confidence to make a film in a context that wasn't her own, which explains her intrepid choice of Uganda as a location. 'Until now I have made films that rely on authenticity – not just in my own vision but in those of the people of the place. Most films about Africa – no matter where they are set – are filmed in Kenya or Zimbabwe because it's supposed to be "easier", but I thought if this character is dreaming about Uganda, why shouldn't we do it there. We used the pocket of Indians who had not left as our extras. So they became witnesses to the re-creation of their own history, and their reactions were how we knew we were on the right track.'

Nair's visit to Uganda yielded more than a desired touch of authenticity, for it was there that she met her husband. 'I had heard of him; he was a political writer and academic who had written a very moving piece on the Asian expulsion from the country. Then when I arrived in Uganda we got together. I fell in love with the country and with him.'

Whether working in a country which is hardly a regular film location or dealing with street urchins turned film stars, Nair is at her best in conditions unusual for most Hollywood directors. Ironically, it was filming in the US that she found the greater trial. 'I felt so much more at home in Uganda, where you can just pick someone from the crowd and shout, "Hey you, in the red shirt, come up front!", than in the US, where every car that slips into the frame has to be paid for by the hour. It's much harder to breathe life into a frame there.'

Like most of the up-and-coming black directors, Nair is happiest generating her own projects, working outside the mainstream. But when asked whether she places herself within the 'New Black Film' banner, she appears taken aback. 'I must say I haven't thought about it – I haven't defined my work that closely – but certainly if I were going to place myself anywhere I'd rather be associated with them than with the mainstream.'

Her role models might be eclectic – from Martin Scorsese to Jane Campion to African novelists – but she certainly shares many of the black film-makers' practical concerns. Shooting black and brown skins, for instance. Until the innovative work of cinematographer Ernest Dickerson for Spike Lee, the complexities of shooting black and brown skins didn't take up much air-time among film practitioners. No one seemed to question the fact that Hollywood cinematography is designed to flatter one particular group. Nair argues that lighting dark skins is a special challenge: 'My cinematographer, Ed Lachman, did a lot of tests beforehand to discover how to light, so the characters emerged looking as they really are. In the love scene I wanted it to be almost monochromatic – just about the skins – so that the sensuality of the two colours emerges.

'*Mississippi Masala* will work on the basis of being hybrid in every dimension. The music, the scenery, even the actors, who came from a variety of traditions. Some, like Sharmila Tagore, are from Indian musicals; Roshan Seth is from the Royal Shakespeare Company; others, like Denzel Washington, are from Hollywood; and there's Sarita Choudhury, who has never acted before. The challenge is to weave these people together and use their particularities to make a composite universe which feels real but does not turn them into quasi-Indians like Alec Guinness in *A Passage to India*.'

First published in the 'Guardian/Sight and Sound' London Film Festival supplement, 1991.

Walter Donohue

Against crawling realism: Sally Potter on 'Orlando'

In the 70s and 80s, Sally Potter was a controversial figure in British independent cinema, making films that blended narrative invention with theoretical and formalist concerns. Her 1979 short *Thriller* has long been a staple on film courses for its deconstruction of opera's sexual politics through a re-reading of *La Bohème*. She followed it up with her feature debut *The Gold Diggers* (1983) with Julie Christie, and *The London Story*, a Technicolor spy musical. More recently, Potter has worked in television: making *Women in Soviet Cinema* (1988) and *Tears, Laughter, Fear and Rage* (1986), a four-part series on the politics of emotions.

Potter's feature *Orlando* is produced by her own company Adventure Pictures, which she formed with Christopher Sheppard. A free reading of Virginia Woolf's historical fantasia, *Orlando* represents Potter's first venture into more mainstream narrative, but it also continues some of her past concerns. Her Russian connection carries on in the co-production deal with Lenfilm and the use of a Russian crew that included Elem Klimov's cinematographer Alexei Rodionov. Potter also co-wrote the score with David Motion; her past work as a composer includes the song cycle *Oh Moscow*, and she has also run her own dance ensemble, the Limited Dance Company. All these diverse concerns find their way into *Orlando*, which with its elaborate staging and exuberant cultivation of artifice gives a new twist to the British costume drama.

Walter Donohue was the film's story editor. (*Sight and Sound*)

Location: Blackbird Yard, Ravenscroft Road, and like birds alighting on a field Sally Potter and I are sitting here in her workroom in the renovated London shoe factory where one draft after another of the script of her new film *Orlando* was exposed, criticised, knocked into shape. Almost a year since the troop set off for St Petersburg to film the Frost Fair sequences, this interview took place.

Walter Donohue: It's strange to be sitting again at this table where so many of our script discussions took place. Can you describe something of the process of adapting Virginia Woolf's novel into your own film?

Sally Potter: It was a process of reading, re-reading and reading again; writing, rewriting and writing again. Cutting characters, stripping things right back to the bone. I did endless skeleton diagrammatic plots, all to find the guiding principle and then reconstruct the story from the inside out. I also went back to research Woolf's sources. And then, finally, I put the book away entirely for at least the last year of writing and treated the script as something in its own right, as if the book had never existed. I felt that by the time we were getting ready to shoot I knew the book well enough, was enough in touch with its spirit, that it would have been a disservice to be slavish to it. What I had to find was a live, cinematic form, which meant being ruthless with the novel. I learnt that you have to be cruel to the novel in order to be kind to the film.

Where did your interest in 'Orlando' begin?

When I first read *Orlando* as a teenager, I remember watching it as a film. And from the first moment I considered doing an adaptation, I thought I could see it, even if parts were out of focus. The book has a live, visual quality to it – which was affirmed in Woolf's diaries, where she said that what she was attempting with *Orlando*, unlike her other books, was an 'exteriorisation of consciousness'. She was finding images for a stream of consciousness, instead of using a literary monologue.

But the single idea that was sustaining enough for me to live with the project for so long was immortality, or the question: what is the present moment? And the second idea was the change of sex, which provides the more obvious narrative structure, and is a rich and lighter way of dealing with the issues between men and women. The more I went into this area, and tried to write a character who was both male and female, the more ludicrous maleness and femaleness became and the more the notion of the essential human being – that a man and woman both are – predominated.

Clearly, here was just a character called Orlando: a person, an individual, a being who lived for 400 years, first as a man and then as a woman. At the moment of change, Orlando turns and says to the audience, 'Same person, different sex.' It's as simple as that.

But Orlando – a character who is both a man and a woman – has to be embodied in an actor. And you chose a woman to play this part. How did you deal with the maleness and femaleness of the characterisation?

We worked primarily from the inside out and talked all the time about Orlando as a person rather than as a man or a woman. Then there was a mass of small decisions which added up to a policy about how to play the part – for instance, we decided on no artificial facial hair for Orlando the man. Whenever I've seen women playing men on screen, it's been a mistake to try to make the woman look too much like a man, because you spend your time as a viewer looking for the glue, the joins between the skin and the moustache. I worked on the assumption that the audience was going to know from the beginning that here was a woman playing a man, and so the thing to do was to acknowledge it and try to create a state of suspended disbelief.

I was attracted to Tilda Swinton for the role on the basis of seeing her in Peter Wollen's film *Friendship's Death*, where she had a cinematic presence that wasn't aligned to what our cinematographer Alexei Rodionov called 'crawling realism', and in the Manfred Karge play *Man to Man*, in which there was an essential subtleness about the way she took on male body language and handled maleness and femaleness. Tilda brought her own research and experience to bear on the part; as her director I worked to help her to achieve a quality of transparency on the screen. The biggest challenge for both of us was to maintain a sense of the development of the character even when we were shooting out of continuity and with the ending still uncertain. The intention was that there would be a seamless quality about the development that would carry that suspended disbelief about maleness, femaleness and immortality.

The idea of suspended disbelief – was direct address to camera one of the devices used to maintain this?

The speeches of Orlando to the audience took many forms during the writing, and during the shooting they were the hardest things to get right. The phrase I used to Tilda was 'golden thread': we were trying to weave a golden thread between Orlando and the audience through the lens of the camera. One of the ways we worked in rehearsal was to have Tilda address those speeches directly to me, to get the feeling of an intimate, absolutely one-to-one connection, and then to transfer that kind of address into the lens. Part of the idea was also that direct address would be an instrument of subversion, so that set against this historical pageant is a complicity with the audience about the kind of journey we're on. If it worked, I hoped it would be funny; it would create a connection that made Orlando's journey also the audience's journey; and most important, it would give the feeling that although Orlando's journey lasted some 400 years and was set in the past, this was essentially a story about the present.

The function of the voiceover at the beginning and end is to dispatch with certain issues as neatly as possible – for instance, the film begins with Orlando's voice saying, 'There can be no doubt about his sex.' I also wanted to state that though Orlando comes from a certain background, which has certain implications, he is separated from this background by a kind of innocence. One is born into a class background, but that can change.

Was there any governing idea behind the transitions from one period to another?

I tried to find a way of making transitions through a characteristic of the period (dress, poetry, music), that could launch us into the next section. And what I found was that you can be much bolder than I ever thought in the way you jump, cinematically, from one period to another. Ironically, the most striking transition is where Orlando enters the maze in the eighteenth century and emerges into the Victorian era, which was the one I hadn't worked out in the script and was still struggling with in the shoot. The decision to effect the transition by having Orlando enter the maze was made simply because there was a maze at the location which I knew I wanted to use; its final form was found in the cutting room.

Perhaps we could discuss one or two of the myriad aspects of the craft of film-making – such as framing?

Framing is the magic key, the door through which you're looking. The quest in shooting *Orlando* was not just for a frame or possible place to put the camera, but for the only place. This became my driving visual obsession. To transcend the arbitrariness of where you put the camera became a joint process between Alexei and myself. And one of his great strengths as a cinematographer is that he won't settle for an obvious or easy visual solution. He's trying to peel back

Questions of immortality: Sally Potter
gives a new twist to the costume
drama in 'Orlando' (1993)

the layers and find this transparent place – and this search for the right frame became a parallel process to trying to achieve a transparency of performance.

Technically, we worked with a monitor, and every frame was adjusted – up, down, right, left – until there was a frame which he and I agreed was *the* frame. If we couldn't agree it was an unhappy moment, and a lot of energy was spent on that kind of tussling. Alexei's intention is to be a mediumistic cinematographer; he says that the greatest compliment Klimov paid him after *Come and See* was that Klimov felt as if he had shot the film himself. That's a very ego-free statement for a cinematographer to make, and for me it was an incredible gift, as well as a challenge that was initially almost too great to meet, because it put the gaze back on me: what did I really want? I didn't always know what I wanted; I was groping to start with. But by the end of the shoot I felt that Alexei and I had one eye.

You're credited, with David Motion, with the music for the film. How did that come about?

A lot of people commented that sound was often mentioned in the script. And I wanted a sound-effect structure and score that would mirror the scale of the film. Our policy during the mix was to make a broad dynamic range and then highlight certain evocative or pointed sounds – such as the peacock's cry when Orlando is walking down the gallery of long white drapes, or the sound of the ice cracking, or of rain taking over the soundtrack.

As far as the music is concerned, I originally wanted to use Arvo Part's *Cantus*, which I had been listening to over and over again. I even got permission, but it became clear that to use it would create as many problems as it would solve – it was a piece in its own right that couldn't be cut or repeated. So I started on a journey to find out what it was about that piece of music that was appropriate to the film, and then to look for another way of achieving this. What I discovered was that a lot of the music I had been listening to for pleasure, and as a sort of spiritual reference for the film, was based on an A-minor triad, or the related C-major triad. This seemed too much of a coincidence, so I drew up a chart of the score and we mapped out a structure based on the A-minor triad and related keys. And the more I got to think about the score, the more I was hearing the music in my head. So eventually we decided to go into a studio to record what I was hearing using my own voice. I recorded an 8-track voice piece for each of the major cues and David Motion wrote instrumental parts around them. Some of the voice parts were lost, but others became the background to the cues, or were fitted around sections he had written and arranged. Fred Frith then improvised some guitar lines around the cues. The end song was written slightly differently: I wrote the lyrics and suggested the key; David provided some musical cues on tape; Jimmy Somerville wrote the vocal tune and then David arranged it. It was a score that was made possible through the use of a sampler and the editorial capacity that machine gives you. It was a score that was constructed rather than composed in the usual way.

The novel ends in 1928, but in order to be faithful to the idea of making the film contemporary, it had to finish in 1993. How did you devise the end?

It reached its final form after everything else had been shot. What became clear was that the correct way to approach it was not just to stick an ending on the story, but to think myself into Virginia Woolf's consciousness. What might she have done with the story had she lived until 1993? It was a strange game, a sort of second-guessing that consisted in me re-reading what she had written after *Orlando*; her thoughts on issues post-1928. It seemed clear that I had to refer to the First and Second World Wars and the effect they had on consciousness. And because the book itself is almost a commentary on the history of literature as the vehicle for consciousness, there had to be a cinematic equivalent of what had happened to that kind of consciousness post-war. In other words, the fracturing of that consciousness and the arrival of the electronic age.

What do you want the audience to feel when they've reached the end?

I hope they are thrilled by the rush into the present, by the notion that finally we are here, now. And a feeling of hope and empowerment about being alive and the possibility of change – which comes through the words of the song and the expression on Orlando's face. I want people to feel humanly recognised, that their inner landscape of hope and desire and longing has found some kind of expression on screen. A gut feeling of release and relief and hope.

First published in March 1993 (volume 3, number 3).

Karen Alexander

Julie Dash: 'Daughters of the Dust' and a black aesthetic

Two African-American women directors' films – Leslie Harris' *Just Another Girl on the I.R.T.* and Julie Dash's *Daughters of the Dust* – have challenged popular misconceptions about black cinema. Their respective distributors vied for the claim of 'first feature by an African-American woman to gain national distribution', and though Dash's film won that race, both movies speak loudly against the new black male hegemony of the HipHop or YoHo school. Leslie Harris fits the urban contemporary mould better, and her challenge to it is simpler, pushing the boys aside to produce the first HipHop film where black women are not mere sexual sideshows or threats to black manhood. The difference Julie Dash makes is deeper, if harder to define, a difficulty unwelcome to journalists who mix cocktails like the 'Godard meets HipHop' tag applied to *I.R.T.*

Daughters of the Dust is set in the islands off the South Carolina coast at the turn of the century, where a Gullah family meets for a 'last supper' before most of its members leave for a new life on the mainland. The film is a tale of rootedness and migration, of a family's coming together and its dissolution – and women, as bearers of their culture's African heritage, are the focus of the dramas that unfold.

The matriarchal Nana Peazant uses spiritual means in her struggle to hold on to her departing family. Her rival for spiritual control is Haagar – a member of the Peazants by marriage who is leading its move north, away from the traditions and beliefs of the family's African past. Nana Peazant's granddaughter Eula is pregnant after being raped by a white landowner; Eula's husband Eli is alienated from his wife because he believes the child she is carrying is that of the white rapist. Nana's spiritual power is affirmed when she reconciles Eula and Eli through a ritual of communion with the family's ancestors, in which Eli is assured of his paternity of the unborn child. Yellow Mary, who has returned to the islands with her lover Trula after both have worked in Cuba as prostitutes, is able to stake a claim for inclusion in the family's history, despite her 'outsider' status. The film concludes with a ritual of spiritual regeneration designed by Nana Peazant to preserve the family from the dangers it will face in the cities of the north.

Daughters of the Dust is an extraordinarily seductive costume drama, on the surface far removed from the concern with contemporary urban life that has dominated the work of the latest wave of black film-makers. But we should remember that a costume drama – if viewed not simply as an excuse to dress up in Tuscany – is also a telling of history, and the re-telling of history is a fundamental concern of almost all significant black cinema and culture. Spike Lee's *Malcolm X* and Isaac Julien's *Looking for Langston* could each be dismissed as costume drama, but each is also a history lesson. The same is true of Lee's forthcoming *Crooklyn*, about growing up in Brooklyn in the 70s, and of Julien's *Young Soul Rebels*, set in London in 1977. In both cases, visualising the past provides a much needed historical context for the situation of black people in the present.

In Dash's film, the costumes, hairstyles and customs depicted are a corrective history lesson in a culture where nineteenth-century black people are usually dressed according to the codes of *Gone with the Wind* and the like. Hiding or distorting black people's history has denied us images of them, and *Daughters of the Dust* works powerfully to recover these from the past, at the same time introducing the cinemagoing public to a powerful black aesthetic.

Before *Daughters of the Dust*, Dash was best known for *Illusions* (1982), a 40-minute drama set in 40s Hollywood and shot in glittering black and white. The film was acknowledged by Isaac Julien as an inspiration for *Looking for Langston*. Dash and Julien have both been accused of making films that are 'too beautiful', as if a 'black aesthetic' mustn't be too 'aesthetic'. *Illusions* and *Daughters of the Dust* are part of Dash's projected series of history pieces, each set at a pivotal moment in the lives of African-American women in different periods. The series is to end with a futuristic film called *Bone, Ash and Rose*, set in 2050.

The Gullah people depicted in *Daughters of the Dust* are descendants of slaves who managed to survive on the sea islands and were able to retain close spiritual ties with the West African cultures from which they were stolen. The non-linear narrative evokes story-telling in the Griot manner of West African oral cultures, in which memories and objects are invested with meanings from which the story is woven: 'The Griot will come to a birth, a wedding or funeral and, over a period of days, will recount the family's history, with the stories going off at a tangent, weaving in and out and in and out,' explains Dash. 'I decided that *Daughters of the Dust* should be told that way.' This narrative structure evolved with the project: 'Originally *Daughters of the Dust* was to be a silent film, but as American Playhouse became involved they insisted on dialogue, and as I expanded the dialogue I introduced the Unborn Child as a character and a narrative voice. So the story has two points of view: that of a child who has not yet been born, and of a great-grandmother who has seen it all and who can also see the coming of the child in the future. I realised the story had to be told in a non-western way.'

Characters too reject western conventions. 'If this story is told in a non-western way,' says Dash, 'then my characters cannot be motivated by the Greek archetypes and Gods that are the foundation of western drama. The Unborn Child, for instance, is Elegba: one foot in this world, one in the other. Although Elegba is usually depicted as male, I made him female because I figured he has the power to be anyone in his role as mediator between the sacred and secular worlds.'

The situation of a group of African-American women at the turn of one century resonates for African-American women at the turn of another, and we can measure the progress made over those 100 years. There are also links and discrepancies across space, across the 'Black Atlantic', between the roles assigned men and women in West African cultures and those assumed by the women Dash depicts. 'In this new world, it is the women who have become the Griots of their culture, even though in the old world it was a male thing passed down through the family,' says Dash. 'Here it's the women who carry the scraps of memory. White sociologists look at it and say it's a matriarchal society, but there's more to it than that. It's as though in the desperate situation in which they found themselves, the women deliberately took on the role of oral historians; they took it upon themselves to be the ones who remember.'

Critical response to *Daughters of the Dust* picked up on the extraordinary visual qualities of its cinematography, but the film is also highly literary. Dash's preoccupation with non-linear, memory and voices from the past or from other worlds echoes themes pursued by several contemporary African-American women writers. The film uses fragments of Paule Marshall's *Praisesong for the Widow*, and other authors are an acknowledged influence. 'It was the literature of black women in the early 70s that inspired me to become a filmmaker of dramatic narratives. Before that I made documentaries, but after reading Toni Cade Bambara, Alice Walker, Toni Morrison, I wanted to tell those kinds of stories. I see myself as a disciple of black women writers. They made me whole.'

Dash has a project to remake Michel Deville's *La Lectrice*, substituting a black heroine absorbed in the classics of black literature: 'This is something I can't get done in Hollywood. They love the project, but they say it's "too literary". I told them, "Just because it's about literature doesn't make it literary." And then they look at me with a blank stare.'

The current wooing of Julie Dash by Hollywood producers will be an interesting test of the adaptability of the independent sector to the marketplace. But Dash's determination to continue to work in the formats and genres that suit her means that it will never be a matter of assimilation. What we can hope for is the exposure of a sophisticated black cinema aesthetic to wider audiences.

First published in September 1993 (volume 3, number 9).

Julie Dash: 'The photographer Mr Snead (above) represents the mainland, the future, science, technology and magic. I'm always amazed no one asks "Why is he using a flash in daylight?" This shot starts out at normal speed then goes into slow motion, so the puff from the flash is exaggerated and becomes like a memory.'

Below: 'Yellow Mary, who knows from experience what awaits the Peazants on the mainland, kisses the talisman Nana Peazant has made – a Bible entwined with moss – to protect the family on their journey. Yellow Mary has returned from a more sophisticated life, but she still kisses the talisman in homage to its strength.'

Above: 'This is Mr Snead photographing the Peazant men on the beach. Through the lens he sees the Unborn Child posing next to her father, but when he looks at them without the lens he can't see her. She allows him a glimpse of her to suggest that there are things beyond the worldly science he and the magic of his camera represent.'

Below: 'This is a Christian scene in a new context. A lot of African Americans became baptists when they reached the new world because baptism provided a camouflage for West African religious practices, such as the worship of water gods. These characters are less focused than the Peazants, who know where their beliefs came from.'

Above: 'These are the hands of Daddy Mac holding a turtle inscribed with signs from the Kongo system of life and death. He is blessing the family before they eat. Such symbols are visual proof of the persistence of a language, cosmology and a world view, despite the confines of being an African captive into slavery.'

Below: 'This is a flashback to an indigo-processing plant where the Unborn Child watches her ancestors at work. The colour, which is in the bow in her hair and the hands of the ancestor, is my way of signifying slavery, rather than by whipmarks or scars, which are images that I believe have lost their power.'

Above: 'The actor playing Eli, in a genuine trance, is gazing at the figurehead floating in the water. The figurehead is a mock-up we took from the prow of a slave ship. It had a terrible power. Before seeing it, I had never realised how cruel it was to have a figurehead of an African warrior guiding a slave ship.'

Below: 'Young Nana, with dust on her hands, is questioning the fertility of the land, in what we assume is a flashback. But the scene is really in the present: the whole film is a flashforward. The film starts out during the period of slavery. The dust is in the past and "Daughters of the Dust" means the daughters of the past.'

Stella Bruzzi

Jane Campion: costume drama and reclaiming women's past

At the beginning of *The Piano*, Ada (Holly Hunter), a mute Scottish woman, arrives in New Zealand with her nine-year-old daughter Flora. They disembark on a remote beach, where they are left by the sailors who accompanied them to await Ada's new husband Stewart (Sam Neill), a rich local landowner. Their strung-out possessions are silhouetted in a flimsy line against the evening sun. Another silhouetted, skeletal structure comes into shot: a tent, made from Ada's hoops and underskirts, in which they shelter for the night.

The Piano ends with a parallel scene as Ada, having left Stewart, returns to the beach and boards a boat with Flora, her lover Baines (Harvey Keitel) and the possessions she arrived with. To preserve the equilibrium of the boat she orders her prized piano to be discarded. As it is tipped overboard, her foot is caught in the unravelling rope and she is dragged under. Her upturned hoops and skirts billow out against the luminous water. At this point, as at others through the film, Ada appears to be trapped and defeated by her clothes. At the last moment, however, she disentangles herself and swims to the surface, leaving her shoe behind; she has, as her voiceover says, 'chosen life'. Her clothes, as elsewhere, work for her.

The Piano is not a simple women's film about a woman's past, but rather a cryptic and evocative exploration of how women's sexuality, clothes and lives interconnect. It is set in New Zealand in the mid-1800s, and though the exact dates of events are never specified, the age which the costumes, morality and gender relations evoke is central to the way the film tackles its theme. Why has director Jane Campion chosen to frame the story of Ada's sexual and emotional awakening in terms of the last century? The Victorian age is seen today as synonymous with the oppression of female sexuality; everything from the voluminous clothes to the many laws which deprived wives of financial autonomy legitimised a patriarchy which kept women in check. In order to express themselves, women were constrained to invent male pseudonyms, to 'ghost' music and art for husbands and brothers, to create elaborate metaphors for their experiences. Their voices were often heard only indirectly: they fabricated unruly, angry alter egos, such as Charlotte Brontë's 'mad woman in the attic' or the monstrous creation of Mary Shelley's *Frankenstein*, or codified their anger against male brutality, as did Artemesia Gentileschi in her violent depiction of *Judith Beheading Holofernes*.

In such a male-dominated history, the experiences of women have been almost entirely obscured, and women since have invaded the past to liberate the female imagination and sexuality as well as to help them to make sense of the present. Since the 70s women have been unearthing forgotten literary works, creating an alternative cultural canon, reinterpreting male texts and forefronting experiences deemed peripheral. The desire to articulate this forgotten past is perhaps the common impulse behind such ostensibly diverse works as Jean Rhys' prequel to Jane Eyre, *Wide Sargasso Sea*, A. S. Byatt's *Possession*, Sally Potter's film version of *Orlando* – and Jane Campion's *The Piano,* which empowers Ada with a 1990s strength and self-knowledge that enables her to transcend the limitations of such disempowered nineteenth-century heroines as Emily Brontë's Catherine.

The two most pervasive models of reclamation of the past used by women film-makers could be termed the 'liberal' and the 'sexual'. The liberal method concentrates on finding a political and ideological affinity between the struggles of women in the present and figures from the past. Campion's film about New Zealand writer Janet Frame, *An Angel at My Table*, Margarethe von Trotta's film biography *Rosa Luxemburg*, and the feminist revivals of Ibsen's plays stem from a liberal impulse to utilise the juxtaposition between past and present to illuminate both. The 'sexual' model, by contrast, foregrounds the personal, more hidden aspects of past women's lives – their dormant passions, their sexual frustrations and the process of denial which governed their relationships with (primarily) men. Although both types of looking back involve costume, in liberal films these are merely signifiers to carry information about country, class and period. Films interested in the emotive aspects of the past imbue the clothes themselves with sensuality, so they become essential components of the sexual dialogue.

The pioneering Australasian women's film of the 70s was Gillian Armstrong's *My Brilliant Career* (1979), a feminist reworking of the traditionally male genre of the liberal history movie – Stanley Kramer's *Inherit the Wind*, Fred Zinnemann's *A Man for All Seasons* and so on. *My Brilliant Career*, a quintessential feminist fairy tale, is based on Miles Franklin's semi-biographical novel about Sybylla Melvyn, a teenage girl from the Bush who chooses a career over a husband. The headstrong Sybylla embodies the struggle for independence and emancipation which was taking place in Australia during the 1890s, but she is equally a construct of the late 1970s – a case of the second women's movement making sense of the first. *My Brilliant Career* was an important feel-good movie for women of my generation, who in 1979 were much the same age as Sybylla was in the late 1890s. Women were still uncertain about what it was they wanted, but were sure that it was not what was on offer. As Sybylla puts it: being 'a wife out in the Bush, having a baby every year.'

More crucial to liberal movies than the superficial authenticity of meticulously costumed films such as Christine Edzard's *Little Dorritt* or *The Fool* is a broad awareness of contemporary events, which form a discrete backdrop to the narrative. *My Brilliant Career* spans five years; Sybylla's voiceover states that the film begins in 'Possum Gully, Australia 1897', and at the end we are told that *My Brilliant Career* was published in 'Edinburgh, 1901'. Australia (far in advance of Britain, which did not grant women the vote until after the First World War) was then in the midst of a successful movement for universal suffrage; two states, South and Western Australia, had already changed the electoral system, while Sybylla's native New South Wales was on the verge of doing so. Sybylla epitomises the exhilaration of this era – her anticipation as she stares into the dawn horizon after posting her manuscript is almost tangible.

The liberal film discerns patterns or draws out meanings which at the time may have been obscured. Sybylla is both historical and contemporary, her struggle (with herself, her family and men) both parochial and perennial. *My Brilliant Career* thus operates as a metaphor for a universal female dilemma. Sybylla remains such a positive role model for women (and paradoxically attractive to all the men in the film) because she pursues her own goals rather than those society would impose. Though she is repeatedly warned that 'loneliness is a terrible price to pay for independence,' she ultimately refuses all proposals of marriage and puts her own aspirations first. The straightforwardness of Sybylla's choice might in a modern context – such as the much untidier world of Armstrong's latest film *The Last Days of Chez Nous* – appear woefully naive. Placed within a historical context, however, the dilemma and decision gain strength from their very simplicity. The liberal analogy film functions best when the metaphor is less complex than the issues it raises about present-day society. Thus Sybylla's 'wildness of spirit' and pursuit of a 'career' – which at the start could be almost anything that got her out of the Bush – were points of identification for 1970s women with more specific concerns.

The Piano offers a more elliptical way of examining the past – one based on complex, hard-to-define emotions and attractions rather than concrete events. This is not to say that *The Piano* is apolitical, but that unlike *My Brilliant Career*, which carries its political commentary through its plot, *The Piano* does so through clothes and sexuality. Films which use sexuality to explore women's unspoken pasts are more personal, more challenging, more dangerous than their liberal counterparts. It is difficult to envisage women objecting to an uncomplicated liberal film like *My Brilliant Career*, but a sexual film such as Liliana Cavani's *The Night Porter* (1974), which examines Nazism through the sado-masochistic relationship between Max, an ex-camp officer, and Lucia, a survivor, frequently repels its audiences. Cavani confronts us with an ambiguous and unpalatable sexual history in which a woman chooses to re-enter a violent relationship that eventually leads to her death. Perhaps the film says the unsayable: that Lucia is not Max's victim, but his equal; that brutal sexuality is not simply a male construct.

Campion's innovation in *The Piano* is to discover a language which articulates a radical opposition to the restrictions imposed on nineteenth-century women through the very means by which those restrictions are usually manifested – clothes. Throughout the film clothes function as agents to liberate rather than to constrain. Visually this is suggested by recurrent images that demonstrate how clothes are constructed, drawing a distinction between the harsh frames – Ada's hoops and the wired angel wings of Flora's Bluebeard costume – and the softness and fluidity of the fabrics stretched over them. Both Ada and Flora are seen adjusting to their clothes, exploring and adapting them and finally learning to feel comfortable in them. To return briefly to the mad woman in the attic and Frankenstein's monster: both Charlotte Brontë and Mary Shelley were impelled to create metaphors which externalised the internal 'demons' of their anger; Campion in *The Piano* finds a way for Ada to express herself through (rather than despite of) her Victorian persona.

Campion's reclamation of women's sexual pasts is exhilarating, but Ada's eventual liberation is presented as an arduous struggle against the systematic denial of the existence of female desire. As wife to Stewart and lover to Baines, she represents conflicting aspects of Victorian womanhood. On the one hand she is the trapped, unwilling wife – a New Zealand Madame Bovary with apparently as much chance of escape or fulfilment from her stifling bourgeois marriage. She is also, in her refusal to speak, representative of what the medical profession branded a 'hysterical' woman; catatonia, anorexia, chronic fatigue and other forms of self-imposed sensory deprivation were commonplace among dissatisfied and desperate Victorian wives, the majority of whom were regarded as dysfunctional rather than as unhappy. Through the elaborate clothes-language she formulates with Baines, however, Ada engineers her escape from Stewart, drudgery and sexual repression – Campion's modern and radical reassessment of the options available to women in the 1850s.

Clothes traditionally signify restraint and conformity; they have covered our nakedness and hidden our shame. Joe Orton's black farce *What the Butler Saw*, for example, concludes with Rance's weary nod in the direction of respectability: 'Let us put on our clothes and face the world.' The Victorians were obsessed with hiding anything that could be deemed suggestive of sex or nakedness, daubing fig leaves on to Adams and Eves and covering the bare legs of tables. The sexuality of Victorian women was repressed or presumed not to exist at all; Queen Victoria herself was so convinced that female sexuality was a dutiful response to men's demands that she denied the possibility of lesbianism.

Victorian women's clothes, as much as the way they were treated, made them inactive and vulnerable. At the start of Caryl Churchill's 1979 play *Cloud Nine*, set in a 'British colony in Africa in Victorian times', the colonial's wife, Betty, complains to her husband because her servant has refused to get the book she requested, having snapped: 'Fetch it yourself. You've got legs under that dress.' *Cloud Nine* is an elaborate dissection of the sexual underworld of Victorian society. Largely through the use of cross-dressing, Churchill challenges and ridicules the accepted notions of Victorian morality and behaviour by inverting the assumption that what people look like and wear are straightforward indicators of who they are or what they are feeling. So Betty, the embodiment of what 'a wife should be', is played by a bearded man, her son by a woman, her insignificant daughter by a rag doll. Throughout Act I characters are rarely permitted to have sex with either the individual or the gender they desire, and the action culminates in the face-saving marriage between the lesbian governess and the intrepid gay explorer. Queen Victoria's model household is a fantasy, a flimsy front for confused morals and anarchic sexuality. Churchill's solution is to liberate the characters by transporting them into the permissive 1970s, because only now, *Cloud Nine* intimates, can clothes be truly compatible with gender and sexuality. In this instance, as in the final sequences of Potter's *Orlando*, the analogy between present and past is made explicit through direct juxtaposition.

The Piano enters into a much more complex dialogue with women's sexual histories, since the present-day consciousness remains embedded exclusively within the nineteenth-century narrative. The sexual experiences of the three protagonists – Ada, Baines and Stewart – are markedly different; Stewart, the stiff, bourgeois gentleman, represents respectability and ignorance, while Ada and Baines epitomise radicalism and liberation. Stewart, like head of household Clive in *Cloud Nine*, is frustrated by how far he is from unlocking the 'mystery' of sexuality and remains unable to break free of his social and gender stereotype. He is left stranded, yearning but unable to deal with the reality of closeness. We do not feel for Clive as his servant cocks his rifle and aims at him, but Stewart's isolation is painful. By the end, he realises that with Baines Ada has discovered an intimacy from which he, frozen in his social role, will always be excluded. At this point, the only option he can see is violence: he hurls Ada against the wall and hacks off her finger when she refuses to deny her love for Baines.

Stewart's first appearance in the film – at the head of the welcoming party to greet his new wife – is in his muddied formal dark suit and top hat. He is embarrassed and puzzled to discover Ada and

Flora sheltering under the hoops and underskirt, and awkwardly commences his rehearsed greeting. Images of a furtive, frustrated gentleman at a peep show spring to mind as Campion distances him from the female sexuality he can never understand or get close to through a series of classic male voyeur images: squinting through a camera eyepiece at Ada posing unhappily in her wedding dress, or sneaking a glance at her making love to Baines through the cracks in the walls or between the floorboards.

Stewart is clearly identified as a rigid masculine figure marooned in what becomes a feminine world. For much of the time he inhabits a different film from Ada. Stewart's sensibility and world view is closer to that of another Australasian Victorian costume drama, Peter Weir's *Picnic at Hanging Rock* (1975), in which three schoolgirls mysteriously disappear while on a Valentine's Day picnic. Here female sexuality is also consistently symbolised through clothes, but the film is built on the mystery rather than the attainment of female sexuality. Unable to articulate their desire, the men become deviant voyeurs, transferring their sexual desire from the girls to their virginal dresses. Thus the dirty scrap of lace which the youthful Michael discovers during the search is invested with sexually charged significance, as is the fact that one girl is subsequently found 'intact' minus her corset. *Picnic at Hanging Rock* is the crystallisation of the Victorian man's perception of intimacy as unobtainable, bewildering, and fascinating.

In *The Piano*, Stewart's predicament is more ambiguous. Denied intimacy, he ultimately unleashes his pent-up sexuality by attempting to rape Ada in the woods. Ada struggles, falls over her skirts and is pulled to the ground. She seems defeated, but is eventually saved by her cumbersome, all-enveloping clothes. Stewart's aggression is deflected by the symbol of Victorian femininity – the hooped skirt – and she escapes. In one of the few scenes when he is alone with his wife, Ada awakens Stewart's desire by skimming his chest with the back of her hand, but when he asks to touch her she recoils. The following night, as Ada strokes his back and buttocks, it is Stewart who wants to stop. What sets Stewart apart from the men in *Picnic at Hanging Rock* is that he reaches the painful point of realising that there is more to sexual contact than sneaking glimpses, frustrated brutality and being touched.

Much of *The Piano* depicts a life which conforms to Stewart's masculine perception. New Zealand may have been the first country to

**Reviewing the past: Ada (Holly Hunter)
and Flora (Anna Paquin) in Jane
Campion's 'The Piano' (1993)**

grant women the vote, but little of this liberalism is manifest in the first part of the film. Often Ada is as quintessentially the Victorian woman as Stewart is the Victorian man; on the beach in the first scene, for example, she looks like a doll beneath the exaggerated hugeness of her travelling outfit and lampshade bonnet. Women's clothes are presented as constricting, ugly, absurd; the multiple skirts which trip Ada and Flora as they trudge through the mud, and which make it ludicrously difficult for Aunt Morag to relieve herself when 'caught short' in the woods. Clothes seem liberating only when they come off, as when Flora dances and cartwheels across the beach in her petticoat. That is, until Ada starts to fall in love with Baines.

In this relationship, the modernity of Campion's response to the past dominates, the potential for sexual expression is realised, and clothes are no longer socially determined. Physically Baines is Stewart's opposite: he never appears dressed as a colonial master and his face is pricked with Maoriesque markings. It is this unconventionality which frees Ada.

The relationship begins when Baines saves Ada's prized piano by intimating a desire to learn how to play. The instrument is brought to his hut, and Stewart tells Ada she is to instruct him. Baines' fascination is not with learning, but with watching Ada play, so a bizarre bargain is struck whereby Ada is allowed to play and win back her piano, while he is permitted to watch, to touch and gradually to unclothe her. As spectators it is clear that we are entering – or rather intruding on – an intensely private world. This intrusion begins one evening after the piano has arrived at Baines' hut: Baines gets up from his bed, removes his shirt and, naked, uses it indulgently to dust the piano, circling it, judging it, getting to know it. Baines considers himself alone, we really shouldn't be there, but we are intrigued by the ritual.

In this formal Victorian world, Harvey Keitel's proud nakedness is both shocking and liberating. Convention is inverted as the man is constructed as a sexual being before the woman. We the audience find ourselves privy to a private dialogue which imbues clothes with a potency beyond the bounds of fetishism and makes what follows an elaborate seduction rather than a cheap strip. This is due partly to the scenes' curious rhythm, a slow but relentless evolution as Ada reworks and refines repeated musical refrains while Baines tells her when to stop, what garment to remove or when he wants to kiss her or lie with her in response to a complex set of rules agreed beforehand. The rich obscurity of the clothes-language is counterbalanced by an incongruous matter-of-factness that puts the relationship on a different plane from anything else in the film.

The language has to do with the sensuality of clothes: how they feel, smell and look, not just what they might signify, as in *Picnic at Hanging Rock*. Thus Baines' rapture can be contained within the minute act of smelling and burying his face in one of Ada's garments while she remains wrapped in her music. Campion's fascination with clothes is reminiscent of that described by the seventeenth-century poet and priest Robert Herrick, whose illicit passion for Julia is displaced on to her clothes – her lace is 'erring', and beneath her 'tempestuous petticoat' lurks 'a careless shoe-string in whose tie/I see a wild civility.' Herrick creates a clothes-eroticism so enticing that Julia becomes insignificant.

In *The Piano*, the point is not that the clothes are substitutes for Ada, but that they are part of her and her body's sensuality. Perhaps the film's most erotically charged moment is when Baines, crouched under the piano, discovers a tiny hole in Ada's stocking and slowly caresses it, skin touching skin. Later, when Ada is sitting at the piano in just her bodice and skirt, Baines stands behind her naked to the waist and glides his hands across her bare shoulders. Again the camera acts in collusion with the characters, skirting around them as Baines circles Ada, picking up the charge between them. Ada and Baines are gradually becoming equals, as the traditional striptease relationship of one person clothed watching another undress is supplanted. When they eventually have sex, they undress together.

Why is this secret language not ludicrous like the adolescent heavings of *Picnic at Hanging Rock* or the misguided gay advances of *Cloud Nine*? The strength of the affair in the *The Piano* lies in Ada's responsiveness; she is no longer the passive Victorian woman, acted upon rather than acting. At first she remains wary and resentful of Baines' bargain, yet she gradually discovers that the relationship can offer her the freedom she, with her mute defiance, had been holding out for. Yet this is not an easy realisation: when Ada returns to Baines' hut having already acknowledged that she loves him, she slaps his cheek and pummels his chest before they kiss, as if she needs to repel him as she repelled Stewart. Then they have sex.

The relationship with Baines is the catalyst to Ada's sensual awakening. When she arrived in New Zealand her piano was her only liberation; she had not spoken since she was six and she had been married off to a stranger. Through *The Piano* Ada discovers the means to articulate what she wants – firstly through constructing an intimacy around clothes, through choosing Baines over Stewart, choosing not to be drowned by her sinking piano, and finally choosing to learn to speak when she and Baines have started a new life together in Nelson. The closing image is of a woman attached to the piano by a taut rope like a graceful helium balloon; beautiful in death but silent. But however momentarily enticing this ocean death may be, Ada chooses to reject it and to live. Jane Campion's *The Piano* is primarily but not exclusively Ada's liberation; it is also the reclamation of women's desires, the sexual personae which the past silenced.

First published in October 1993 (volume 3, number 10).

Compiled by Pat Coward
Actors' filmographies

Catherine Deneuve

Born 22 October 1943, Paris, France

1958 *Les Collégiennes.*
　Dir: André Hunebelle
1959 *Les Petits Chats.* Dir: Jacques Villa
1960 *Les Portes claquent.*
　Dir: Jacques Poitrenaud
L'Homme à femmes.
　Dir: Jean-Gérard Cornu
1961 *Les Parisiennes,* episode: *Sophie.*
　Dir: Marc Allegret
1962 *Et Satan conduit le bal.*
　Dir: Grisha Dabat
Le Vice et la vertu (Vice and Virtue).
　Dir: Roger Vadim
1963 *Les Parapluies de Cherbourg*
　(The Umbrellas of Cherbourg).
　Dir: Jacques Demy
Les Plus Belles Escroqueries du monde,
　episode: *L'Homme qui vendit la tour*
　Eiffel. Dir: Claude Chabrol
Vacances portugaises. Dir: Pierre Kast
1964 *La Chasse à l'homme*
　(The Gentle Art of Seduction/Male Hunt).
　Dir: Edouard Molinaro
Un monsieur de compagnie (Male
　Companion). Dir: Philippe de Broca
Le constanza della ragione.
　Dir: Pasquale Festa Campanile
1965 *Repulsion.* Dir: Roman Polanski
Le Chant du monde. Dir: Marcel Camus
La Vie de château.
　Dir: Jean-Paul Rappeneau
Les Créatures. Dir: Agnès Varda
Das Liebeskarussell, episode: *Angela*
　(Who Wants to Sleep, episode: Angela).
　Dir: Rolf Thiele
1966 *Les Demoiselles de Rochefort*
　(The Young Girls of Rochefort).
　Dir: Jacques Demy
Belle de jour. Dir: Luis Buñuel
1967 *Manon 70.* Dir: Jean Aurel
1968 *Benjamin ou les mémoires d'un*
puceau. Dir: Michel Deville
Mayerling. Dir: Terence Young
La Chamade. Dir: Alain Cavalier
April Fools. Dir: Stuart Rosenberg
La Sirène du Mississippi (Mississippi
　Mermaid). Dir: François Truffaut
1970 *Tristana.* Dir: Luis Buñuel
Peau d'Ane (Donkey Skin/The Magic Donkey).
　Dir: Jacques Demy
1971 *Ça n'arrive qu'aux autres*
　(It Only Happens to Others).
　Dir: Nadine Trintignant
Liza. Dir: Marco Ferreri
1972 *L'Evénement le plus important*
　depuis que l'homme a marché sur la lune
　(A Slightly Pregnant Man).
　Dir: Jacques Demy
Un flic (Dirty Money).
　Dir: Jean-Pierre Melville
Langlois. Dirs: E. Hershon, R. Guerra, doc
1973 *Touche pas à la femme blanche.*
　Dir: Marco Ferreri
1974 *Fatti di gente per bene/La Grande*
　Bourgeoise. Dir: Mauro Bolognini
L'Agression aka *Sombres vacances*
　(Aggression). Dir: Gérard Pirès
La Femme aux bottes rouges.
　Dir: Juan Buñuel
Zig-Zig. Dir: Laszlo Szabo
1975 *Le Sauvage (The Savages/Lovers Like*
　Us). Dir: Jean-Paul Rappeneau
Hustle. Dir: Robert Aldrich
1976 *Si c'était à refaire.*
　Dir: Claude Lelouch
Anima persa/Ames perdues. Dir: Dino Risi
1977 *Casotto (The Beach Hut).*
　Dir: Sergio Citti
March or Die. Dir: Dick Richards
Ils sont grands ces petits. Dir: Joël Santoni
1978 *L'Argent des autres.*
　Dir: Christian de Chalonge
Ecoute voir... Dir: Hugo Santiago
1979 *A nous deux (An Adventure for Two).*
　Dir: Claude Lelouch
Courage fuyons. Dir: Yves Robert
1980 *Le Dernier Métro (The Last Metro).*
　Dir: François Truffaut
Je vous aime. Dir: Claude Berri
1981 *Le Choix des armes.*
　Dir: Alain Corneau

Hôtel des Amériques. Dir: André Téchiné
Le Choc. Dir: Robin Davis
1982 *L'Africain.* Dir: Philippe de Broca
1983 *The Hunger.* Dir: Tony Scott
1984 *Le Bon Plaisir.* Dir: Francis Girod
Fort Saganne. Dir: Alain Corneau
Paroles et musique. Dir: Elie Chouraqui
1985 *Speriamo che si femmina!/Esperons que si sait une fille (Let's Hope It's a Girl).*
Dir: Mario Monicelli
1986 *Le Lieu du crime.* Dir: André Téchiné
1987 *Agent Trouble.*
Dir: Jean-Pierre Mocky
1988 *Un drôle d'endroit pour un rencontre (A Strange Place to Meet).*
Dir: François Dupeyron
1989 *Fréquence meurtre.*
Dir: Elisabeth Rappeneau
Helmut Newton: Frames from the Edge.
Dir: Adrian Maben, doc
1991 *La Reine blanche.*
Dir: Jean-Loup Hubert
1992 *Contre l'oubli*, segment: *El Salvador.*
Dir: Chantal Akerman, doc
1993 *Ma saison préférée.*
Dir: André Téchiné
Les Demoiselles ont eu 25 ans.
Dir: Agnes Varda, doc
Indochine. Dir: Régis Wargnier

Marlene Dietrich

Born 27 December 1901, Berlin, Germany
Died 6 May 1992, Paris, France

1923 *Der kleine Napoleon*, aka *So sind die Männer (The Little Napoleon).*
Dir: Georg Jacoby
Tragödie der Liebe (Tragedy of Love).
Dir: Joe May
Der Mensch am Wege (Man by the Roadside).
Dir: Wilhelm Dieterle
1924 *Der Sprung ins Leben (Leap into Life).*
Dir: Johannes Guter
1925 *Die freudlose Gasse (The Joyless Street/The Street of Sorrow).*
Dir: Georg Wilhelm Pabst
1926 *Manon Lescaut.*
Dir: Arthur Robinson

Eine DuBarry von Heute (Modern DuBarry).
Dir: Alexander Korda
Madame wünscht keine Kinder (Madam Wants No Children).
Dir: Alexander Korda
Kopf hoch, Charly! (Heads Up, Charlie!).
Dir: Dr Willi Wolff
1927 *Der Juxbaron (The Imaginary Baron).*
Dir: Dr Willi Wolff
Sein grösster Bluff (His Greatest Bluff).
Dir: Harry Piel
Wenn ein Weib den Weg verliert (Café Electric). Dir: Gustav Icicky
1928 *Prinzessin Olala (The Art of Love).*
Dir: Robert Land
1929 *Ich Küsse ihre Hand, Madame (I Kiss Your Hand, Madam).* Dir: Robert Land
Die Frau, nach der Man sich sehnt (Three Loves). Dir: Kurt Bernhardt
Das Schiff der verlorenen Menschen (The Ship of Lost Men). Dir: Maurice Tourneur
Gefahren der Brautzeit (Dangers of the Engagement). Dir: Fred Sauer
1930 *Der blaue Engel (The Blue Angel).*
Dir: Josef von Sternberg
Morocco. Dir: Josef von Sternberg
1931 *Dishonored.*
Dir: Josef von Sternberg
1932 *Shanghai Express.*
Dir: Josef von Sternberg
Blonde Venus. Dir: Josef von Sternberg
1933 *Song of Songs.*
Dir: Rouben Mamoulian
1934 *The Scarlet Empress.*
Dir: Josef von Sternberg
1935 *The Devil is a Woman.*
Dir: Josef von Sternberg
1936 *Desire.* Dir: Frank Borzage
I Loved a Soldier. Dir: Henry Hathaway, unfinished
The Garden of Allah.
Dir: Richard Boleslawski
1937 *Knight without Armour.*
Dir: Jacques Feyder
Angel. Dir: Ernst Lubitsch
1939 *Destry Rides Again.*
Dir: George Marshall
1940 *Seven Sinners.* Dir: Tay Garnett
1941 *The Flame of New Orleans.*
Dir: René Clair

Manpower. Dir: Raoul Walsh
1942 *The Lady is Willing.*
  Dir: Mitchell Leisen
The Spoilers. Dir: Ray Enright
Pittsburgh. Dir: Lewis Seiler
1944 *Follow the Boys.*
  Dir: Eddie Sutherland,
  guest appearance
Kismet. Dir: William Dieterle
1946 *Martin Roumagnac.*
  Dir: George Lacombe
1947 *Golden Earrings.*
  Dir: Mitchell Leisen
1948 *A Foreign Affair.* Dir: Billy Wilder
1949 *Jigsaw.* Dir: Fletcher Markle,
  guest appearance
1950 *Stagefright.* Dir: Alfred Hitchcock
1951 *No Highway (Highway in the Sky).*
  Dir: Henry Koster
1952 *Rancho Notorious.* Dir: Fritz Lang
1956 *Around the World in Eighty Days.*
  Dir: Michael Anderson,
  guest appearance
1957 *The Monte Carlo Story.*
  Dir: Samuel A. Taylor
1958 *Witness for the Prosecution.*
  Dir: Billy Wilder
Touch of Evil. Dir: Orson Welles
1961 *Judgement at Nuremberg.*
  Dir: Stanley Kramer
1962 *Black Fox.*
  Dir: Louis Clyde Stoumen,
  doc, narrator
1964 *Paris When It Sizzles.*
  Dir: Richard Quine
1978 *Schöner Gigolo – Armer Gigolo*
  (Just a Gigolo). Dir: David Hemmings
1984 *Marlene.* Dir: Maximilian Schell,
  doc, voice only

Jodie Foster

Born 19 November 1962, Los Angeles,
  California, US

1972 *Napoleon and Samantha.*
  Dir: Bernard McEveety
Menace on the Mountain.
  Dir: Vincent McEveety, TVM
1973 *Kansas City Bomber.*

  Dir: Jerrold Freedman
1973 *Tom Sawyer.* Dir: Don Taylor
One Little Indian. Dir: Bernard McEveety
1974 *Alice Doesn't Live Here Anymore.*
  Dir: Martin Scorsese
Smile, Jenny, You're Dead.
  Dir: Jerry Thorpe, TVM
1975 *Echoes of a Summer*
  aka *The Last Castle.* Dir: Don Taylor
1976 *Taxi Driver.* Dir: Martin Scorsese
Bugsy Malone. Dir: Alan Parker
Freaky Friday. Dir: Gary Nelson
The Little Girl Who Lives Down the Lane.
  Dir: Nicolas Gessner
1977 *Candleshoe.* Dir: Norman Tokar
Moi, fleur bleue (Stop Calling Me Baby!).
  Dir: Eric Le Hung
Casotto (The Beach Hut). Dir: Sergio Citti
1978 *Movies Are My Life.*
  Dir: Peter Haydon, doc
1979 *Foxes.* Dir: Adrian Lyne
1980 *Carny.* Dir: Robert Kaylor
1982 *O'Hara's Wife.*
  Dir: William Bartman
1983 *Svengali.*
  Dir: Anthony Harvey, TVM
1984 *Les Sang des autres (The Blood of*
  Others). Dir: Claude Chabrol
The Hotel New Hampshire.
  Dir: Tony Richardson
1987 *Siesta.* Dir: Mary Lambert
Five Corners. Dir: Tony Bill
1988 *Mesmerized.* Dir: Michael Laughlin,
  unreleased
Stealing Home. Dir: Steven Kampmann
The Accused. Dir: Jonathan Kaplan
1989 *Backtrack (Catchfire).* Dir: Alan
  Smithee, aka Dennis Hopper
1991 *The Silence of the Lambs.*
  Dir: Jonathan Demme
Little Man Tate. Dir: Jodie Foster
Shadows and Fog. Dir: Woody Allen
1993 *Sommersby.* Dir: Jon Amiel

Television series, appearances
(unless otherwise indicated)
1969, 1970 *Mayberry R.F.D.*
1969, 1970, 1971 *The Courtship of Eddie's*
  Father
1969, 1971, 1972 *Gunsmoke*

1969 *Julia*
1970 *Nanny and the Professor*
Daniel Boone
1971, 1972 *My Three Sons*
1972 *Ironside*
Bonanza
Ghost Story
My Sister Hank, pilot
The Paul Lynde Show
1972–74 *The Amazing Chan and the Chan Chan*, animated, voice only
1973 *The Partridge Family*
Kung Fu
The New Adventures of Perry Mason
Love Story
Bob and Carol and Ted and Alice, regular cast
1974 *Paper Moon*, regular cast
1975 *Medical Center*

ABC Afterschool Specials
1973 *Rookie of the Year*
Alexander
1975 *The Secret Life of T. K. Dearing*

Lillian Gish

Born 14 October 1896, Springfield, Ohio, US
Died 27 February 1993, Manhattan, New York, US

1912 *An Unseen Enemy*.
    Dir: D. W. Griffith
Two Daughters of Eve. Dir: D. W. Griffith
In the Aisles of the Wild. Dir: D. W. Griffith
The One She Loved. Dir: D. W. Griffith
The Painted Lady. Dir: D. W. Griffith
The Musketeers of Pig Alley.
    Dir: D. W. Griffith
My Baby. Dir: Frank Powell
Gold and Glitter. Dir: Frank Powell
The New York Hat. Dir: D. W. Griffith
The Burglar's Dilemma. Dir: D. W. Griffith
A Cry for Help. Dir: D. W. Griffith
1913 *Oil and Water*. Dir: D. W. Griffith
The Unwelcome Guest. Dir: D. W. Griffith
The Stolen Bride. Dir: Tony O'Sullivan
A Misunderstood Boy. Dir: D. W. Griffith
The Left-Handed Man. Dir: D. W. Griffith

The Lady and the Mouse.
    Dir: D. W. Griffith
The House of Darkness. Dir: D. W. Griffith
Just Gold. Dir: D. W. Griffith
A Timely Interception. Dir: D. W. Griffith
Just Kids. Dir: Dell Henderson
The Mothering Heart. Dir: D. W. Griffith
During the Round Up. Dir: D. W. Griffith
An Indian's Loyalty. Dir: Frank Powell
*A Woman in the Ultimat*e.
    Dir: D. W. Griffith
A Modest Hero. Dir: D. W. Griffith
So Runs the Way. Dir: D. W. Griffith
The Madonna of the Storm.
    Dir: D. W. Griffith
The Blue or the Gray.
    Dir: William Christy Cabanne
The Conscience of Hassan Bey.
    Dir: William Christy Cabanne
Men and Muslim. Dir: D. W. Griffith
The Battle at Elderbush Gulch.
    Dir: D. W. Griffith
1914 *The Green-Eyed Devil*.
    Dir: James Kirkwood
The Battle of the Sexes. Dir: D. W. Griffith
The Hunchback.
    Dir: William Christy Cabanne
The Quicksands.
    Dir: William Christy Cabanne
Home, Sweet Home. Dir: D. W. Griffith
A Fair Rebel. Dir: Paul Powell (?)
Judith of Bethulia. Dir: D. W. Griffith
Silent Sandy. Dir: James Kirkwood
The Escape. Dir: D. W. Griffith
The Rebellion of Kitty Belle.
    Dir: William Christy Cabanne
Lord Chumley. Dir: James Kirkwood
Man's Enemy. Dir: Frank Powell
The Angel of Contention. Dir: Jack O'Brien
The Wife. Dir: unknown
The Tear that Burned. Dir: Jack O'Brien
The Folly of Anne. Dir: Jack O'Brien
The Sisters. Dir: William Christy Cabanne
His Lesson. Dir: Donald Crisp, extra
1915 *The Birth of a Nation*.
    Dir: D. W. Griffith
The Lost House.
    Dir: William Christy Cabanne
Enoch Arden (As Fate Ordained).
    Dir: William Christy Cabanne

Captain Macklin. Dir: Jack O'Brien
Souls Triumphant. Dir: Jack O'Brien
The Lily and the Rose. Dir: Paul Powell
1916 *Daphne and the Pirate*.
   Dir: William Christy Cabanne
Sold for Marriage.
   Dir: William Christy Cabanne
An Innocent Magdalene. Dir: Allan Dwan
Intolerance. Dir: D. W. Griffith
Diane of the Follies.
   Dir: William Christy Cabanne
Pathways of Life.
   Dir Dir: William Christy Cabanne
Flirting with Fate.
   Dir: William Christy Cabanne
The Children Pay. Dir: Lloyd Ingraham
1917 *The House Built Upon Sand*.
   Dir: Edward Morrissey
1918 *Hearts of the World*.
   Dir: D. W. Griffith
The Great Love. Dir: D. W. Griffith
A Liberty Bond, short. Dir: D. W. Griffith
The Greatest Thing in Life.
   Dir: D. W. Griffith
The Romance of Happy Valley.
   Dir: D. W. Griffith
1919 *Broken Blossoms*. Dir: D. W. Griffith
True Heart Susie. Dir: D. W. Griffith
The Greatest Question. Dir: D. W. Griffith
1920 *Way Down East*. Dir: D. W. Griffith
1921 *Orphans of the Storm*.
   Dir: D. W. Griffith
1923 *The White Sister*. Dir: Henry King
1924 *Romola*. Dir: Henry King
1926 *La Bohème*. Dir: Henry King
The Scarlet Letter. Dir: Victor Seastrom
   (Victor Sjöström)
1927 *Annie Laurie*. Dir: John S. Robertson
The Enemy. Dir: Fred Niblo
1928 *The Wind*. Dir: Victor Seastrom
   (Victor Sjöström)
1930 *One Romantic Night*.
   Dir: Paul L. Stein
1933 *His Double Life*. Dirs: Arthur
   Hopkins, William C. de Mille
1942 *The Commandos Strike at Dawn*.
   Dir: John Farrow
1943 *Top Man*. Dir: Charles Lamont
1946 *Miss Susie Slagle's*. Dir: John Berry
Duel in the Sun. Dir: King Vidor

1948 *Portrait of Jennie (Jenny)*.
   Dir: William Dieterle
1955 *The Cobweb*. Dir: Vincent Minnelli
The Night of the Hunter.
   Dir: Charles Laughton
1958 *Orders to Kill*. Dir: Anthony Asquith
1960 *The Unforgiven*. Dir: John Huston
1966 *Follow Me, Boys!*. Dir: Norman Tokar
Warning Shot. Dir: Buzz Kulik
1967 *The Comedians*. Dir: Peter Glenville
1969 *Arsenic and Old Lace*.
   Dir: Robert Scheerer, TVM
1970 *Henri Langlois*. Dirs: Elia Hershon,
   Roberto Guerra, doc
1975 *DW: Feature Film Years*.
   Dir: Merrill Brockway, TV doc
1976 *Twin Detectives*.
   Dir: Robert Day, TVM
1978 *A Wedding*. Dir: Robert Altman
Swedenborg: The Man Who Had to Know.
   Dirs: Harvey Bellin, Tom Kieffer
Sparrow. Dir: Jack Sold, TVM
1981 *Johnny Appleseed and the
   Frontier Within*.
   Dir: Harvey Bellin, Tom Kieffer
Thin Ice. Dir: Paul Aaron, TVM
1983 *Hobson's Choic*.
   Dir: Gilbert Cates, TVM
1984 *Hambone and Hillie*. Dir: Roy Watts
Lillian Gish. Dir: Jeanne Moreau, TV doc
1985 *Sweet Liberty*. Dir: Alan Alda
1987 *The Whales of August*.
   Dir: Lindsay Anderson
1993 *Lillian Gish: An Actor's Life for Me*.
   Dir: Terry Saunders, doc

Television drama
1949 *The Late Christopher Bean* (*The Philco
   Television Playhouse*). Dir: Fred Coe
1951 *The Birth of the Movies* (*The Philco
   Television Playhouse*). Dir: Delbert Mann
Ladies in Retirement (*Robert Montgomery
   Presents*). Dir: Norman Felton
Detour (*Pulitzer Playhouse*).
   Dir: Frank Telford
The Joyous Season (*Celanese Theater*).
   Dir: Alex Segal
1952 *The Autobiography of Grandma Moses*
   (*The Schlitz Playhouse of the Stars*).
   Dir: Joseph Scibetta

1953 *The Trip to Bountiful*
(*Goodyear Television Playhouse*).
Dir: Vincent J. Donehue
1954 *The Quality of Mercy*
(*Robert Montgomery Presents*).
Dir: Daniel Petrie
The Laphams of Boston (*US Steel*).
Dir: Alex Segal
The Corner Druggist (*The Campbell
Soundstage*). Dir: Mark Daniels
1955 *I, Mrs. Bibb* (*The Kraft Television
Theatre*). Dir: Richard Dunlap
The Sound and the Fury (*Playwrights '56*).
Dir: Vincent J. Donehue
1956 *The Day Lincoln Was Shot*
(*Ford Star Jubilee*). Dir: Delbert Mann
Morning's at Seven (*Alcoa Hour*).
Dir: Alex Segal
1960 *The Grass Harp* (*Play of the Week*).
Dirs: Ward Baker, Jack Kuney
1961 *The Spiral Staircase* (*Theater 62*).
Dir: Boris Sagal
1963 *Body in the Barn*
(*The Alfred Hitchcock Hour*).
Dir: Joseph Newman

Television series
1962 *The Defenders*, episode *Grandma TNT*.
Dir: Elliot Silverstein
1963 *Mr. Novak*, episode *Hello Miss
Phipps!*. Dir: Don Medford
The Breaking Point, episode *The Gnu, Now
Almost Extinct*
1964 *The Defenders*, episode *Stowaway*.
Dir: Vincent J. Donehue
1975 *The Silent Years*.
Dir: Paul Killiam, doc
1979 *Hollywood*.
Dirs: Kevin Brownlow, David Gill, doc
1981 *The Love Boat*, episode I*saac's
Teacher*. Dir: Bob Sweeney
1986 *The Adventures of Huckleberry Finn*.
Dir: Peter H. Hunt, mini-series

Filmography courtesy of 'Film Dope'

Whoopi Goldberg

Born 13 November 1949, Manhattan,
New York, US

1985 *The Color Purple*.
Dir: Steven Spielberg
1986 *Jumpin' Jack Flash*.
Dir: Penny Marshall
1987 *Burglar*. Dir: Hugh Wilson
Fatal Beauty. Dir: Tom Holland
1988 *The Telephone*. Dir: Rip Torn
Clara's Heart. Dir: Robert Mulligan
1989 *Homer and Eddie*.
Dir: Andrei Konchalovsky
Kiss Shot. Dir: Jerry London, TVM
1990 *Ghost*. Dir: Jerry Zucker
1991 *Wisecracks*. Dir: Gail Singer, doc
The Long Walk Home. Dir: Richard Pearce
Soapdish. Dir: Michael Hoffman
1992 *Sister Act*. Dir: Emile Ardolino
The Player. Dir: Robert Altman
Sarafina!. Dir: Darrell James Roodt
1993 *Made in America*.
Dir: Richard Benjamin

Television series
1986 *Moonlighting*, episode
Camille, guest appearance
1988 *D. C. Follies*, episode
Whoopi Goldberg Visits
1988–92 *Star Trek: The Next Generation*,
appearances in second, third, fourth
and fifth series
1990 *A Different World*, guest appearance
Tales From the Crypt, episode *Dead Wait*
1990–1 *Bagdad Café*, regular cast
1990–3 *Captain Planet and the Planeteers*,
first, second and third series,
animated, voice only

Television specials include
1985 *Whoopi Goldberg: Direct from
Broadway*
1986 *The American Film Institute Salute
to Billy Wilder*
1987 *The American Comedy Awards*
Carol, Carl, Whoopi and Robin
(*A Carol Burnett Special*)
Happy Birthday Hollywood
Scared Straight: 10 Years Later, doc

Up All Nite (A Pointer Sisters Special)
Funny, You Don't Look 200
Comic Relief
1988 *Comedy Tonight with*
  Whoopi Goldberg
Free to Be... A Family
Pee-Wee's Playhouse Christmas Special
Freedom Fest: Nelson Mandela's 70th
  Birthday
Fontaine... Why Am I Straight?
Comic Relief II
1989 *My Past Is My Own*
  (Schoolbreak Special)
The Debbie Allen Special
Comic Relief III
1990 *Hot Rod Brown (Tales from the Whoop)*
Bob Hope's All Star Tribute to Oprah Winfrey
  (The Oprah Winfrey Show series)
15th Annual Circus of the Stars
Motown 30: What's Goin' On
Whoopi Goldberg and Billy Connolly in
  Performance
Comic Relief IV
1991 *Chez Whoopi*
Blackbird Fly, dramatised doc
The Greatest Hits of Comic Relief
1992 *The Magical World of Chuck Jones*
Comic Relief V
The Whoopi Goldberg Show

Gong Li

Born 31 December 1965, Shenyang,
  Liaoning Province, China

Selected filmography
1987 *Hong gaoliang (Red Sorghum)*.
  Dir: Zhang Yimou
1989 *Dai hao meizhou bao (Code Name*
  'Cougar'). Dir: Zhang Yimou
1990 *Ju Dou (Secret Love, Hidden Faces)*.
  Dir: Zhang Yimou
Tseun yung (A Terra-cotta Warrior).
  Dir: Tung Yee Ching
1991 *Dahong denglong gaogao gua (Raise*
  the Red Lantern). Dir: Zhang Yimou
1992 *Mengxing shifen (Mary from Beijing)*.
  Dir: Sylvia Chang
Qui Ju da guansi (The Story of Qiu Ju).
  Dir: Zhang Yimou

Pan Yu Liang (Pan Yu Liang, A Woman
  Painter) (The Story of Art).
  Dir: Huang Shuqin
1993 *Tang Bai Fu (Flirting Scholar)*.
  Dir: Lee Lik-chee
Bawang bie ji (Farewell to My Concubine).
  Dir: Chen Kaige

Audrey Hepburn

Born 4 May 1929, Brussels, Belgium
Died 20 January 1993, Tolochenaz,
  Switzerland

1951 *One Wild Oat*.
  Dir: Charles Saunders
Laughter in Paradise. Dir: Mario Zampi
Young Wives' Tale. Dir: Henry Cass
The Lavender Hill Mob.
  Dir: Charles Crichton
Nous irons à Monte Carlo. Dir: Jean Boyer
  (English language version: *Monte Carlo*
  Baby. Dir: Jean Boyer, Lester Fuller)
1952 *Secret People*.
  Dir: Thorold Dickinson
1953 *Roman Holiday*. Dir: William Wyler
1954 *Sabrina (Sabrina Fair)*.
  Dir: Billy Wilder
1956 *War and Peace*. Dir: King Vidor
Funny Face. Dir: Stanley Donen
1957 *Love in the Afternoon*.
  Dir: Billy Wilder
1959 *The Nun's Story*.
  Dir: Fred Zinnemann
Green Mansions. Dir: Mel Ferrer
1960 *The Unforgiven*. Dir: John Huston
1961 *Breakfast at Tiffany's*.
  Dir: Blake Edwards
1962 *The Children's Hour (The Loudest*
  Whisper). Dir: William Wyler
1963 *Charade*. Dir: Stanley Donen
1964 *Paris When It Sizzles*.
  Dir: Richard Quine
My Fair Lady. Dir: George Cukor
1966 *How to Steal a Million*.
  Dir: William Wyler
1967 *Two for the Road*.
  Dir: Stanley Donen
Wait Until Dark. Dir: Terence Young
1976 *Robin and Marian*.

Dir: Richard Lester
1979 *Bloodline* aka *Sidney Sheldon's Bloodline*. Dir: Terence Young
1982 *They All Laughed*.
Dir: Peter Bogdanovich
1987 *Love Among Thieves*.
Dir: Robert Young, TVM
1989 *Always*. Dir: Steven Spielberg

Television drama
1952 *Rainy Day in Paradise Junction* (*CBS Television Workshop*)
1957 *Mayerling* (*Producers Showcase*).
Dir: Anatole Litvak

Television specials
1970 *A World of Love*. Dir: Clark Jones
1989 *The AFI Salute to Gregory Peck*.
Dir: Lou Horvitz
1989 *The Barbara Walters Special*
Lerner and Loewe: Broadway's Last Romantics. Dir: John Musilli
1991 *Gardens of the World*.
Dir: Bruce Franchini
The Fred Astaire Songbook.
Dir: David Heeley

Hattie McDaniel

Born 10 June 1895, Wichita, Kansas, US
Died 26 October 1952, Hollywood, California, US

1932 *The Golden West*. Dir: David Howard
Blonde Venus. Dir: Josef von Sternberg
Hypnotized. Dir: Mack Sennett
Washington Masquerade (*Mad Maskerade*).
Dir: Charles Brabin
1933 *The Story of Temple Drake*.
Dir: Stephen Roberts
I'm No Angel. Dir: Wesley Ruggles
1934 *Judge Priest*. Dir: John Ford
Operator 13 (*Spy 13*).
Dir: Richard Boleslawski
Lost in the Stratosphere.
Dir: Melville Brown
Imitation of Life. Dir: John Stahl
Babbitt. Dir: William Keighley
Little Men. Dir: Phil Rosen
Fate's Fathead

(*Charley Chase Comedy* series), short
The Chases of Pimple Street (*Charley Chase Comedy* series), short
1935 *The Little Colonel*. Dir: David Butler
Travelling Saleslady. Dir: Ray Enright
China Seas. Dir: Tay Garnett
Alice Adams. Dir: George Stevens
Music Is Magic. Dir: George Marshall
Another Face. Dir: Christy Cabanne
Okay Toots! (*Charley Chase Comedy* series), short
The Four Star Boarder (*Charley Chase Comedy* series), short
Anniversary Trouble (*Our Gang* series), short
1936 *Next Time We Love* (*Next Time We Live*). Dir: Edward H. Griffith
Gentle Julia. Dir: John Blystone
The Singing Kid. Dir: William Keighley
Show Boat. Dir: James Whale
The First Baby. Dir: Lewis Seiler
Hearts Divided. Dir: Frank Borzage
High Tension. Dir: Allan Dwan
The Bride Walks Out. Dir: Leigh Jason
Star for a Night. Dir: Lewis Seiler
Postal Inspector. Dir: Otto Brower
Valiant Is the Word for Carrie.
Dir: Wesley Ruggles
Libeled Lady. Dir: Jack Conway
Can This Be Dixie?. Dir: George Marshall
Reunion (*Hearts in Reunion*).
Dir: Norman Taurog
Arbor Day (*Our Gang* series), short
1937 *Racing Lady*. Dir: Wallace Fox
Don't Tell the Wife. Dir: Christy Cabanne
The Crime Nobody Saw.
Dir: Charles Barton
The Wildcatter. Dir: Lewis D. Collins
Saratoga. Dir: Jack Conway
Over the Goal. Dir: Noel Smith
Forty-Five Fathers. Dir: James Tinling
True Confession. Dir: Wesley Ruggles
Nothing Sacred. Dir: William Wellman
1938 *Battle of Broadway*.
Dir: George Marshall
The Shopworn Angel. Dir: H. C. Potter
Carefree. Dir: Mark Sandrich
The Mad Miss Manton. Dir: Leigh Jason
The Shining Hour. Dir: Frank Borzage
Everybody's Baby. Dir: Malcolm St. Clair

1939 *Zenobia* (*Elephants Never Forget*).
   Dir: Gordon Douglas
Gone with the Wind. Dir: Victor Fleming
1940 *Maryland*. Dir: Henry King
1941 *The Great Lie*.
   Dir: Edmund Goulding
Affectionately Yours. Dir: Lloyd Bacon
They Died With Their Boots On.
   Dir: Raoul Walsh
1942 *The Male Animal*.
   Dir: Elliott Nugent
In This Our Life. Dir: John Huston
George Washington Slept Here.
   Dir: William Keighley
1943 *Johnny Come Lately* (*Johnny Vagabond*). Dir: William K. Howard
Thank Your Lucky Stars. Dir: David Butler
1944 *Since You Went Away*.
   Dir: John Cromwell
Janie. Dir: Michael Curtiz
Three Is a Family. Dir: Edward Ludwig
Hi Beautiful (*Pass to Romance*).
   Dir: Leslie Goodwin
1946 *Janie Gets Married*.
   Dir: Vincent Sherman
Margie. Dir: Henry King
Song of the South. Dir: Harve Foster
Never Say Goodbye. Dir: James V. Kern
1947 *The Flame*. Dir: John H. Auer
1948 *Mickey*. Dir: Ralph Murphy
1949 *Family Honeymoon*.
   Dir: Claude Binyon
The Big Wheel. Dir: Edward Ludwig

Television series
1950 *Beulah*

Tilda Swinton

Born 1961, Scotland

1986 *Caravaggio*. Dir: Derek Jarman
Zastrozzi. Dir: David Hopkins, TV series
The Open Universe. Dir: Klaus Wyborny
Untitled. Dir: Christoph Schlingensief
1987 *Aria: Segment 9: Charpentier's 'Depuis le jour'*. Dir: Derek Jarman
Friendship's Death. Dir: Peter Wollen
The Last of England. Dir: Derek Jarman
1988 *Degrees of Blindness*.

   Dir: Cerith Wyn-Evans
1989 *War Requiem*. Dir: Derek Jarman
Play Me Something. Dir: Timothy Neat
A Call to Arms. Dir: Cordelia Swann
1989–90 *Your Cheatin' Heart*.
   Dir: Michael Whyte, TV series
1990 *The Garden*. Dir: Derek Jarman
1991 *Edward II*. Dir: Derek Jarman
Hamlet (*Shakespeare: The Animated Tales* series). Dir: Natalia Orlova, TV, voice only
1992 *Man to Man*. Dir: John Maybury
The Party – Nature Morte.
   Dir: Cynthia Beatt
Sara Maitland (*Obsessions* series).
   Dir: Steve Billinger, TV, narrator
1993 *Wittgenstein*. Dir: Derek Jarman
Orlando. Dir: Sally Potter

Directors' filmographies

Chantal Akerman

Born 6 June 1950, Brussels, Belgium

1968 *Saute ma ville*, short
1971 *L'Enfant aimé, ou je joue à être une femme mariée*, short
1972 *Hotel Monterey*
La Chambre, short
1973 *Le 15/18*. Co-director
Hanging Out Yonkers, unfinished
1974 *Je tu il elle* (*I... You... He... She*)
1975 *Jeanne Dielman, 23 Quai de Commerce, 1080 Brussels*
1977 *News from Home*
1978 *Les Rendez-vous d'Anna*
1980 *Dis-moi*
1982 *Toute une nuit* (*All Night Long*)
Les Chemins de retour, doc
1983 *Les Années 80*
L'Homme à la valise
Pina Bausch, aka *Un jour Pina a demandé*, TV doc
1984 *J'ai faim, j'ai froid*, episode in *Paris vu par... 20 ans après*

Family Business, short
New York, New York bis, short
Lettre d'un cinéaste, TV
1985 *Golden Eighties*
1986 *Letters Home*, short
Le Marteau, short
Mallet Stevens, short
1988 *Histoires d'Amérique: Food, Family and Philosophy (American Stories)*
1991 *Nuit et jour (Night and Day)*
1992 *Contre l'oubli*, segment: *El Salvador*, doc

Jane Campion

Born 1955, Wellington, New Zealand

1981 *Tissues*, short
1982 *Peel*, short
1984 *A Girl's Own Story*, short
Passionless Moments, short. Co-director
1985 *After Hours*, short
1986 *Two Friends*, TVM
Dancing Daze Episode 5, TV series
1989 *Sweetie*
1990 *An Angel at My Table*
1993 *The Piano*

Julie Dash

Born 1952, New York, US

1973 *Working Models of Success*, doc
1977 *Diary of an African Nun*, short
1978 *Four Women*, short
1982 *Illusions*, short
1983 *We Are Mothers Too Early*, short
1988 *Breaking the Silence*, short
1989 *Preventing Cancer*, short
Phyliss Wheatly, YWCA, short
1990 *Relatives*, TV short
1991 *Praise House*, TV short
Daughters of the Dust
1992 *Lost in the Night*, music video

Doris Dörrie

Born 1955, Hanover, Germany

1976 *Ob's Stürmt oder Schneit*, doc. Co-director
1977 *Ene, mene, mink*, short
1978 *Der erste Walzer*, short
Hättest was Gescheits gelernt (If Ya'd Only Learned Something Practical), TV doc
1979 *Paula aus Portugal*, TVM
1980 *Katharin Eiselt, 85, Arbeiterin*, TV doc
1981 *Von Romantik keine Spur: Martina (19) wird Schäferin Dazwischen*, TVM
Unter lauter Schafen, TV doc
1983 *Mitten in Herz (Straight Through the Heart)*
1984 *Im Innern des Wals (In the Belly of the Whale)*
1985 *Männer (Men)*
1986 *Paradies (Paradise)*
1987 *Ich und er (Me and Him)*
1989 *Geld (Money)*
1991 *Happy Birthday Türke! (Happy Birthday)*
1993 *Keiner liebt mich*

Mira Nair

Born 1957, Orissa, India

1979 *Jama Masjid Street Journal*, doc
1982 *So Far from India*, doc
1985 *India Cabaret*, doc
1987 *Children of Desired Sex*, doc
1988 *Salaam Bombay!*
1991 *Mississippi Masala*

Pratibha Parmar

Born 1957, India

1983 *Reframing Aids*, doc
1986 *Emergence*, doc
1988 *Sari Red*, short
1989 *Memory pictures*, doc
1990 *Bhangra Jig*, TV short
Flesh and Paper, TV doc
Khush (Out series), TV doc
1991 *A Place of Rage (Critical Eye series)*, TV doc

1992 *Double the Trouble, Twice the Fun*
(*Out* series), TV doc
1993 *Warrior Marks – Genital Mutilation
and Sexual Maiming of Women*
(*Critical Eye* series), TV doc

Sally Potter

Born 1949

1979 *Thriller*, short
1983 *The Gold Diggers*
1987 *The London Story*
1986 *Tears, Laughter, Fear and Rage*,
TV series
1988 *Women in Soviet cinema: I Am an Ox,
I Am a Horse, I Am a Man, I Am a Woman*
(*Women Call the Shots* series), TV doc
1993 *Orlando*

Leni Riefenstahl

Born 22 August 1902, Berlin, Germany

As actress
1926 *Der Heilige Berg* (*The Holy Mountain*).
Dir: Dr Arnold Fanck
1927 *Der grosse Sprung*
(*The Great Leap/Gita, the Goat Girl*).
Dir: Dr Arnold Fanck
1929 *Das Schicksal derer von Habsburg* (*The
Fate of the Hapsburgs/The Destiny of the
House of Hapsburg*). Dir: Rudolf Raffé
Die weisse Hölle vom Piz Palü (*The White Hell
of Pitz Palü*). Dir: Dr Arnold Fanck (re-
edited with a sound track in 1935)
1930 *Stürme über dem Montblanc*
(*Storm over Mont Blanc/Avalanche*).
Dir: Dr Arnold Fanck
1931 *Der weisse Rausch* (*The White Frenzy*).
Dir: Dr Arnold Fanck
1932 *Das blaue Licht* (*The Blue Light*).
Dir: Leni Riefenstahl
1933 *S.O.S. Eisberg* (*S.O.S. Iceberg*).
Dir: Dr Arnold Fanck
1954 *Tiefland* (*Lowlands*).
Dir: Leni Riefenstahl

As director
1932 *Das blaue Licht* (*The Blue Light*)
1933 *Sieg des Glaubens*
(*Victory of Faith*), doc
1935 *Triumph des Willens*
(*Triumph of the Will*), doc
Tag der Freiheit: Unsere Wehrmacht
(*Day of Freedom: Our Armed Forces*), doc
1938 *Olympia, I Teil Fest der Völker;
II Teil Fest der Schönheit* (*Olympia, Part 1
Festival of Nations; Part 2 Festival of
Beauty*), doc
1954 *Tiefland* (*Lowlands*)
1970s *Die Nubas* (*The Nubas*), doc,
unfinished

Monika Treut

Born 1954, Münchengladbach,
Germany

1980 *Berlinale 80*, short. Co-director
Space Chaser, short. Co-director
1981 *Ich brauche unbedingt
Kommunikation* (*I Really Need
Communication*), short
Kotz-Bitchband, short
Die Frau von Übermorgen, short.
Co-director
1983 *Bondage*, doc
1985 *Verführung: Die grausame Frau*
(*Seduction: The Cruel Woman*).
Co-director
1988 *Jungfrauenmaschine* (*Virgin Machine*)
1989 *Annie*, doc
1991 *My Father Is Coming*
1992 *Max*, doc
Dr. Paglia, doc
Female Misbehaviour, compilation of
Bondage, Annie, Max and *Dr. Paglia*
1993 *Erotique*

Compiled by Linda Ruth Willams

Select bibliography

This bibliography offers
suggestions for further reading
in areas related to the major
concerns of this book, organised
thematically in sections. In
addition to the books and articles
listed here, interested readers are
encouraged to consult the range of
journals which regularly publish
pieces on gender and cinema, such
as *Camera Obscura, Cineaste, Ciné-
Tracts, Feminist Review, Film/Literature
Quarterly, Jump Cut, Monthly Film
Bulletin, New Formations, O.L.R.,
P.M.L.A., Screen, Sight and Sound,
Signs, Wide Angle* and *Women:
A Cultural Review*. This bibliography
contains English-language
publications only.

Feminist criticism and theory

Basic collections

Brunsdon, Charlotte (ed): *Films for
Women*, London: British Film Institute,
1986

Doane, Mary Ann, Mellencamp,
Patricia, and Williams, Linda (eds): *Re-
vision: Essays in Feminist Film Criticism*,
Frederick, Maryland: American Film
Institute/University Publications of
America, 1984

Erens, Patricia (ed): *Sexual Stratagems:
The World of Women in Film*, New York:
Horizon Press, 1980

— (ed): *Issues in Feminist Film Criticism*,
Bloomington: Indiana University
Press, 1991

Kay, Karyn and Peary, Gerald (eds):
*Women and the Cinema: A Critical
Anthology*, New York: Dutton, 1977

Kuhn, Annette: *Women's Pictures:
Feminism and Cinema*, London:

Routledge & Kegan Paul, 1982

Kuhn, Annette, with Susannah
Radstone (eds): *The Women's Companion
to International Film*, London: Virago,
1990

Penley, Constance (ed): *Feminism and Film
Theory*, New York and London:
Routledge/British Film Institute, 1988

Pribram, E. Deidre (ed): *Female Spectators:
Looking at Film and Television*, London
and New York: Verso, 1988

Screen (ed): *The Sexual Subject: A Screen
Reader in Sexuality*, London and New
York: Routledge, 1992

Feminist criticism in the 70s

Baynes, Sylvia: 'Feminist Film Criticism',
in *Alternative Cinema*, February 1979

Bergstrom, Janet: 'Rereading the Work
of Claire Johnston', in *Camera Obscura*
3–4, 1979, reprinted in *Feminism and
Film Theory*, edited by Constance
Penley, New York and London:
Routledge/British Film Institute, 1988

Bovenschen, S.: 'Is There a Feminine
Aesthetic?', in *New German Critique* 10,
1977

Citron, Michelle, *et al*: 'Women and
Film: A Discussion of Feminist
Aesthetics', in *New German Critique*,
13, 1978

Cook, Pam, and Johnston, Claire:
'The Place of Woman in the Cinema
of Raoul Walsh', in *Raoul Walsh*,
Edinburgh Film Festival Publication,
1974, reprinted in *Feminism and Film
Theory*, edited by Constance Penley,
op. cit.

Haskell, Molly: *From Reverence to Rape:
The Treatment of Women in the Movies*,
Harmondsworth: Penguin, 1974

Johnston, Claire: *Notes on Women's
Cinema*, Screen pamphlet, London:
SEFT, 1973

— 'Towards a Feminist Film Practice:
Some Theses', in *Edinburgh Film Festival
Magazine* 1, Edinburgh Film Festival
Publication, 1976, reprinted in *Movies
and Methods Volume II*, edited by Bill
Nichols, Berkeley and London, 1985

Mellen, Joan: *Women and Their Sexuality in the New Film*, New York: Horizon Press, 1973

Mulvey, Laura: 'Visual Pleasure and Narrative Cinema', in *Screen* 16, 3, Autumn 1975, and 'Afterthoughts on "Visual Pleasure and Narrative Cinema" inspired by *Duel in the Sun*', in *Framework* 6, 1981, both also collected in *Visual and Other Pleasures*, Bloomington: Indiana University Press, 1989

Women and Film: back issues of U.S. journal published between 1972 and 1975

General feminist texts

Alford, Lynne, and Thomas, Sian (eds): *Women in Soviet Cinema*, London: Pandora, 1991

Attwood, Lynne: *Red Women on the Silver Screen*, London: Pandora, 1993

Berry, Chris (ed): *Perspectives on Chinese Cinema*, London: British Film Institute, 1991

Butler, Judith: *Gender Trouble: Feminism and the Subversion of Identity*, New York: Routledge 1990

Camera Obscura: 'Special Issue: Television and the Female Consumer', *Camera Obscura* 16, 1988

Creed, Barbara: 'From Here to Modernity – Feminism and Postmodernism', in *Screen* 28, 2, Spring 1987

Davis, Susan, and Maxwell, Anne: 'Some Notes Towards a Feminist Film Criticism', in *Alternative Cinema* 11, 4, Summer 1983–4

de Lauretis, Teresa: 'Guerrilla in the midst: women's cinema in the 80s', in *Screen* 31, 1, Spring 1990

— *Technologies of Gender: Theories of Theory, Film, and Fiction*, Bloomington: Indiana University Press, 1987

— (ed): *Feminist Studies/Critical Studies*, Bloomington: Indiana University Press, 1986

Fischer, Lucy: 'Shot/Countershot: An Intertextual Approach to Women's Cinema', in *Journal of Film and Video* 41, 4, Winter 1989

Gaines, Jane, and Herzog, Charlotte (eds): *Fabrications: Costume and the Female Body*, London and New York: Routledge, 1991

Gledhill, Christine: 'Recent Developments in Feminist Criticism', in *Film Theory and Criticism: Introductory Readings*, edited by Gerald Mast and Marshall Cohen, Oxford and New York: Oxford University Press, 1985

Kaplan, E. Ann: *Women and Film: Both Sides of the Camera*, New York and London: Methuen, 1983

Knight, Julia: *Women and the New German Cinema*, London: Verso, 1990

Koch, Gertrud: 'Why Women Go To Men's Films', in *Feminist Aesthetics*, edited by Gisela Ecker, London: The Women's Press, 1985

Kuhn, Annette: *The Power of the Image*, London and New York: Routledge, 1985

Lawrence, Amy: *Echo and Narcissus: Women's Voices in Classical Hollywood Cinema*, Berkeley and London: University of California Press, 1991

Levitin, Jacqueline: 'The Western: Any Good Roles for Feminists?', in *Film Reader* 5, 1982

Mayne, Judith: *The Woman at the Keyhole: Feminism and Women's Cinema*, Bloomington and Indianapolis: Indiana University Press, 1990

McCreadie, Marsha: *Women on Film: The Critical Eye*, New York: Praeger, 1983

Modleski, Tania: *Feminism Without Women: Culture and Criticism in a "Postfeminist" Age*, New York and London: Routledge, 1992

— *The Women Who Knew Too Much: Hitchcock and Feminist Theory*, New York and London: Methuen, 1988

Neale, Stephen: 'Sexual Difference in Cinema', in *Sexual Difference*, special issue of *Oxford Literary Review* 8, 1–2, 1986

Rayns, Tony and Meek, Scott: *BFI Dossier No. 3: Electric Shadows: 45 Years of Chinese*

Cinema, London: British Film Institute, 1980

Rich, B. Ruby: 'In the Name of Feminist Film Criticism', in *Movies and Methods Volume II*, edited by Bill Nichols, Berkeley and London, 1985

Schlesinger, Philip, *et al*: *Women Viewing Violence*, London: British Film Institute, 1992

Showalter, Elaine: *Sexual Anarchy: Gender and Culture in the Fin de Siècle*, London: Bloomsbury, 1991

Thumim, Janet: *Celluloid Sisters: Women and Popular Cinema*, Basingstoke and London: Macmillan, 1992

Vincendeau, Ginette: 'Women's Cinema, Film Theory and Feminism in France', in *Screen* 28, 4, Autumn 1987

Welsch, Janice R.: 'Introduction: Feminist Film Criticism', in *Film Criticism* xiii, 2, Winter 1989

Williamson, Judith: *Deadline at Dawn: Film Criticism 1980–1990*, London: Marion Boyars, 1992

The female gaze

Browne, Nick: 'The Spectator-in-the-Text: The Rhetoric of *Stagecoach*', in *Narrative, Apparatus, Ideology: A Film Theory Reader*, edited by Philip Rosen, New York: Columbia University Press, 1986

Camera Obscura: special edition on *The Spectatrix*, 20–1, 1989, edited by Janet Bergstrom and Mary Ann Doane

Coons, Rachel: 'Body Heat: Who is the victim of the Gaze?', in *Focus* 6, Spring 1986

Cunningham, Donna S.: 'The Vertigo of Visual Pleasure', in *Focus* 9, 1989

de Lauretis, Teresa: 'Film and the Visible', in *How Do I Look?*, edited by Bad Object-Choices, Seattle: Bay Press, 1991

Doane, Mary Ann: 'Film and the Masquerade: Theorising the Female Spectator', in *Screen* 23, 3–4, 1982

— 'Masquerade reconsidered: Further Thoughts on the Female Spectator', in *Discourse* 11, 1, Fall–Winter 1988–9

— 'Misrecognition and Identity', in *Ciné-Tracts* 3, 3, Fall 1980

Draper, Ellen: 'Zombie Women When the Gaze is Male', in *Wide Angle* 10, 3, 1988

Gamman, Lorraine, and Marshment, Margaret (eds): *The Female Gaze: Women as Viewers of Popular Culture*, London: The Woman's Press, 1988

Grosz, Elizabeth: 'Voyeurism/ Exhibitionism/The Gaze', in *Feminism and Psychoanalysis: A Critical Dictionary*, edited by Elizabeth Wright, Oxford and Cambridge, Mass.: Basil Blackwell, 1992

Hansen, Miriam: *Babel & Babylon: Spectatorship in American Silent Film*, Cambridge, Mass. and London: Harvard University Press, 1991

Kaplan, E. Ann: 'Is the Gaze Male?', in *Desire: The Politics of Sexuality*, edited by Ann Snitow, Christine Stansell, and Sharon Thompson, London: Virago, 1983. This collection is published by Monthly Review Press in the US as *Powers of Desire: The Politics of Sexuality*, 1983

Mayne, Judith: *Cinema and Spectatorship*, London and New York: Routledge, 1993

Waldman, Diane: 'Film Theory and the Gendered Spectator: The Female or the Feminist Reader?', in *Camera Obscura* 18, 1988

W5 Group: 'Female Spectatorship', in *The Independent Eye* 10, 2, Winter 1989

Psychoanalysis, semiotics and feminism

Bersani, Leo: 'Sexuality and Aesthetics', in *October* 28, Spring 1984

Burgin, Victor, Donald, James, and Kaplan, Cora (eds): *Formations of Fantasy*, London and New York: Methuen, 1986

Cowie, Elizabeth: 'Fantasia', in *m/f* 9, 1984, pp. 70–105

de Lauretis, Teresa: *Alice Doesn't: Feminism, Semiotics, Cinema*, Bloomington: Indiana University Press, 1984

Doane, Mary Ann: *Femmes Fatales: Feminism, Film Theory, Psychoanalysis*, New York and London: Routledge, 1991

Heath, Stephen: 'Sexual Difference', in *Screen* 19, 3, Autumn 1978

— 'The Turn of the Subject', in *Explorations in Film Theory: Selected Essays from Ciné-Tracts*, edited by Ron Burnett, Bloomington: Indiana University Press, 1991

Kaplan, E. Ann (ed): *Psychoanalysis and Cinema*, London and New York: Routledge, 1990

Lesage, Julia: 'The Human Subject – You, He, or Me? Or, The Case of the Missing Penis', in *Jump Cut* 4, 1974

Metz, Christian: *Psychoanalysis and Cinema: The Imaginary Signifier*, translated by Celia Britton, Annwyl Williams, Ben Brewster and Alfred Guzzetti, Basingstoke and London: Macmillan, 1990, first published 1975

Penley, Constance: *The Future of an Illusion: Film, Feminism, and Psychoanalysis*, London and New York: Routledge, 1989

Rodowick, D. N.: *The Difficulty of Difference: Psychoanalysis, Sexual Difference and Film Theory*, London and New York: Routledge, 1992

Rose, Jacqueline: *Sexuality in the Field of Vision*, London: Verso 1986

— 'Response', in *Camera Obscura* 20–1

Silverman, Kaja: *The Subject of Semiotics*, Oxford and New York: Oxford University Press, 1983

— *The Acoustic Mirror: The Female Voice in Psychoanalysis and Cinema*, Bloomington: Indiana University Press, 1988

Studlar, Gaylyn: 'Masochism and the Perverse Pleasures of the Cinema', in *Movies and Methods Volume II*, edited by Bill Nichols, Berkeley and London: University of California Press, 1985

Walker, Janet: 'Psychoanalysis and Feminist Film Theory: The Problem of Sexual Difference and Identity', in *Wide Angle* 6, 3, 1984

Stars and their audiences

Allen, Jeanne Thomas: 'The Film Viewer as Consumer', in *Quarterly Review of Film Studies* 5, 4, 1980

Barthes, Roland: 'The Face of Garbo', in *Mythologies*, New York: Hill and Wang, 1972

Baxter, Peter: 'On the Naked Thighs of Miss Dietrich', in *Movies and Methods, Volume II*, edited by Bill Nichols, Berkeley and London: University of California Press, 1985

Clarke, Jane, and Simmonds, Diana: *Move Over Misconceptions: Doris Day Reappraised*, London: British Film Institute, 1980

De Beauvoir, Simone: 'Brigitte Bardot and the Lolita Syndrome', in *Women and the Cinema*, edited by Karyn Kay and Gerald Peary, New York: Dutton 1977

De Cordova, Richard: *Picture Personalities: The Emergence of the Star System in America*, Urbana and Chicago: University of Illinois Press, 1990

Donald, James: 'Stars', in *The Cinema Book*, edited by Pam Cook, London: British Film Institute, 1985

Dyer, Richard: *Stars*, London: British Film Institute, 1979

— *Heavenly Bodies: Film Stars and Society*, New York: St Martin's Press, 1986

— and Vincendeau, Ginette (eds): *Popular European Cinema*, London and New York: Routledge, 1992

Eckert, Charles: 'The Carole Lombard in Macy's Window', in *Fabrications: Costume and the Female Body*, edited by Jane Gaines and Charlotte Herzog, New York: Routledge, 1990

Gish, Lillian: *The Movies, Mr Griffith and Me*, New York: Prentice Hall 1969

Gledhill, Christine (ed): *Stardom: Industry of Desire*, London and New York: Routledge 1991

Hamilton, Marybeth: 'A little bit spicy, but not too raw: Mae West, pornography and popular culture', in *Sex Exposed: Sexuality and the Pornograpy Debate*, edited by Lynne Segal and

Mary McIntosh, London: Virago, 1992

Hansen, Miriam: 'The Return of Babylon: Rudolph Valentino and Female Spectatorship (1921–1926)', in *Babel & Babylon: Spectatorship in American Silent Film*, Cambridge, Mass. and London: Harvard University Press, 1991

Hayward, Susan: 'The Star as National Signifier', in *French National Cinema*, London and New York: Routledge, 1993

Jackson, Carlton: *Hattie: The Life of Hattie McDaniel*, New York and London: Madison Books, 1990

Kobal, John: *People Will Talk: Personal Conversations with the Legends of Hollywood*, London: Aurum Press, 1991

Matthews, Peter: 'Garbo and Phallic Motherhood – A "Homosexual" Visual Economy', in *Screen* 29, 3, Summer 1988

Mayne, Judith: 'Star-Gazing', in *Cinema and Spectatorship*, London and New York: Routledge, 1983

Spoto, Donald: *Dietrich*, London: Bantam, 1992

Steinem, Gloria: *Marilyn*, London: Victor Gollancz, 1987

Studlar, Gaylyn: *In the Realm of Pleasure: Von Sternberg, Dietrich and the Masochistic Aesthetic*, Urbana: University of Illinois Press, 1988

Sexuality, colonialism and black cinema

Attile, Martina: 'Black Women and Representation', in *Undercut* 14–15, Summer 1985

Bhabha, Homi K.: 'The Other Question: The Stereotype and Colonial Discourse', in *The Sexual Subject: A Screen Reader in Sexuality*, edited by *Screen*, London and New York: Routledge, 1992

Bobo, Jacqueline: 'Black Women in Fiction and Nonfiction: Images of Power and Powerlessness', in *Wide Angle* 13, 3–4, July–October 1991

Bogle, Donald: *Toms, Coons, Mulattoes, Mammies and Bucks: An Interpretive History of Blacks in American Films*, New York: Viking Press, 1973

Bourne, Stephen: 'Hattie McDaniel and Butterfly McQueen in Hollywood', in *Artrage*, Autumn 1989

Brown, Jane D., and Campbell, Kenneth: 'Race and Gender in Music Videos: The Same Beat but a Different Drummer', in *Journal of Communication* 36, 1, Winter 1986

Cham, Mbye B., and Andrade-Watkins, Claire (eds): *Blackframes: Critical Perspectives on Black Independent Cinema*, Cambridge, Mass.: MIT Press, 1988

Dagle, Joan: 'Effacing Race: The Discourse on Gender in *Diva*', *Post Script* 10, 2, Winter 1991

Diawara, Manthia (ed): Special Issue of *Wide Angle* 13, 3–4, July–October 1991, on black cinema

Friedman, Lester D. (ed): *Unspeakable Images: Ethnicity and the American Cinema*, Urbana and Chicago: University of Illinois Press, 1991

Gibson-Hudson, Gloria J.: 'African American Literary Criticism as a Model for the Analysis of Films by African American Women', in *Wide Angle* 13, 3–4, July–October 1991

Holmlund, Christine Anne: 'Displacing Limits of Difference: Gender, Race and Colonialism in Edward Said and Homi Bhabha's Theoretical Models and Marguerite Duras's Experimental Films', in *Quarterly Review of Film and Video* 13, 1–3, 1991

— 'Visible Difference and Flex Appeal: The Body, Sex, Sexuality, and Race in the *Pumping Iron* Films', *Cinema Journal* 28, 4, Summer 1989

hooks, bell: *Black Looks: Race and Representation*, Turnaround Press, 1993

Mapp, Edward: 'Black Women in Films: A Mixed Bag of Tricks', in *Black Films and Film-Makers: A Comprehensive Anthology from Stereotype to Superhero*, edited by Lindsay Patterson, New York: Dodd, Mead & Co, 1975

Mercer, Kobena: 'Just looking for

trouble: Robert Mapplethorpe and fantasies of race', in *Sex Exposed: Sexuality and the Pornography Debate*, edited by Lynne Segal and Mary McIntosh, London: Virago, 1992

—, and Julien, Isaac: 'Race, Sexual Politics and Black Masculinity: A Dossier', in *Male Order: Unwrapping Masculinity*, edited by Rowena Chapman and Jonathan Rutherford, London: Lawrence & Wishart, 1988

Pines, Jim: *Blacks in Films: A Survey of Racial Themes and Images in the American Film*, London: Studio Vista, 1975

—, and Willemen, Paul (eds): *Questions of Third Cinema*, London: British Film Institute, 1989

Reid, Mark A.: *Redefining Black Film*, Berkeley and London: University of California Press, 1993

Stam, Robert, and Spence, Louise: 'Colonialism, Racism and Representation: An Introduction', in *Movies and Methods, Volume II*, edited by Bill Nichols, Berkeley and London: University of California Press, 1985

Tomaselli, Keyan: *The Cinema of Apartheid*, London and New York: Routledge, 1989

Yearwood, Gladstone L. (ed): *Black Cinema Aesthetics*, Athens, Ohio: Center for Afro-American Studies, 1982

Race, gender and spectatorship

Bobo, Jacqueline: 'The Color Purple': Black Women as Cultural Readers', in *Female Spectators: Looking at Film and Television*, edited by E. Diedre Pribram, London and New York: Verso, 1988,

— 'Black Women's Responses: *The Color Purple*', in *Jump Cut* 33, 1988

Butler, Cheryl B.: '*The Color Purple* Controversy: Black Woman Spectatorship', in *Wide Angle* 13, 3–4, July–October 1991

Diawara, Manthia: 'Black Spectatorship: Problems of Identification and Resistance', in *Screen* 29, 4, Autumn 1988

Gaines, Jane: 'White Privilege and

Looking Relations: Race and Gender in Feminist Film Theory', in *Cultural Critique* 4, 1986 and *Screen* 29, 4, Autumn 1988

Mayne, Judith: 'White Spectatorship and Genre-Mixing', in *Cinema and Spectatorship*, London and New York, 1993

Gender and genre

Melodrama and the 'woman's film'

Barton, Palmer R.: 'The Successful Failure of Therapy in *Now Voyager*: The Women's Picture as Unresponsive Symptom', in *Wide Angle* 8, 1, 1986

Byars, Jackie: *All That Hollywood Allows: Re-reading Gender in 1950s Melodrama*, Chapel Hill and London: University of North Carolina Press, 1991

Cook, Pam, 'Melodrama and the Women's Picture', in *BFI Dossier No. 18: Gainsborough Melodrama*, edited by Sue Aspinall and Robert Murphy, London: British Film Institute, 1983

— 'Duplicity in *Mildred Pierce*', in *Women in Film Noir*, edited by E. Ann Kaplan, London: British Film Institute, 1978

Doane, Mary Ann: *The Desire to Desire: The Woman's Film of the 1940s*, Bloomington: Indiana University Press, 1987

Gledhill, Christine (ed): *Home is Where the Heart Is: Studies in Melodrama and the Woman's Film*, London: British Film Institute, 1987

—, and Kaplan, Ann E.: 'Dialogue on Stella Dallas and Feminist Film Theory', in *Cinema Journal* 25, 4, Summer 1986

Holdstein, Deborah H.: 'Women's Pictures: The Perfect Moment', in *Jump Cut* 32, 1987

Jacobs, Lea: '*Now, Voyager*: Some Problems of Enunciation and Sexual Difference', in *Camera Obscura* 7, 1981

— *The Wages of Sin: Censorship and the Fallen Woman Film, 1928–1942*, Madison: University of Wisconsin Press, 1991

Kaplan, E. Ann: 'The Case of the Missing

Mother: Maternal Issues in Vidor's *Stella Dallas*', in *Heresies*, 16, 1983

— (ed): *Women in Film Noir*, London: British Film Institute, 1978

Kuhn, Annette: 'Women's Genres', in *The Sexual Subject: A Screen Reader in Sexuality*, edited by *Screen*, London and New York: Routledge, 1992

La Place, Maria: 'Bette Davis and the Ideal of Consumption: A Look at *Now Voyager*', in *Wide Angle* 6, 4, 1985

Madden, David: 'Marble Goddesses and Mortal Flesh: Notes for an Erotic Memoir of the Forties', in *The Film Journal* 2, 1, 1972, special issue on Sexuality.

Mayne, Judith: 'Early Cinema and Women's Films', in *The Woman at the Keyhole: Feminism and Women's Cinema*, Bloomington: Indiana University Press, 1990

Modleski, Tania: '"Never to be thirty-six years old": *Rebecca* as female Oedipal drama', in *Wide Angle* 5, 1, 1982

Nelson, Joyce: '*Mildred Pierce* Reconsidered', in *Movies and Methods, Volume II*, edited by Bill Nichols, Berkeley and London: University of California Press, 1985

Taylor, Helen: *Scarlett's Women: Gone with the Wind and its female fans*, London: Virago, 1989

Williams, Linda: 'Something Else Besides a Mother: *Stella Dallas* and the Maternal Melodrama', in *Cinema Journal* 24, 1, 1984

Waldman, Diane: '"At Last I Can Tell It to Someone!": Feminine Point of View and Subjectivity in the Gothic Romance Film of the 1940s', in *Cinema Journal* 23, 2, 1983

Horror, science fiction and 'exploitation'

Bergstrom, Janet: 'Androids and Androgyny', *Camera Obscura* 5, 1986

Buntzen, Lynda K.: 'Monstrous Mothers: Medusa, Grendel, and now *Alien*', in *Film Quarterly* XL, 3, Spring 1987

Burgin, Victor, Donald, James, and Kaplan, Cora (eds): *Formations of Fantasy*, London: Methuen, 1986

Clover, Carol J.: *Men, Women and Chain Saws: Gender in the Modern Horror Film*, London: British Film Institute, 1992

Cook, Pam, 'The Art of Exploitation, or How to Get into the Movies', in *Monthly Film Bulletin*, December 1985

Creed, Barbara: *The Monstrous-Feminine: Women in the Horror Film*, London and New York: Routledge, forthcoming

Hillier, Jim, and Lipstadt, Aaron: *BFI Dossier No. 7: Roger Cormans' New World*, London: British Film Institute, 1981

Kuhn, Annette (ed): *Alien Zone: Cultural Theory and Contemporary Science Fiction Cinema*, London and New York: Verso, 1990

Modleski, Tania: 'The Terror of Pleasure: the contemporary horror film and postmodern theory', in *Studies in Entertainment: Critical Approaches to Mass Culture*, edited by Tania Modleski, Bloomington: Indiana University Press, 1986

Neale, Stephen: '*Halloween*: suspense, aggression, and the look', in *Framework* 14, 1981

— 'Issues of Difference: *Alien* and *Blade Runner*', and, Mellencamp, Patricia: 'Uncanny feminism: The Exquisite Corpses of Cecelia Condit, both collected in *Fantasy and the Cinema*, edited by James Donald, London: British Film Institute, 1989

Penley, Constance, *et al*: *Close Encounters: Film, Feminism and Science Fiction*, Minneapolis: University of Minnesota Press, 1991

Wide Angle: special edition on 'The Fantastic', 10, 3, 1988

Pornography

Barrowclough, Susan, 'Not A Love Story', in *Screen* 23, 5, Nov/Dec 1982

Brown, Beverley, 'A Curious Arrangement', *Screen* 23, 5, Nov/Dec 1982

Chester, Gail, and Dickey, Julienne: *Feminism and Censorship: The Current Debate*, Bridport: Prism Press and New

York: Avery Publishing, 1988

Dicaprio, Lisa: 'Not A Love Story: The Film and the Debate' and 'Interview with Bonnie Klein' in *Jump Cut* 30, March 1985

Dworkin, Andrea: *Pornography: Men Possessing Women*, London: The Women's Press and New York: Perigree Books, 1981

Feminists Against Censorship: *Pornography and Feminism: The Case Against Censorship*, edited by Gillian Rodgerson and Elizabeth Wilson, London: Lawrence & Wishart, 1991

Fuentes, Annette, and Schrage, Margaret: 'Deep Inside Porn Stars: Interview with Veronica Hart, Gloria Leonard, Kelly Nichols, Candida Royalle, Annie Sprinkle and Veronica Vera', in *Jump Cut* 32, 1987

Gibson, Pam Church, and Gibson, Roma (eds): *Dirty Looks: Women, Pornography, Power*, London: British Film Institute, 1993

Hansen, Christian, Needham, Catherine, and Nichols, Bill: 'Skin Flicks: Pornography, Ethnography, and the Discourses of Power', in *Discourse* 11.2, Spring–Summer 1989

McClintock, Anne: 'Gonad the Barbarian and the Venus Flytrap: Portraying the female and male orgasm', in *Sex Exposed: Sexuality and the Pornography Debate*, edited by Lynne Segal and Mary McIntosh, London: Virago, 1992. Also see other essays in this collection for important discussions of sexuality and power.

Merck, Mandy: *Perversions: Deviant Readings*, London: Virago 1993

Pajaczkowska, Claire: 'Images and Pornography', in *Explorations in Film Theory: Selected Essays from Ciné-Tracts*, edited by Ron Burnett, Bloomington: Indiana University Press, 1991

Russ, Joanna: 'Pornography and the Doubleness of Sex for Women', in *Jump Cut* 32, 1987

Soble, A.: *Pornography: Marxism, feminism and the future of sexuality*, New Haven:

Yale University Press, 1986

Vance, Carole S. (ed): *Pleasure and Danger: Exploring Female Sexuality*, London: Routledge & Kegan Paul, 1984

Williams, Linda: *Hard Core: Power, Pleasure and the "Frenzy of the Visible"*, London: Pandora, 1990

— 'Pornographies on/scene, or diff'rent strokes for diff'rent folks', in *Sex Exposed*, edited by Lynne Segal and Mary McIntosh, *op. cit.*

Sexualities

Lesbian and gay cinema

Bad Object-Choices (ed): *How Do I Look? Queer Film and Video*, Seattle: Bay Press, 1991

Bourne, Stephen: 'Where There Was Once Silence: Representations of Black lesbians and gays in British cinema', in *Square Peg* 15, 1987

Dyer, Richard (ed): *Gays and Film*, London: British Film Institute, 1977

— *Now You See It: Studies on Lesbian and Gay Film*, London and New York: Routledge, 1990

— 'Male Gay Porn: Coming to Terms', in *Jump Cut* 30, March 1985

— 'Believing in Fairies: The Author and The Homosexual', in *Inside/Out: Lesbian Theories/Gay Theories*, edited by Diana Fuss, New York and London: Routledge, 1991

Gallagher, Brian: 'Sexual Warfare and Homoeroticism in Billy Wilder's *Double Indemnity*', *Literature/Film Quarterly* 15, 4, 1987

Holmlund, Christine Anne: 'When is a Lesbian Not a Lesbian? The Lesbian Continuum and the Mainstream Femme Film', in *Camera Obscura* 25–6, 1991

Mayne, Judith: 'The Critical Audience', in *Cinema and Spectatorship*, London and New York: Routledge, 1993

— 'A Parallax View of Lesbian Authorship', *Inside/Out: Lesbian Theories/Gay Theories*, edited by Diana Fuss, *op. cit.*

Russo, Vito: *The Celluloid Closet: Homosexuality in the Movies*, New York: Harper & Row, 1981

Weiss, Andrea: 'From The Margins: New Images of Gays in the Cinema', in *Cineaste* 15, 1, 1986

— 'A Queer feeling when I look at you: Hollywood stars and lesbian spectatorship in the 1930s', in *Stardom: Industry of Desire*, edited by Christine Gledhill, London and New York: Routledge, 1991

— *Vampires & Violets: Lesbians in the Cinema*, London: Jonathan Cape, 1992

White, Patricia: 'Female Spectator, Lesbian Specter: The Haunting', in *Inside/Out: Lesbian Theories, Gay Theories*, edited by Diana Fuss, *op. cit.*

Wood, Robin: 'Responsibilities of A Gay Film Critic', in *Movies and Methods, Volume II*, edited by Bill Nichols, Berkeley and London: University of California Press, 1985

Masculinities

Barton, Palmer R.: 'A Masculinist reading of Two Western Films: *High Noon* and *Rio Grande*', in *Journal of Popular Film and Television* 12, 4, Winter 1984–5

Butler, Judith: 'The Force of Fantasy: Feminism, Mapplethorpe, and Discursive Excess', in *Differences* 2, 1990

Chapman, Rowena, and Rutherford, Jonathan (eds): *Male Order: Unwrapping Masculinity*, London: Lawrence & Wishart, 1988

Chow, Rey: 'Male Narcissism and National Culture: Subjectivity in Chen Kaige's *King of the Children*', in *Camera Obscura* 25–6, 1991

Cohan, Steven: 'Masquerading as the American Male in the Fifties: Picnic, William Holden and the Spectacle of Masculinity in Hollywood Film', *Camera Obscura* 25–6, 1991

—, and Hark, Ina Rae (eds): *Screening the Male: Exploring Masculinities in Hollywood Cinema*, New York and London: Routledge, 1993

Cook, Pam: 'Masculinity in Crisis?', in *Screen* 23, 3–4, September–October 1982

Creed, Barbara: 'Phallic Panic: Male hysteria and Dead Ringers' in *Screen* 31, 2, Summer 1990

Dyer, Richard: 'Don't Look Now: The Male Pin-Up', in *The Sexual Subject: A Screen Reader in Sexuality*, edited by *Screen*, London and New York: Routledge, 1992

Jardine, Alice, and Smith, Paul: *Men in Feminism*, New York: Methuen, 1987

Jeffords, Susan: 'The Big Switch: Hollywood Masculinity in the 90s', in *Film Theory Goes to the Movies*, edited by Jim Collins, Hilary Radner and Ava Preacher Collins, New York and London: Routledge, 1993

Kirkham, Pat and Thumim, Janet (eds): *You Tarzan: Masculinity, Movies and Men*, London: Lawrence & Wishart, 1993

Kroker, Arthur and Marilouise (eds): *The Hysterical Male: New Feminist Theory*, Basingstoke and London: Macmillan, 1992

Krutnik, Frank: *In a Lonely Street: Film Noir, Genre, Masculinity*, London and New York: Routledge, 1991

Limbacher, James L.: *Sexuality in World Cinema*, two volumes, New Jersey and London: The Scarecrow Press, 1983

Mellen, Joan: *Big Bad Wolves: Masculinity in the American Film*, New York, 1977

Meyer, Richard: 'Rock Hudson's Body', in *Inside/Out: Lesbian Theories, Gay Theories*, edited by Diana Fuss, New York and London: Routledge, 1991

Middleton, Peter: *The Inward Gaze: Masculinity and Subjectivity in Modern Culture*, London and New York: Routledge 1992

Neale, Stephen: 'Masculinity as Spectacle: Reflections on Men and Mainstream Cinema', in *Screen* 24, 6, 1983

Ross, Andrew: 'Masculinity and *Miami Vice*', in *Sexual Difference*, special issue of *Oxford Literary Review* 8, 1–2, 1986

Sedgwick, Eve Kosofsky: *Between Men: English Literature and Homosocial Desire*, New York: Columbia University Press, 1985

Segal, Lynne: *Slow Motion: Changing Masculinities, Changing Men*, New Jersey: Rutgers University Press/London: Virago, 1990

Silverman, Kaja: *Male Subjectivity at the Margins*, New York and London: Routledge, 1992

Vincendeau, Ginette: 'Community, Nostalgia and the Spectacle of Masculinity – Jean Gabin', in *Screen* 26, 6, Nov–Dec 1985

Waugh, Tom: 'Men's Pornography: Gay vs. Straight', in *Jump Cut* 30, March 1985

Williams, Linda Ruth: 'Putting on his glory: Lawrence's male spectacles', in *Sex in the Head*, Hemel Hempstead: Harvester-Wheatsheaf and Detroit: Wayne State University Press, 1993

Women film-makers

Acker, Ally: *Reel Women: Pioneers of the Cinema 1896 to the Present*, London: Batsford, 1991

Barrowclough, Susan: 'Chantal Akerman: adventures in perception', *Monthly Film Bulletin* 51, 603, April 1984

Benjamin, Julie, and MacLean, Alison: 'Revolving Clotheslines and Morris Minors: A Discussion of New Zealand Film-Making with Gaylene Preston', in *Alternative Cinema* 11, 4, Summer 1983–4

Blonski, Annette, Cunningham, Sophie, and Verhoeven, Debby: 'No-Funds Situation', *Cinema Papers* 67, January 1988

Brophy, Chris: 'So You Want to be a Camerawoman: Australian Film Industry Profile of Jan Kenny', in *Metro* 67, 1985

Cameron-Wilson, James: 'Tights! Camera! Action! Female Film Directors', in *Film Review*,

February 1990

Chell, Samuel L.: 'Dorothy Arzner's *Dance, Girl, Dance*: Regendering the Male Gaze', in *Cineaction* 24–5, 1991

Citron, Michelle: 'Women's Film Production: Going Mainstream', in *Female Spectators: Looking at Film and Television*, edited by E. Diedre Pribram, London and New York: Verso, 1988

Cook, Pam: 'Approaching the Work of Dorothy Arzner', in *Feminism and Film Theory*, edited by Constance Penley, New York and London: Routledge/British Film Institute, 1988

— 'Breaking Down the Myths: Feminist Film Distribution Today', in *Monthly Film Bulletin* 53, 624, January 1986

Coolidge, Martha: 'Dialogue on Film: Martha Coolidge', in *American Film* ix, 8, June 1984

Curtis Fox, Terry: 'Unearthed Directors', in *Focus* 8, Autumn 1972

Dash, Julie: *Daughters of the Dust: The Making of an African American Woman's Film*, New York: The New Press, 1992

Elsaesser, Thomas: 'Public Bodies and Divided Selves: German Women Film-Makers in the 80s', *Monthly Film Bulletin* 54, 647, December 1987

Gibbons, Luke: 'The Politics of Silence: Anne Devlin, Women and Irish cinema', in *Framework* 30–31, 1986

Haffter, Petra: 'The Association of Women Film Workers', in *Jump Cut* 30, March 1985

Heck-Rabi, Louise: *Women Filmmakers: A Critical Reception*, New Jersey: Scarecrow Press, 1984

Horton, Robert: 'Life Upside Down: Jodie Foster directs', in *Film Comment* 27, 1, Jan–Feb 1991

Houston, Beverley: 'Missing in Action: Notes on Dorothy Arzner', in *Wide Angle* 6, 3, 1984

Hu, Sang: 'The Ascendancy of China's Women Directors', in *China's Screen* 1, 1986

Jackson, Lynne, and Jaehne, Karen: 'Eavesdropping on female Voices: A *Who's Who* of Contemporary Women

Film-Makers', in *Cineaste* 16, 1–2, 1987–8

Johnston, Claire (ed): *Dorothy Arzner: Towards a Feminist Cinema*, London: British Film Institute, 1975

— 'Women's Cinema as Counter-Cinema', from *Notes on Women's Cinema*, London: SEFT, 1973, collected in 'Feminist Criticism', section of *Movies and Methods: An Anthology*, edited by Bill Nichols, London and Berkeley: University of California Press, 1976

Larkin, Alile Sharon: 'Black Women Film-makers Defining Ourselves: Feminism in Our Own Voice' in *Female Spectators: Looking at Film and Television*, ed. Diedre Pribram, *op. cit.*

Lucia, Cynthia: 'Redefining Female Sexuality in the Cinema: An Interview with Lizzie Borden', in *Cineaste* 19, 2–3, 1993

Martin, Angela: 'Chantal Akerman's Films: a Dossier', in *Feminist Review* 3, 1979

McAfee, Lynda: 'Woman with a Movie Camera', in *Focus* 9, 1989

Murray, Scott (ed): *Back of Beyond: Discovering Australian Film and Television*, Sydney: Australian Film Commission, 1988

Pilling, Jayne (ed): *Women & Animation: A Compendium*, British Film Institute Exhibition and Distribution Division, 1993

Quart, Barbara Koenig: *Women Directors: The Emergence of a New Cinema*, New York: Praeger, 1988

Springer, Claudia: 'Black Women Film-Makers', in *Jump Cut* 29, March 1984

Suter, Jacquelyn: 'Feminine Discourse in Christopher Strong' in *Feminism and Film Theory*, edited by Constance Penley, *op. cit.*

Weiss, Andrea: 'Transgressive Cinema: Lesbian Independent Film', in *Vampires & Violets: Lesbians in the Cinema*, London: Jonathan Cape, 1992

Contributors' notes

Karen Alexander is a critic and film-maker who has contributed to several books on film.

Carole Angier is the author of *Jean Rhys: Life & Work* and wrote the screenplay of Jean Rhys' *Wide Sargasso Sea* (1993, director John Duigan). She has made a BBC documentary on German director Edgar Reitz, and wrote all 10,656 English subtitles for Reitz's *Die Zweite Heimat*. She is currently working on a biography of Primo Levi.

Stephen Bourne is an archivist and consultant on the history of black entertainers. He has contributed to television documentaries on Adelaide Hall and the Nicholas Brothers and compiled *Salutations*, a radio series celebrating the achievements of black entertainers and musicians in Britain from the 20s to the 50s.

Stella Bruzzi lectures in film and television at Royal Holloway, University of London. She has also taught at Bristol and Manchester, and worked in the BBC's Music and Arts Department. Her current research interests include k. d. lang and a book about women and the media.

Carol J. Clover teaches medieval studies and film at the University of California, Berkeley. Her most recent book is *Men, Women and Chain Saws: Gender in the Modern Horror Film* (BFI Publishing/Princeton University Press, 1992). She is currently working on a book about trial movies.

Manohla Dargis writes regularly for *Village Voice* and has a special interest in avant-garde cinema.

Walter Donohue was story editor for Sally Potter's *Orlando*, John Boorman's *Where the Heart Is*, Peter Greenaway's *A Zed and Two Noughts* and *Drowning By Numbers* and Wim Wenders' *Paris, Texas* and *Until the End of the World*. He is film books' editor for Faber & Faber, London.

Richard Dyer is Professor of Film Studies at the University of Warwick. His books include *Heavenly Bodies*, *Now You See It*, *Only Entertainment*, *The Matter of Images* and *Brief Encounter*.

Thomas Elsaesser is Professor at the University of Amsterdam and Chair of the Department of Film and TV Studies. His essays on film theory, history, genre and national cinema have appeared in over 50 collections. Recent books as author and editor include *Early Cinema: Space Frame Narrative* (1990) and *Writing for the Medium: Television in Transition* (1993).

Lizzie Francke lectures on film at Middlesex University and writes for the *Guardian* and other newspapers and journals. She is author of *Script Girls: Women Writers in Hollywood*, to be published in 1994 by BFI Publishing.

Marjorie Garber is Professor of English and Director of the Center for Literary and Cultural Studies at Harvard University. She is the author of *Vested Interests: Cross-Dressing and Cultural Anxiety* (Routledge, 1992; Penguin, 1993) as well as of three books on Shakespeare. She has recently co-edited a collection of essays on cultural studies, popular culture and the news, *Media Spectacles* (Routledge, 1993).

Julia Knight lectures in media studies at the University of Luton. She is author of *Women and the New German Cinema* (Verso, 1992).

Gertrud Koch is Professor in Film Studies at the Ruhr University, Bochum. She has published books on the work of Herbert Marcuse, Siegfried Kracauer, representation and sexual difference, and the visual construction of Jewishness. She is co-publisher of the journals *Babylon – Beiträge zur jüdischen Gegenwart* and *Frauen und Film*.

Irene Kotlarz has lectured in animation history at the National Film and Television School and Royal College of Art. She has directed four international animation festivals and has programmed and produced documentaries on the subject. She is currently executive producer at Speedy Films in London.

Angela McRobbie is Principal Lecturer in Sociology at Thames Valley University and author of *Postmodernism and Popular Culture* (Routledge, 1994).

Michael O'Pray is Senior Lecturer in the School of Fine Art at the University of East London. He has edited *Andy Warhol: Film Factory* and, with Jayne Pilling, *Into the Pleasure Dome, the Films of Kenneth Anger*. He is currently working on books about Derek Jarman and Adrian Stokes and film aesthetics.

Berenice Reynaud writes for *Cahiers du cinéma*, *Screen*, *Village Voice*, *Afterimage* and *Cinemaya* (Bombay), among others. A correspondent for the Créteil Women's Film Festival and San Sebastian Film Festival, she has curated many film/video programmes. She teaches at the California Institute of the Arts.

B. Ruby Rich lives in San Francisco and New York. She is a Contributing Writer to *Elle* magazine, film/video reviews editor for *GLQ: A Journal of Lesbian and Gay Studies*, and a frequent contributor to *Village Voice*. She is currently Visiting Professor at the University of California, Berkeley, and is completing a book of essays on women, film and sexuality.

Andrea Stuart is a journalist, broadcaster and occasional academic. She is currently working on a book about women entertainers, to be published in 1994 by Jonathan Cape.

Amy Taubin is a regular film and television writer for *Village Voice* and frequent contributor to *Mirabella*. She is currently writing a book about *Taxi Driver* for BFI Publishing. Her experimental film *In the Bag* (1981) is in the collection of the Museum of Modern Art, New York. From 1983 to 1987 she was the film and video curator of The Kitchen, New York City.

Ginette Vincendeau is Senior Lecturer in Film Studies at the University of Warwick. She co-edited *French Film, Texts and Contexts* (1990) and *Popular European Cinema* (1992) and is co-author of *Jean Gabin, Anatomie d'un mythe* (1993). She is currently editing the BFI/Cassell *Encyclopedia of European Cinema*.

Linda Ruth Williams lectures in film and literature at the University of Southampton. She is author of *Sex in the Head: Visions of femininity and film in D. H. Lawrence* (Harvester, 1993) and editor of *The Bloomsbury Guide to Twentieth Century Literature* (1992). She is currently writing a book on psychoanalytic criticism.

Elizabeth Wilson is Professor and Reader in Media Studies at the University of North London. She is author of a number of books on feminism and cultural history, including *Adorned in Dreams: Fashion and Modernity*, *Hallucinations: Life in the Postmodern City* and *The Sphinx in the City*, and has recently published a thriller, *The Lost Time Café*.

Index